Food and Drink Service

Levels 1 and 2

Roy Hayter

Hotel & Catering Training Company

HOTEL & CATERING TRAINING COMPANY

150th YEAR
M
MACMILLAN

First published 1993 by
THE MACMILLAN PRESS LTD
Houndmills, Basingstoke, Hampshire RG21 2XS
and London
Companies and representatives
throughout the world

ISBN 0–333–59502–5

A catalogue record for this book is available from the British
Library

Typeset by the author
and Kate Jennings & Associates, London

Printed in Great Britain by
Scotprint Ltd, Musselburgh

Contents

Acknowledgements

The Hotel & Catering Training Company and The Macmillan Press gratefully acknowledge the contribution made to this book by the following:

Industry liaison, research and supervision of photography

Pam Frediani

Advice with the text

Clive Finch, Visiting Professor, Thames Valley University

Photographic locations

The Brewery Tap, Young & Co, Wandsworth (with the help of Steve Gallagher); Butlin's South Coast World, Bognor Regis; Café Rouge, Putney; Carters Vending, Derby; Clementine Churchill Hospital, Harrow; Conrad Hotel, London; Ealing Hospital, Southall; The Grand, Brighton; La Mancha, Putney; Linden Lodge School, Wimbledon; McDonald's, Wandsworth; Matt's Café, Chelsea Harbour, London; Pizza Express, Clapham; St. Faith's School, Wandsworth; St. John's College, Cambridge; St. Saviour's School, Clapham.

Photographers

Simon Green; Christine Osborne; Simon Hawkins, of Simon Reeve Photography, Cambridge; Keith Turnbull; Martin Brown, of Utal Fisher, Derby.

Illustrations, computer graphics and artwork

Diana Beatty, Kate Jennings, Tom Lines, Pam Frediani, Ian Thompson (original cover design).

Loan of photographs

Birmingham College of Food, Tourism, Creative Studies, photographer Chris Goddard; Cephas Ltd, photographer Mike Rock; Churchill Restaurant, London; Commercial Catering Group Services; Conrad Hotel, London; Decor Style; Equity Cruise Lines; Food from France; Gardner Merchant; Harry Ramsden's, photographer Freddie Walker; The Hotel Intercontinental, Soufflé Restaurant, London; Impact Photos, photographers Mohamed Anson, Jeremy Nicholl, Homer Sykes; The Kobal Collection; Maxon Europe Ltd; The Milk Marketing Board; Network, photographers Frieder Blickle, Wolfgang Kuhz, Barry Lewis, Paul Lowe, Andrej Reiser, Homer Sykes; Orient Express; Remanco; Royal Navy; Smollensky's Balloon; TGI Friday's; Wimpy International Ltd; Catherine Blackie (also picture research).

Supplying examples of procedures, advice and help with the text, and photographs

Clare Walker, *Caterer & Hotelkeeper*; Maggie Tiltman, Avon County School Meals Service; Gerard Basset and Jennifer Murray for wine tasting; Birmingham College of Food, Tourism, Creative Studies; Mike Combe, Butlin's South Coast World; The Butter Council; Rachel Lindner, Catering and Allied Services; Jayne Wagshaw, Champagne Bureau; J.L.Pollet, Chase Restaurants; Ruth Leggett, Chef and Brewer; Julie Duggan, Clementine Churchill Hospital, Harrow; Chris Hillier, Commercial Catering Group Services; Doreen Boulding, Stephen Kyack-Lane, Colin Vickers, Conrad Hotel, London; Alan Blenkinsopp, Norbert Lieder, Michael Phipps, Coppid Beech Hotel, Bracknell; Phil Ruddock, Concetta Wager, Ealing Hospital; Sophie Vallejo, Food from France; Debbie Foster, Forte Heritage; Alan Gomm, Forte Hotels; Dorothy Miller, Fox and Pheasant, Stoke Poges, Chef & Brewer, Country Carvery; Pam Rotherforth, Gardner Merchant; Richard Baker, The Grand, Brighton; Richard Richardson, Harry Ramsden's; Maundy Todd, Holiday Care Services; Rosemary Morrison, Hotel Catering & Institutional Management Association Reference Library; Tim Penrose, Adam Austin, Hudson's Coffee Houses Ltd; Fiona Newstead, Kentucky Chicken Great Britain Ltd; Barrie Larvin for demonstrating the opening of still and sparkling wines (photographs, Pims Photographs) and commenting on section 10; Margaret Nolan, Linden Lodge School, Wimbledon; Maxon Europe Ltd; Verne George, Roy Perrott, Merrychef Ltd; Alfred Thorpe, Milk Marketing Board; David Ford and Jane Price, Old Orleans Restaurant, Thurrock; Kate and Peter Osborne; Mark Lindsell, Rank Leisure; Sqn.Ldr.Brian Jarman, Royal Air Force; Major Nigel Marchant, Royal Logistics Corps (Catering); Lt.Comm.Frederick Radcliffe, Royal Navy; Simon Hawkey, Nigel Bruce, St.John's College, Cambridge; Chris Gooch, Sankey Vending; The Tea Council; Chris Maguire, Travellers Fare Ltd; Visa Napery Fabrics; Diana Blewitt, Wandsworth Council Contracts Division; C.Jeffries, Whitbread Inns; Brigadier Andrew Paviour, Geoffrey Spence, Wine and Spirit Education Trust.

Piloting/commenting on the text

Academy of Food & Wine Service Working Group: Saverio Buchicchio of Dormy House Hotel; Roger Capisano; Silvano Giraldin of Le Gavroche representing Les Arts de la Table; Phil Hamilton of Academy of Food & Wine Service; Nicholas Leach of Ind Coope-Taylor Walker; Brian Turner of Turners representing Académie Culinaire de France.

Executive of the Academy of Food & Wine Service: David Battersby, Jeremy Bennett, Rodney Briant-Evans, Phil Hamilton, Nick Scade.

Project Advisory Group of the Academy of Food & Wine Service: Barry Cole, Director of The Osborne Hotel, representing the Master Innholders; Jenny Harvey of Hospitality & Leisure Manpower, adviser to the project and Harry Murray, Executive Director of The Imperial Hotel, also representing the Master Innholders.

Gary Wood, Birmingham College of Food, Tourism, Creative Studies; Elaine Foulds, Brooklands College, Weybridge; Hamish Cobban, Telford College, Edinburgh.

Claire Wilson, Mike Fellowes, HCTC Marketing Department; Gill Pittard, Award-Making Division; Alison McFadden (Research); Susan Yates (Coordinator); Mark Ashby, Geraldine Barker (Coordinator), Fiona Friebell, Rhian Lawton, Karen O'Connor, Jenny Thornton, HCTC Central; June Barclay, Geraldine Barker, Ros Gillies (Coordinator), Jill Smyth, Fiona Young, HCTC Scotland; Kay Backham (Coordinator), Judith Hogg, Dee Houlden, Mike Petty, Graham Richards, HCTC Southern & Western.

Other information sources used in the text

John Artis Ltd; Remanco; Automatic Vending Association of Britain; Brewers' Society; Janet Williams, Coin-A-Drink; Carters Vending; The Health and Safety Executive; National Restaurant Association; Staines Catering Equipment Ltd; The Ravenhead Co. Ltd.

Every effort has been made to trace all the copyright holders. If any have been inadvertently overlooked, the publishers will be pleased to make the necessary arrangement at the first opportunity.

About this book

Introduction

This book will help you work towards the NVQs/SVQs in *Serving Food and Drink:* Table/tray, Counter, Take-away (level 1), and Restaurant (level 2). All the core and optional units are covered in detail to give you the maximum choice of areas in which to develop your skills and competence.

The structure

The main part of the book is broken down into 13 sections. As you can see from the contents page, many sections cover two NVQ/SVQ units, one from each level, while others deal with a unit or units which occur at one level only.

Finding your way within sections

Headings show clearly what is covered in any *double page opening* in the book. At the top:

- on the left-hand side is the *section number and title*
- on the right-hand side is the *number and title of the NVQ/SVQ unit(s)* which the information relates to.

Range checklists

These are given at the end of each section. They will help you monitor your progress. To avoid repetition, *laid down procedures* have been excluded. These include relevant:

- legislation regarding health and safety, hygiene, licensing, consumer protection, weights and measures
- establishment procedures.

What assessment for NVQ/SVQ is about

Your NVQ/SVQ assessor will concentrate on whether or not you can demonstrate a range of skills in the service of food and drink. What is important is that you are competent in these skills, not how you have acquired them.

There is no one correct way of setting a table, for example, or pouring a drink. Where your workplace has laid down procedures designed to meet the needs of your customers, it is these which you should follow. That is why so many of the NVQ/SVQ performance criteria refer to:

- customer requirements being correctly identified
- work carried out with minimum disturbance to customers.

It will help to bear this in mind when you study the steps that are given throughout this book.

Food and drink service has been compared to a theatrical performance, with the restaurant your stage, and your customers the audience.

There will be certain procedures to follow in your workplace, and these will take into account the various laws and regulations on health, hygiene, safety, consumer protection, etc.

Your customers have certain expectations of their meal. Your employers seek to meet those expectations with an efficient, successful operation.

Your role is to meet both sets of expectations. This means becoming familiar with your workplace procedures – and a book of this sort can only seek to underline and perhaps explain those, not try and replace them.

You will not be expected to learn huge amounts of facts to gain your NVQ/SVQ. As part of your assessment, you may be asked questions about work activities which your assessor is unable to see you doing in the workplace. You will also be questioned to check that you have the necessary *underpinning knowledge*, which in food and drink service is largely concerned with the reasons behind good practice, for example:

- why a constant stock of food service items has to be maintained
- why waste must be handled and disposed of correctly
- why menus should be checked before use.

Industry examples

Throughout the book examples are given of checklists and procedures from a wide range of hotel and catering companies and organisations, and extracts from *Caterer & Hotelkeeper*, an industry magazine. These show how the details of serving food and drink vary according to customer needs and workplace practices.

Activities: ACTION boxes

These appear throughout the book to help you reinforce your understanding of the text, and to relate general procedures to the requirements of your workplace. They also act as progress checks, so that you and your assessor have a better idea of what has been covered, and what has not.

At the end of the book, in *Answers to activities,* you will find guidance to each activity, as well as discussion points and some further, related activities – the activities are numbered to provide a cross-reference point. In *Further activities*, more challenging exercises are provided, if you wish to develop your skills beyond levels 1 and 2.

To get the best value from the activities, discuss your completed work with a supervisor or manager at work, or a tutor from your college or training centre.

Glossary and Index

To make the text accessible to people working in all types of establishment, at all levels of the market, industry jargon is used as little as possible. Should you come across words you are not familiar with, turn to the *Glossary*.

The *Index* will also point you in the right direction if you can't find information where you expect it to be.

Key features

On the first page of each section you will find a statement of the units and element titles which the section relates to.

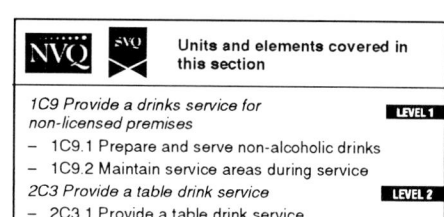

The contents guides will help you see at a glance how the information is organised in relation to the NVQ/SVQ elements.

Contents guide	Page
Preparing service areas and equipment	28
Clearing after service	30
Preparing dining areas for table service	31
Preparing for tray service	35
Range checklist	36

At the top right-hand side of every double page opening, is the *number and title of the NVQ/SVQ unit(s)* which the information on the pages relates to.

1C2 Provide a table or tray service

2C2 Provide a table service

If a double page opening is to do with a level 1 unit only, there will be nothing in the lower space. If it is to do with level 2 only, there will be nothing in the upper space.

If some of the text on a page relates to both levels, while some relates to level 2 only, this is indicated by the appropriate symbols alongside the heading.

Preparing and serving drinks   LEVELS 1 + 2

Serving alcoholic drinks   LEVEL 2

Tick off once you are confident you can meet the performance criteria for each item in the range. You should aim to cover the whole range, although your assessor only needs to observe your work in a specific number of areas.

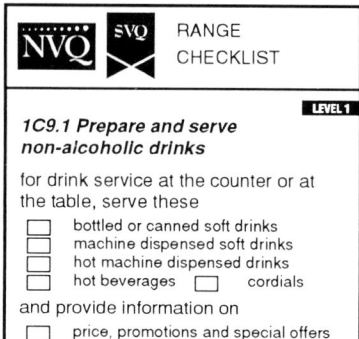

Maintaining customer care   LEVELS 1 + 2

Your job – or the job you are training for – involves much more than serving food and drink. Just as important is the way you relate to people – the people you are working with, the people you are serving – whether you know them as customers, clients, colleagues, guests, staff, students, patients or pupils.

Your skill is in helping customers enjoy themselves. And because each customer is different, with a different set of needs, you have a key role to play in deciding how best to meet those needs.

Our mission

We are dedicated to standards of excellence in every aspect of our business.

HUDSON'S
A Tradition of Excellence

Quality products and quality service combined with theatrical panache, style and the old values of respect, politeness and dignity make Hudson's the success that it is.

Our philosophy is really very simple, but making it work takes the best effort of everyone in the team. Our prime objective is to SATISFY THE CUSTOMER – because the customer is the most important single factor in our business.

Your role   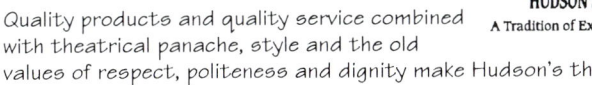 CATERING AND ALLIED

We're in the theatrical business. We put on a 'performance' whereby the food is beautifully cooked 'backstage' and attractively presented 'front of house'. Staff are pleasant and helpful and everywhere is spotlessly clean.

But, like any show, there has to be more. There has to be a touch of magic, of style and imagination. We must create an aura of well-being around our customers from the moment they step into our restaurant.

This means bringing something special to the job over and above the basic courtesies of listening to clients, advising them and giving them the benefits of our experience.

This is where you come in – the reason we are successful is because we are different. And this is because we encourage you to add your own touch of individuality to the performance.

How can you achieve this?

Through training, through being part of a dynamic team, through developing your particular skills, by taking opportunities to move into other areas or other restaurants and by recognising that it is your unique talents that make us special.

 **Units and elements covered in this section**

LEVEL 1   **LEVEL 2**

G3 Deal with customers
– G3.1 Maintain customer care
– G3.2 Deal with customer complaints
– G3.3 Deal with customer incidents

Contents guide

Customers will feel the atmosphere immediately they enter the premises. And whether it's a good atmosphere or a bad one depends very much on the mood and attitude of staff.

Colleagues should support each other. If someone is under pressure it may be possible for another to help.

Greeting customers

You will know from your own experiences as a customer, the difference made by a warm, friendly greeting from the person serving you.

Your own greeting to customers should always be polite and courteous. There are very few instances where a smile will not be appreciated.

The precise words you use to greet customers will depend on the time of day, the style and rules of your establishment. For some 'Good evening madam' (or sir) will be expected, for others 'Welcome to Jo's' will be right.

It makes customers feel very welcome when you use their name, 'Good morning, Mr Hamilton', perhaps because you remember them from previous visits, or because you have taken the trouble to check the reservations book.

If you expect to be serving at a function or event attended by Royalty, Government, Civil or Church dignitaries, find out first the correct form of addressing such people. It's one occasion when knowing the person's name is not much help (except perhaps when you tell your friends about the event afterwards).

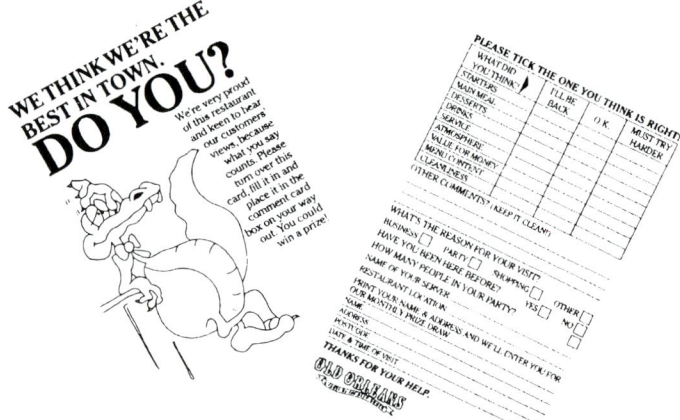

Prominently displayed on tables, or provided with the bill at the end of the meal, customer comment cards are a way of saying to customers 'We want to provide what you want, and welcome your views on how well we are doing'.

The exact words you use to greet customers are probably less important than how you say them. Try and convey warmth in your voice, with the smile on your face, with the look in your eyes.

ACTION 1

These are some of the things written about customer service in industry journals. Tick the appropriate box or boxes (i.e. if you agree and the statement applies to your workplace). Discuss the issues raised, and your response with your manager or tutor, and colleagues.

	Agree	Strongly disagree	Relevant to your workplace
Cleanliness of the restaurant and quality of the food are *the* two considerations when choosing a restaurant.	☐	☐	☐
When I come into your restaurant, make me happy. Make me feel good about spending my money.	☐	☐	☐
Treat customers as guests, the same way you would treat them in your own home.	☐	☐	☐
Get to the customers within 60 seconds of them coming into the restaurant. Once they are seated, allow a further 60 seconds at the most before serving them, even if it is only to say 'I'll be right with you'.	☐	☐	☐
Understanding why a customer is eating in the restaurant is the clue. E.g. the romantic couple in the corner are not there to be entertained by your razor-sharp wit.	☐	☐	☐
Customers cannot judge the time. If they have to wait 2 minutes, in their minds it becomes 10. Leave them for 5 minutes and they will say they have been waiting for 30.	☐	☐	☐
A happy customer will tell 3 people. An unhappy one will tell at least 20.	☐	☐	☐
You should throw your personality at the table you are serving.	☐	☐	☐
The impression conveyed to customers should be that nothing is too much trouble.	☐	☐	☐
Up to 95% of dissatisfied customers who do complain will become loyal customers if their complaints are handled well and quickly.	☐	☐	☐
Giving good customers extra large portions, and the choice cuts, is good customer care.	☐	☐	☐

Anticipating customer needs

If the shop assistant greets you in a friendly manner – you feel welcome. If the assistant also makes helpful suggestions regarding the products you want to buy – you feel you really are getting quality service.

Your customers will respond in the same positive way when you anticipate their needs. For example, by:

- pointing to the salad counter if you hear them say 'It's too hot for roast pork'

- suggesting a dish which can be prepared quickly, if they seem to be in a hurry

- finding out what food customers have ordered, before you approach them to take their drinks order

- removing the flowers from the table if they are trying to work on business papers

- explaining that you can do children's portions

- producing the bill when they are ready for it.

What affects customers' choice of where to eat

Time – how long they have available.

Money – what they are prepared to spend.

Reason for the meal – need something to eat, children are hungry, convenience, social, to relax, impulse, business, celebration, desire to impress.

Location/distance prepared to travel – this will depend on availability of transport, car parking and time.

Food preference – type of food they wish to eat (including vegetarian, ethnic, something they can't get at home).

Facilities of restaurant – many people prefer restaurants where they do not have to sit too close to other customers.

Atmosphere – quiet dinner, or a lively cabaret show.

Time of day – are the preferred restaurants open, what sort of meals/food are available at the particular time.

Familiarity or personal recommendation – if a customer has a favourite restaurant or restaurant chain, then there may be no reason to consider any other option. *The strength of any restaurant business lies in its reputation – you are only as good as the last meal you served.*

ACTION   2

A recent survey of adults who eat out in table service restaurants showed that crumbing the table down, and refilling glasses frequently were regarded as less important than the knowledge and helpfulness of the service staff.

Discuss with your colleagues how the findings of The Butter Council's survey match up with what you know about your customers. For example, do your customers prefer a formal approach, or to be treated like a friend? Ask your manager if you can do a small survey of your own.

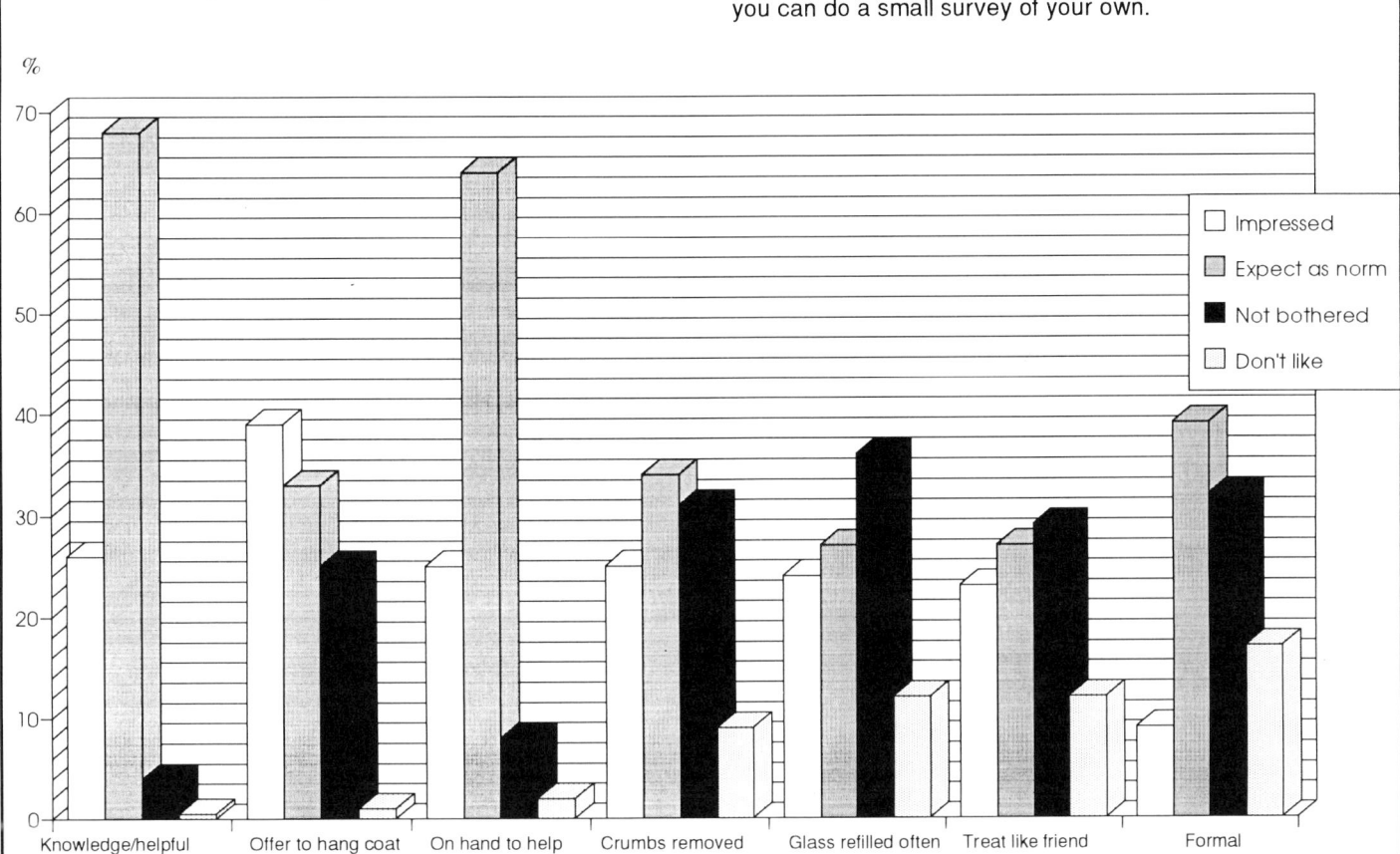

Answering customer enquiries

Are you irritated by the response 'Don't know' when you ask a shop assistant where else you can find a product which has sold out? Are you impressed when the assistant goes to special lengths to find out how you can get spare parts for a product you bought at the shop years ago?

Your customers will react in a similar way when you respond to their enquiries:

- whether it be about the menu – which they will expect you to know about

- or if it's worth seeing the film which is on at the local cinema.

But this doesn't mean customers expect you to double as a film critic, or to know everything about everything. What customers do appreciate is when you:

- show an interest and pride in your job, in the place you work for, and in the locality where you work

- make an effort to help and show initiative

- can point customers in the right direction if they don't have the information themselves.

Customers appreciate staff who make an effort to help.

Answering the telephone

A ringing telephone can be frightening – especially if it is not your normal duty to answer it, and there is no one else available. The phone can also be intrusive – when it starts ringing and you are busy doing something else.

Nevertheless how you answer the telephone will make a considerable impression on the caller. You may win a new customer. You may lose an existing customer.

1 Pick up the receiver promptly.
2 Say good morning/afternoon/evening, followed by the name of the establishment, then 'May I help you?' (It may be workplace policy also to state your name.)
3 Write down the name of the caller and the main points of the conversation. Repeat these to make sure you have understood correctly.
4 At the end, thank the caller – by name if possible.
5 Pass on any information you need to without delay.
6 If the caller has a query which you cannot answer yourself, ask the person to hold while you find out the necessary information, or inform him or her that you will transfer the call to (name the person) who can help.
7 If the call is for someone else, pass it on, telling the caller what you are doing. If the person required is not available, offer to take a message. Then make sure the written message reaches the relevant person.
8 Never leave the caller waiting any longer than is absolutely necessary and keep the person informed at all times about the steps you are taking to help. Remember the caller cannot see what is going on and could soon become anxious or angry.
9 When taking a message, be sure to write down: name of caller, name of person to receive the message, day and time of call, the message itself, telephone number of the caller if relevant, and your own name, as the person who took the call.

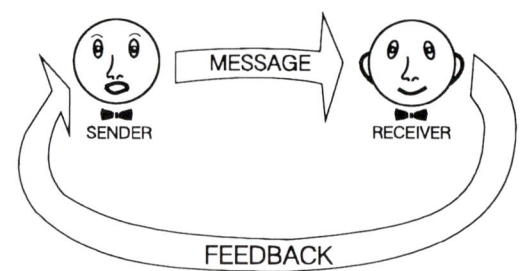

Successful communication

Be specific and to the point – don't dance all round the subject, so the receiver is left wondering exactly what the point of the conversation is.

Use commonly understood words – your customers don't want to know about your grasp of industry jargon.

Time what you are going to say – do not give information about the dessert course before customers have eaten their main course.

Pay attention to what is being said in reply – if a customer says he or she doesn't want wine because of driving later, remember this and suggest non-alcoholic drinks where appropriate, e.g. at the end of a formal dinner, for the toasts.

Ask the person to repeat what has been said – if you are unclear about any detail. Alternatively, repeat what has been said yourself, so the other person can confirm or correct the details.

Speak clearly – restaurants are often noisy. Pay attention to the words you use and the way you pronounce and articulate them. Adjust the tone, speed, pitch and volume of your voice to suit the circumstances.

Your selling role

Serving food and drink is about satisfying customers' needs and expectations. Whatever type of establishment you work in, selling is part of this process, although your role may be:

- at a very general level – if you are serving behind a buffet, for which customers have paid a fixed price, the emphasis will be on promoting the establishment as a whole by giving good service

- a naturally helpful response to an unspecific customer request – 'Coffee please', when several varieties are available: 'Would you like espresso, cappuccino or filter coffee?'

- part of the service routine – 'Burger please', when the usual accompaniment is fries: 'Would you like fries with your burger?'

- to mention specific dishes – 'Good morning, Mrs MacNutt, here is the menu. The soup of the day is carrot with orange and a hint of coriander – quite delicious.'

One of the skills of selling is to know when not to. With experience, you will find it easier to recognise the customer who wants a specific product or service, or who cannot easily afford to spend more. Both will resent encouragement to pay for something else.

Selling through service

Dealing with food in a public house is not so much a question of serving food as selling products to people.

This needs a positive approach and is a skill to be acquired.

You are a sales person. You need a:
- thorough knowledge of the menu
- background to new or unusual specials
- pleasant attitude as this creates a pleasant attitude in the house
- lively interest in what customers want.

Make the first approach to the customer, don't wait to be asked.

The different ways in which you can help sell your establishment's services and products can be thought of as 8 groups. To each of the examples given below, add a second which relates more closely to your own workplace.

 OBSERVING ... parents with a restless child: 'Shall I bring a small plate of chips while you decide what to order?'

 LISTENING ... to the customer you hear say 'I have been so impressed by the Chilean wines': 'We have two on our list, Mrs ...'

 THINKING ... by saying to the customer who has asked if the vegetables are organic: 'We also have organic wines'

 KNOWING ... what your establishment offers – to a group on an office outing: 'Would you like details of our party specials?'

 DESCRIBING ... in an attractive way dishes likely to interest the customer : 'The potato spinach pie is made with fresh spinach and new potatoes, thinly sliced. It also has...'

 SUGGESTING ...a range of dishes or drinks when a customer is not specific: 'You can have a mixed or green salad, or there are some speciality salads such as...'

 SUGGESTING ALTERNATIVES ... to the customer who asks for a brandy: 'We have a range of cognacs and Armagnacs'

 SUGGESTING MORE EXPENSIVE ITEMS... to the customer who asks for water: 'We have a range of mineral waters, as well as freshly squeezed fruit juices with lemonade'

Some hospitality companies use quite sophisticated selling routines. For example, asking customers after their meal: 'Would you like a brandy or liqueur with your coffee?' If the reply is 'No, I don't think so', continuing: 'We also have excellent vintage ports, or Madeira, and some unusual malt whiskies.' This makes it much harder for the customer to say 'No', than the question 'Would you like a drink with your coffee?'

Customers with special needs

All your customers are special. But those with mobility and/or communication difficulties have special needs. So do those eating on their own, older people, the very young and children.

Helping wheelchair users

1 If possible, encourage the customer to sit at a table which has plenty of space around it. A wheelchair user could feel uncomfortable if other customers are clearly inconvenienced by his or her presence.

2 Ensure that menus and other information are within easy reach of a wheelchair user.

Don't:

• make decisions on behalf of a wheelchair user unless he/she asks. A wheelchair is merely a form of transport

• move the wheelchair without first consulting the occupant

• discuss the needs or requirements of the wheelchair user with a third party – always direct any questions or comments directly to the wheelchair user.

Helping people who are blind or partially sighted

1 Talk naturally to the customer. Do not conduct the conversation through a third party unless this is obviously preferred.

2 Describe the layout of the restaurant/dining room. Knowing why particular sounds or smells are coming from different parts of the room will help the customer to relax and enjoy the meal.

3 Offer to go through the menu. But don't confuse the person with too many details at once, and do give the price for each item.

4 Touch is the way that blind people see and that is the key to communication. If you just call out: 'Can I help you?' the blind person doesn't know who is being spoken to.

On dining alone

CATERER *& Hotelkeeper*

A friend likes to eat out, but now he often dines alone having recently lost his wife. He describes the typical treatment:

Maître d' (looking pointedly over friend's shoulder): 'Somebody joining you, sir?'

Friend: 'No.'

Maître d': 'You're on your own then, sir?'

Friend: 'Yes.'

Maître d': 'So that's just a table for one then, is it?'

Friend: 'Yes.'

Maître d': 'All right.' (More loudly) 'A table for one.'

My friend is then usually guided to a table which is either surrounded on all sides by large parties of riotous guests or buried deep in the corners of the room where he can too easily be forgotten. As the table is usually set for two, a long delay will then ensue as the waiting staff assume, wrongly, that he is waiting for a companion to arrive.

Then the conversation begins all over again.

Waiter: 'Shall I wait until your friend arrives before giving you the menu?'

Friend: 'No, I'm on my own.'

Waiter: 'On your own?'

Friend: (wearily) 'Yes.'

Waiter: 'So that's just a table for one is it?'

Clare Walker, 3 September 1992

People with disabilities also have abilities. Never make assumptions, e.g. that because a person has limited mobility, he or she is dependent and must be treated as a small child.

Touch to ask the order, then touch again to hand the drink or food over. Having handled a glass the blind person will remember where it is on the table.

5 Tell the chefs that you are serving a customer who cannot see the food. If it is a set menu, ask if the fish or meat can be boned, another vegetable offered in place of peas, and the lettuce leaves chopped.

6 Once you have put the plate down in front of the guest, touch to indicate the guest is being spoken to, and then describe what is on the plate using the hands of a clock: e.g. meat at 12 o'clock, potatoes at 3 o'clock, vegetables at 6 o'clock.

7 Offer to assist, but don't feel snubbed if your offer is rejected.

8 When you present the bill, tell the customer the amount, and ask if you can itemise the different charges. When you return with the change, identify the value of each note so the blind person can fold it in a particular way.

Don't:

• grab your customer and take him or her to the table. Ask or wait for the person to tell you how he/she would like to be guided

• fill cups or glasses to the brim. If you are serving a slice of gâteau, put it in a bowl rather than a flat plate, and provide a spoon and fork to eat it with

• play with or pet guide dogs in the restaurant.

Helping people who are deaf or hard of hearing

1 Speak slowly, clearly and in plain language. Look directly at the customer when you are talking, and keep hands away from your mouth. Avoid standing with your back to a window or bright light which makes it difficult for the person to see your face. Even if the person cannot lip read, seeing the expression on your face as you talk will help understanding.

2 Seat the customer away from loud noises (these can be extremely uncomfortable for people who are deaf or hard of hearing).

Helping people with speech difficulties

1 Avoid correcting the person or trying to take over what the person is saying. When necessary, ask short questions that can be quickly answered or only require a nod of the head or other gesture.

2 Do not pretend to understand something that you don't. If necessary, repeat what you do understand, checking from the person's reactions whether or not you are right.

With thanks to Holiday Care Services and Maundy Todd; Peter and Kate Osborne; Caterer & Hotelkeeper, and Andy Moran, general manager, Belmont Hotel, Llandudno, Giuseppe Belvedere, restaurant manager, Liverpool Moat House.

Looking after the special needs of these children includes providing guidance on each child's dietary requirements to the food serving staff (known as carers). For example: 'Juke Brown: no milk or rice puddings. Can have custard and yogurt. Restrict portions and no second helpings'.

ACTION 4

The photographs show three groups of customers with special needs. Alongside each, note one or two ways in which serving staff (and you if appropriate) could help such customers.

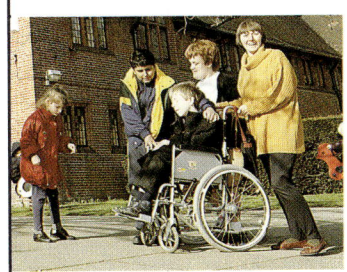

Dealing with complaints
LEVELS 1 + 2

How often do you put up with poor standards in silence, rather than cause a fuss by complaining? You probably do this because you fear the complaint will be badly received, or it is very difficult to get someone to listen to the problem and take action.

Certainly, it can be unpleasant to be at the receiving end of a complaint. The experience can be a very draining one which you remember for a long time.

Try not to take complaints as criticism of you personally. Instead, view them as useful feedback which will help improve standards for all customers.

Dealing well with a complaint will almost certainly win a loyal customer.

Dealing with complaints in a typical fast food or take-away restaurant

Complaints you can usually deal with (depending on company policy) include:

Incorrect order – customer has not left premises
Apologise. Put aside the product which is not required and replace with the correct one. Your supervisor may have to log the wasted item.

Short delay in completing order Apologise. Advise the customer of the waiting time: 'The French fries will be ready in 2 minutes'.

Longer delay in completing order Apologise. Advise the customer of the waiting time and offer an alternative: 'The chicken nuggets will be 10 minutes. Would you prefer a chicken and bacon burger?'

If the customer accepts the alternative, serve the order in the usual way. If the customer prefers to wait, offer a free drink (if this is company policy).

Always ask your manager to deal with customers who complain about:

- wrong change
- something found in the food which shouldn't be there
- any other problem relating to the quality of the food
- incorrect take-away orders not discovered until the customer has returned home.

ACTION 5

Form a group with your colleagues and discuss 3 or 4 of the complaints which appear on both sides of *Caterer & Hotelkeeper's* Top 10. What could be done to improve the situation/avoid the problem? What steps in the various complaints procedures described opposite would have been particularly relevant/helpful in each instance?

Repeat the exercise at intervals of a week or so, until you have discussed each complaint. On each occasion review the progress you have made in improving your understanding of customers' needs.

Top 10

CATERER *& Hotelkeeper*

Complaints from customers about waiting staff	Complaints from waiting staff about their customers
Being asked by the waiter who has ordered what, after the order is taken.	Customers who think that because waiters serve, they must be servile.
Poor assistance in wine selection and service. Glasses not topped up regularly enough.	Customers flicking fingers to get the attention of waiters or waitresses.
No order of service. No recognition of ladies and host.	Customers who reserve a table and don't turn up.
Being interrupted by waiting staff while guests are talking.	Customers who reserve a table for 6 and arrive with 4 or 8.
Customers not being attended to as soon as they walk through the door.	Ladies who place their orders through their partners while ignoring the waiter.
Unfriendly staff or waiters not helpful with minor customer requests.	Customers who eat everything on their plates and complain about the food.
Bread not fresh/warm.	Customers who drink two-thirds of the wine which they have tasted and approved, then complain of it being corked.
Food not cooked to specification.	
Poor quality and temperature of tea/coffee.	Customers who smoke with little regard for fellow diners.
Plates cleared before all guests have finished eating.	Customers who fail to observe dress code.
	Customers who try to intimidate staff by saying: 'Do you know who I am?'

✍ *Source: Restaurant Services Guild*

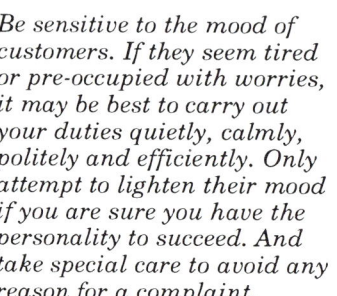

Be sensitive to the mood of customers. If they seem tired or pre-occupied with worries, it may be best to carry out your duties quietly, calmly, politely and efficiently. Only attempt to lighten their mood if you are sure you have the personality to succeed. And take special care to avoid any reason for a complaint.

G3 Deal with customers

General procedure for dealing with complaints

1 Listen to the complaint until the customer has finished speaking. Do not interrupt, even when you know you will be asking the manager to handle the situation.

2 Apologise but do not admit that you or the establishment is to blame.

3 Do not make excuses or blame anyone else.

4 Never argue or disagree. Customers are always right, even when you think they are wrong.

5 Keep calm and remain polite.

6 If appropriate, and it is the procedure in your workplace, consider offering another serving of the same dish (you need to be confident of success the next time), or an alternative (when the customer may need to consult the menu):

– remove the dish from the table

– write out a special check for the new order

– lay a fresh place setting

– collect and serve the new dish as soon as possible

– apologise for the inconvenience

– enquire if the new dish is satisfactory.

7 Never offer something you cannot provide – consider what would happen if the customer accepts your suggestion of a complimentary bottle of wine, and you then discover this is against company policy, and the dispense bar refuses to give you one.

8 Thank the customer for bringing the matter to your attention – said with sincerity, this will show the customer that you are genuine in your efforts to put things right.

9 Report the complaint to your supervisor or complete a workplace complaints form, as appropriate.

Look upon an awkward customer as a challenge. We all have to deal with them from time to time and a lot of awkwardness arises from misunderstanding. *Hudson's*

Remember that a person we regard as 'difficult' is often a person with a collection of ideas that do not agree with our own. *Ritzy*

Complaints, whatever their nature, should be referred to the manager. Delay can only cause confusion and very often the wrong interpretation may be put on a situation if it is not dealt with immediately.

HUDSON'S
A Tradition of Excellence

All complaints received in the restaurant have to be recorded on the investigation forms. This will enable us to produce some kind of pattern.

Chase Restaurants Limited

Within reason, complaints should always be accommodated as in most cases it will create goodwill.

Obnoxious customers will have to be treated with even more care and tact.

Any little remarks from the customers to a chef de rang or commis have to be reported to the manager immediately.

A complaint is an opportunity to turn customer dissatisfaction into satisfaction.

Ritzy

When dealing with a complaint, we are looking to control the conversation with the customer and to empathise, not sympathise. By presenting you with a complaint, a customer wants you to know they are upset, what has upset them, and what is to be done. Given this, we should always:

* pay attention
* make no assumptions
* listen for free information
* acknowledge, respond and inform
* never defend, make excuses or ignore the customer's point of view.

Complaints procedure – Rank Organisation

Standard

Always listen and respond positively.

All complaints must be resolved to the customer's satisfaction.

All complaints should be reported to a member of management.

Benefit

You have transformed dissatisfaction into satisfaction. A customer will remember this and tell others.

Complaints create a hostile atmosphere. When they are resolved, a fun and friendly atmosphere is resumed.

Guide

1 Give the person your full attention. If necessary invite them to a quieter location.

2 Ask them to tell you what the problem is – use a warm and encouraging tone.

3 Listen carefully to what they say.

4 Maintain eye contact and positive body language.

5 Take action to resolve the complaint and inform the customer what you are going to do.

6 If you are unable to satisfy the customer, contact a member of management.

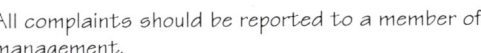

Dealing with incidents

After unexpected things have occurred at work involving you and your customers, do you say to yourself 'If only I had known what to do or say?' This is because there is usually:

- no time to think how you are going to deal with the incident
- no one at hand to help, nor the opportunity to consult books or notes from training sessions.

General procedure

If you have encountered a similar event before, you will be able to use that experience.

1 Keep calm.

2 Establish what has happened.

3 Decide the priorities.

4 Reassure the customer.

5 Know the limits of your authority.

6 Refer matters which fall outside your authority immediately to the relevant person.

7 Report the incident to your manager.

ACTION 6

Because much depends on your personality and perceptions, the way you handle situations may differ from how your colleagues tackle similar situations.

Decide what you would do if some customers in your restaurant started behaving like these two – Bette Midler and Lily Tomlin in *Big Business* (1988). Then ask some of your colleagues and friends what they would do.

ACTION 7

Get together with a number of your colleagues and discuss how you would deal with each of these situations (adapted from *Caterer & Hotelkeeper*).

1 You are on room service duty. One of the hotel guests, a Chinese businessman, phones asking for more tea. When you deliver the tea you discover the guest had been making tea with the pot pourri for the past two days.

2 A large party of customers have enjoyed their dinner, but are cutting it fine to get to the theatre on time. It is raining which means taxis will be hard to find.

Anticipating this, you have the bill ready. But when you present it, one of the group says 'Oh, we must have separate bills. Some of us can claim the expense from our business.' No mention had been made before of separate bills, and you hadn't thought to ask when you took the order.

3 A few days ago I stayed in a 'business-class' hotel. I had with me my three young children.

At breakfast my youngest child, who is 4 years old, complained of a stomach ache and lay down on the floor. As I started to rise to investigate a waitress arrived and said to the child 'If you don't get up off the floor we'll need to take a stick to your bottom.'

Seconds later the child vomited. The waitress departed and I managed to catch further 'deposits' in a napkin. I waited expectantly for the waitress to return with a cloth, but in vain. A minute or so later I saw her taking a breakfast order for another table.

In response to my request for help, she said she could not get her hands dirty while she was serving food.

Letter from William Smart of West Wickham, 19 November 1992

NVQ SVQ RANGE CHECKLIST

LEVEL 1	LEVEL 2

G3.1 Maintain customer care

these groups of customers

☐ adults   ☐ children
☐ those with mobility difficulties
☐ those with communication difficulties

G3.2 Deal with customer complaints

these types of complaints

☐ those which can be resolved within individual's authority
☐ those which cannot be resolved within individual's authority

G3.3 Deal with customer incidents

irregular or unplanned occurrences involving customers to include

☐ lost child
☐ spillages
☐ breakages
☐ lost property

Introduction

You and your colleagues have a responsibility under the law not to endanger your own health and safety, or that of other people who may be affected by the way you work. Customers, contractors, and anyone else with reason to be on the premises, are protected under the law.

Maintaining a safe environment

LEVELS 1 + 2

In spite of all the laws, regulations and effort that go into making workplaces safe, accidents continue to occur. There are many reasons, and you will almost certainly be aware of times when you have:

- been very busy and cut corners
- forgotten to mention to someone that some plates or a dish is very hot, for example
- assumed that because something has been left safe on all the previous occasions you have checked, there is no need to bother this time
- been distracted or called away in the middle of a task, and not remembered until much later that you have left a heating appliance on, or the floor wet
- thought you could find out for yourself how to clean a piece of equipment, and not asked or checked instructions
- been over-tired or careless
- carried sharp implements incorrectly.

Contents guide

Lives could depend on you knowing what to do in the event of an accident, fire or security problem.

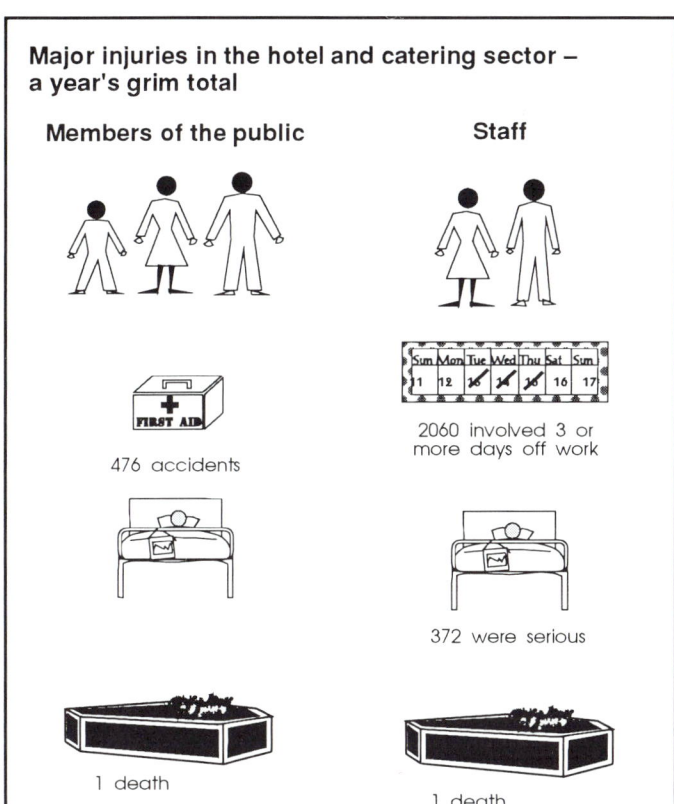

Major injuries in the hotel and catering sector – a year's grim total

Members of the public   **Staff**

476 accidents

2060 involved 3 or more days off work

372 were serious

1 death   1 death

Source: Health and Safety Executive 1991/92 report. The HSE estimate that only 17% of non-fatal injuries in the hotel and catering sector are reported.

 **Units and elements covered in this section**

LEVEL 1   **LEVEL 2**

G1 Maintain a safe and secure working environment
- G1.1 Carry out procedures in the event of a fire
- G1.2 Carry out procedures on discovery of a suspicious item or package
- G1.3 Carry out procedures in the event of an accident
- G1.4 Maintain a safe environment for customers, staff and visitors
- G1.5 Maintain a secure environment for customers, staff and visitors

Accident procedures

`LEVELS 1 + 2`

Your priority should be to get urgent help from a trained first aider. While help is coming, remain calm, and try to keep the casualty warm.

Do not move the casualty unless absolutely necessary. If the accident has been caused by an electric shock, switch off the current at the plug or mains before touching the casualty.

A record must be kept of all accidents which occur in the workplace. If you are involved in, or witness an accident, you will be asked to give certain information by your supervisor or manager. So that you can give useful answers, you might find it helpful to make some notes as soon as possible after the accident, e.g.:

- time of the accident
- where it occurred
- the sequence of events.

Fire procedures

`LEVELS 1 + 2`

You will receive regular training on what to do in the event of a fire in your premises. You may also have specific duties to carry out, e.g. helping to evacuate customers.

Personal safety and safe evacuation of the building are always the main priorities. Because of the dangers, fighting the fire yourself is not generally encouraged.

In general:

1 Remain calm.
2 Walk, don't run.
3 Leave the building by the nearest safe route. Do not use the lift. Do not stop to collect personal belongings.
4 Report to the assembly point outside.
5 Do not re-enter the building until you are told that it is safe to do so by the person in charge.

You can contribute to fire safety by: **Birmingham** COLLEGE OF FOOD TOURISM CREATIVE STUDIES

- observing no-smoking rules
- thoughtfully disposing of matches, cigarette ends, etc.
- keeping flammable materials away from heat sources
- never obstructing fire exits or escape routes
- never misusing fire extinguishers
- never wedging open fire doors
- following fire procedures

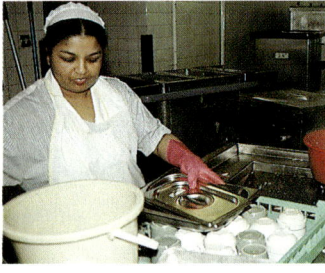

Use the protective clothing that is provided. Be particularly careful when carrying things. Exposure to harmful substances and trips and falls account for many of the accidents which occur.

Calling the emergency services

One day it might be up to you to call the emergency services. Be prepared.

1 Use the nearest telephone.
2 Dial 999. No money is required.
3 Answer the operator's questions clearly:
 – give the number of the telephone you are using so that you can be called back if necessary
 – state which service you want: ambulance, fire brigade or police
 – state the location, nature of the incident, number of people injured and extent of their injuries, if known.
4 Remain on the phone until the operator rings off – to be sure that you have given sufficient information.

If you have to go through an area filled with smoke

- keep low or crawl – the smoke will be less dense
- keep calm. Cover your mouth and nose with a towel. Breathe shallowly through the nose to reduce the risk of taking gulps of smoke
- keep to the walls so you know you are moving in a straight direction
- feel your way using the back (not palm) of your hand – you will be less likely to get cut by anything sharp.

If you discover a fire first

- raise the alarm by operating the nearest fire alarm
- call for help using the procedure laid down.

If this will not put yourself or anyone else in danger

- make sure that colleagues and customers in your work area know there is a fire, and help them to escape
- switch off all electrical and gas appliances
- close all windows and the doors which will not be used during the evacuation
- attack the fire with the equipment provided.

For fires involving	Use
wood, paper, fabrics	water extinguisher, fire hose
electrical equipment	CO_2 extinguisher (black)
oil, polishes, paint	dry powder extinguisher (blue) or foam extinguisher (cream)
flaming pan/guéridon dish	fire blanket

Maintaining a secure environment

LEVELS 1 + 2

If you work in a city centre or airport location, or in the building of a bank or computer firm, for example, there will be strict security measures in place to protect staff and customers. Become familiar with these so that you know and follow procedures covering such matters as:

- wearing of identity badges
- searching of bags when you enter/leave the building
- reporting of suspicious persons
- reporting of suspicious packages
- what to do in the event of a security alert.

General procedure

1 Put equipment and materials in the correct place after use. Storage areas (including lockers for any personal valuables) must always be kept locked.

2 If you have to use an external fire exit door, e.g. to take the rubbish out, make sure the door is properly shut when you return to the building.

3 If you are on closing duties, check that windows and doors are securely shut. Check that everyone has left the premises – thieves sometimes hide in the toilets, emerging when everyone else has gone to help themselves and then break out.

4 Take special care of keys. They should never be left unattended, nor lent to anyone else without the proper procedure being followed.

5 Check that everything is all right during the meal and act immediately on any complaints – this reduces the opportunity a customer may seek for refusing to pay because of unsatisfactory food or service.

6 Check credit cards and cheque payments carefully. Check large denomination notes for forgeries. (See section 4.)

7 Watch that customers do not depart before paying the bill – toilet areas near the restaurant entrance present an opportunity for slipping out unchallenged.

8 Always alert a manager to any suspicious behaviour.

Lost property

When coats, umbrellas, etc. (but not suspicious items or packages – see right hand column) are left behind, hand them promptly to a manager. Say where you found the item, and any other helpful information: owner's name, description, table sat at, arrival/departure time, etc.

Before returning lost property, politely ask for a description of the item. If you feel any doubt about its ownership, or the value is substantial, brief your manager so that he or she can take over.

Customers have the right to security and privacy. In the case of royalty, politicians, dignitaries and other VIP hotel guests (left) and hospital patients (right), special security measures may include the use of a false name or pseudonym. Staff are strictly forbidden from using the real name of the person, and are not allowed to discuss their duties outside work in case information falls into dishonest hands.

Dealing with suspicious items or packages

LEVELS 1 + 2

Any item or package left unattended must be treated with caution. People who leave bombs and similar devices go to great trouble to make sure that the package does not look suspicious. If you are caught unawares you will put your life and the lives of everyone in the vicinity in danger.

Alert your manager or the security officer immediately. Do not touch or attempt to move the object.

Restaurant staff security

FORTE HOTELS

1 On discovering a bag/baggage which has no obvious owner, try and establish its ownership: 'Is that your bag, sir?' and ensure that the item is moved closer to the person. If there is no obvious owner, report it immediately to your supervisor or manager.

2 In the event of a bomb threat, search your area of responsibility.

3 Be aware of any procedures in your establishment regarding bomb threats and evacuation.

 *Alan Gomm, Head of Security*

G1 Maintain a safe and secure working environment

ACTION 8

Safety boxes throughout the book highlight dangers associated with particular tasks or procedures. Here are some more general safety measures. Work through the list honestly and carefully, using these (or similar) symbols for those:

☑ you are very careful about all the time

★ you need to pay more attention to

☒ which do not apply to you.

How to prevent accidents

- ☐ Don't come to work if you are unwell. You'll only become accident prone and spread germs.
- ☐ Wear the correct uniform or work clothing and sensible shoes.
- ☐ Use the proper routes as they are intended, e.g. the *In* or *Out* door. Open and shut doors carefully.
- ☐ Don't run. If carrying something hot or heavy, warn people as you approach them.
- ☐ Look after floor areas. Pick up items and clear up spillages quickly.
- ☐ Use the right equipment, safely and correctly, for the task.
- ☐ Cups and containers for serving food should never be used to store or hold other substances, e.g. disinfectants.

How to prevent falls

- ☐ Watch out for hazards such as customers' bags and feet.
- ☐ Don't store items where they can be tripped over or might fall.
- ☐ Remove used plates to the wash-up area as soon as possible. Never let dirty items pile up on tables and behind counters.
- ☐ Do not allow cables for electrical equipment to trail across floors. If you are using a vacuum cleaner, the area you are working in should be closed off to the public.
- ☐ Carry things in a way that doesn't obstruct your view.
- ☐ Load trays carefully so that items will not fall off.
- ☐ Get help to carry heavy items.

How to prevent burns and scalds

- ☐ Treat hotplates and gas or spirit lamps carefully. Never carry when lit.
- ☐ Take care when using matches, and with lighted candles on tables and buffet displays.
- ☐ Use your service cloth to hold hot plates.
- ☐ Warn customers if plates are very hot.

How to prevent cuts

- ☐ Take special care when handling or putting down anything with a sharp surface, or which might break.
- ☐ Clear up broken glass or china at once – wrap in newspaper or other strong paper before placing in the bin.
- ☐ Glasses: carry by the handle, stem or base, or on a tray.
- ☐ Watch out for broken glass when sorting bottles.
- ☐ Remove from service any chipped or cracked items.
- ☐ Store knives with the blades facing in the same direction.

How to prevent electric shocks

- ☐ Ensure hands are dry when using electrical equipment.
- ☐ Switch off appliances after use. Unplug before cleaning.
- ☐ Do not overload power points. Never pull on plugs or leads.
- ☐ Never use equipment with frayed wires. Do not attempt repairs.

How to prevent fires

- ☐ Ensure ashtrays are available in smoking areas.
- ☐ Clear ashtrays regularly, emptying the contents into a metal bin (ideally with a hinged lid), never a container with paper or other waste which might burn.
- ☐ Watch out for cigarette ends discarded on floors and furniture, behind curtains and under bench seats. Carpets and upholstery can smoulder for a long time before bursting into flame.
- ☐ Don't let rubbish accumulate.
- ☐ Do not overload power points.
- ☐ Take special care when using spirit or gas appliances.
- ☐ Switch off equipment when not in use. Remove plugs from sockets.

 **RANGE CHECKLIST**

LEVEL 1		LEVEL 2

G1.1 Carry out procedures in the event of a fire
☐ all types of fire ☐

G1.2 Carry out procedures on discovery of a suspicious item or package
☐ all bags, packages & parcels left unattended without reason ☐

G1.3 Carry out procedures in the event of an accident
☐ all accidents involving injury to customers, staff and visitors ☐

G1.4 Maintain a safe environment for customers, staff and visitors
☐ items, areas and incidents which threaten the safety of customers, staff and visitors ☐

G1.5 Maintain a secure environment in...
☐ work areas/staff facilities ☐
☐ storerooms and cellars ☐
☐ store cupboards and cabinets ☐
☐ fridges and freezers ☐
☐ private facilities for customers ☐
☐ public areas ☐

and with regard to
☐ lost property ☐

Watch out for hazards such as customers' bags and feet.

Hygiene in serving

Introduction

Food not hygienically prepared and served is:

harmful to health – food poisoning causes discomfort and illness, and, in serious cases, death

disastrous for business – even the best established reputation can be wiped out by the publicity resulting from a case of food poisoning, or a bad report by the Environmental Health Officer (EHO).

Under the Food Safety Act 1990, a problem in your workplace could lead to:

- the premises being closed
- the proprietor or manager being banned from operating another food business
- unlimited fines and two years' imprisonment.

Workplace procedures

Legal requirements are one influence on how you set about doing a task. Customers' needs are another. Workplace procedures bring both these together.

Your own procedures will place considerable importance on hygiene, like the examples reproduced in this section. There are hygiene boxes at relevant points throughout the book. The following points summarise good practice:

1 Keep food at the correct temperature.

2 Keep food covered as much as possible.

3 Use the proper serving equipment not your hands to handle food.

4 Do not order food before it is needed, or too much at one time so that it has to stand around for a long time.

5 Use hot plates to keep hot food hot. Never reheat food which has become cold.

6 Keep raw and cooked food separate.

7 Don't use the same equipment for preparing cooked food and raw food.

8 Keep work surfaces, table tops and floor areas clean and dry at all times.

9 Keep cleaning equipment clean. Use specific cloths for specific cleaning purposes, e.g. red cloths for wiping food surfaces, blue for general dusting.

 **Units and elements covered in this section**

LEVEL 1   **LEVEL 2**

G2 Maintain a professional and hygienic appearance
  – G2.1 Maintain a professional and hygienic appearance

Contents guide

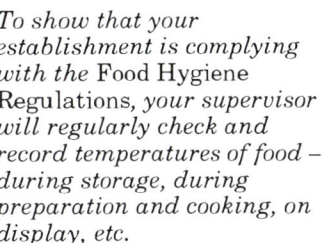

To show that your establishment is complying with the Food Hygiene Regulations, *your supervisor will regularly check and record temperatures of food – during storage, during preparation and cooking, on display, etc.*

At many catering operations a sample is taken daily of each dish, dated and kept for 3 to 5 days in a refrigerator. If there is a suspected case of food poisoning, the sample can be sent away for analysis.

Time

The time delay between the end of preparation and service must be kept to a minimum.

Do not overload counter display units. Aim to sell all items on display within 30 minutes from the time they are put on display.

Temperature

Keep hot food above 63°C.

The ideal temperature for cold display units is 5°C.

Cold food should be kept under refrigeration before going on display.

Service counters and hot plates should be switched on sufficiently early to reach the correct temperature before food is placed in them.

Do not add superfluous decoration which might restrict airflow and impede the efficiency of the display chiller.

Avoiding contamination

Food on display must be adequately protected from the risk of contamination by customers and staff. Smoking must not be allowed in food service areas.

Maintaining a professional and hygienic appearance

LEVELS 1 + 2

How you look will largely influence customers' perception of the hygiene standards of the establishment as a whole. The care taken over your appearance will influence customers' enjoyment of the food, drink, decor, atmosphere – indeed their whole meal experience.

Personal hygiene

1 Keep yourself clean and fresh. The body secretes moisture constantly through sweat glands located all over it. You will perspire more working under pressure in a hot environment. Sweat itself is virtually odourless and normally evaporates quickly. The smell comes from bacteria which live on the perspiration, especially in areas such as the underarms where it cannot evaporate freely. A daily bath or shower is the best protection.

2 Keep yourself healthy. A clear skin and complexion depend largely on adequate sleep, exercise and a balanced diet. You will enjoy your work more, and do a better job, if you are not overtired.

3 Pay special attention to your hands. You depend on them for most tasks. The health of the people eating the food you have served depends on how clean you keep your hands. Your fingernails should be clean, trimmed and free of varnish.

4 In food service and preparation areas, long flowing hair is not acceptable. It might get trapped in machinery and pieces of hair are likely to fall into food. You will find that your hair (and this applies to beards and moustaches as well) absorbs smoke and food smells. Daily washing will keep it clean and in healthy condition.

 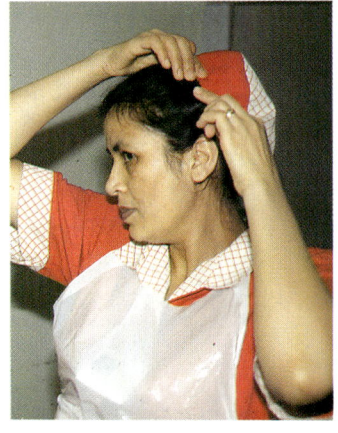

Hairstyles should be neat and away from the face. Long hair should be tied back.

In some workplaces, a head covering forms part of the uniform.

Appearance and personal hygiene checklist

1 Bathe at least once a day and use a good deodorant.

2 Never wear strong perfume or aftershave.

3 Keep hair and uniform tidy at all times. Tie back long hair.

4 Report and cover any cuts or abrasions.

5 Wash hands frequently, before coming on duty and especially after using the toilet or smoking.

6 Keep nails short and free of varnish.

7 Keep make-up to a minimum.

8 Always demonstrate a high standard of personal hygiene, i.e. being clean shaven.

9 Do not display unpleasant personal habits, i.e. chewing gum.

Uniform and hygiene

1 Your first impression stays with the customer. So take pride in your appearance.

2 Your standards reflect the company's – and our standards are very high.

3 You will be issued with a uniform and it is your responsibility to ensure that you have a uniform ready for every shift. You will wash those items that can be washed and those that need dry cleaning will be looked after by Housekeeping.

4 You will be expected to provide your own footwear and maintain it in a suitable condition.

For men
- hair must be clean, trimmed to a length not longer than the bottom of a shirt collar
- moustache or beard must be groomed and trimmed neatly
- aftershave must be applied lightly

For women
- hair must be clean and arranged away from your face
- make-up should be conservative
- perfume should be used sparingly

The nose, mouth and ears

Up to 40% of adults carry staphylococci in the:

nose – coughs and sneezes can carry droplet infection for a considerable distance, and persons with bad colds should not handle open food. Disposable single-use paper tissues are preferable to handkerchiefs. Picking or scratching the nose is not acceptable.

and mouth – food handlers should not eat sweets, chew gum, taste food with the fingers or an unwashed spoon or blow into glasses to polish them. Apart from being aesthetically unacceptable, spitting can obviously result in food contamination, and is illegal.

G2 Maintain a professional and hygienic appearance

Jewellery

5 Remove rings, bracelets, necklaces and earrings before going on duty. If you wear a wedding ring, this may be left on.

Uniform

6 You spend long hours on your feet. Wear comfortable shoes that will not slip, and which will provide protection against spills and dropped objects. Wash your feet every day, and keep your toe nails trimmed. Change socks daily.

7 Once you have changed into uniform, leave your outdoor clothing and footwear in the area set aside for this purpose. Don't take it with you into the restaurant. Respect your uniform.

The Food Hygiene (General) Regulations 1970 *require food handlers to observe personal hygiene rules and use hygienic work methods.*

A crisp, clean uniform creates a favourable impression with customers.

All dining centre staff must wear suitable footwear when in the kitchen or dining centre. Footwear must be in a good state of repair, kept clean and reasonably slip resistant. All footwear must cover the foot, i.e. the toes and heels should be enclosed. The heel of a shoe should not be high or worn down. Socks, stockings or tights must be worn at all times.

Avon COUNTY COUNCIL FOR SERVICES YOU NEED

ACTION 9

You are asked to help liven up a training session on personal hygiene for food serving staff. Use the diagram below to bring out the key points in the most memorable way. You will find plenty of suggestions in the industry examples in this section.

Use the diagram to bring out the good points, e.g. clean teeth and breath, and the positive effects they have on customers. Alternatively, concentrate on bad practices, e.g. greasy hair, crumpled, stained uniform, so that the negative effects on customers can be discussed.

HAIR

COMPLEXION

MOUTH

CLOTHING

BODY CLEANLINESS

FEET

JEWELLERY

FINGERS AND HANDS

G2 Maintain a professional and hygienic appearance

Hygienic habits at work

8 Wash your hands thoroughly before touching food. Use plenty of hot water, and the soap and scrubbing brush which have been provided.

9 Dry your hands well after washing. Use the paper towels, hot air drier or roller towel provided – never a tea towel or service cloth.

10 Hold cutlery by the handle, glasses and cups by the stem or base, plates by the rim. Your fingers should never come into contact with eating surfaces.

11 Do not wash food or service equipment in wash-hand basins, and do not use food sinks for hand washing.

12 If you feel a sneeze coming, or you need to cough, turn away from any food. Hold a disposable paper tissue over your nose and mouth, and wash your hands afterwards.

13 Do not lick your fingers or touch your nose, mouth or hair.

14 Never smoke or spit in food service or preparation areas.

Covering cuts and reporting illness

15 Cover cuts, open sores and wounds with a waterproof dressing.

16 Report *any* illness or infection. Your supervisor will make the judgement of whether it is safe for you to work with food, or not. Don't put other people's health at risk because you don't want to admit to feeling ill.

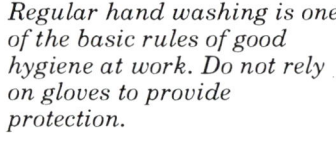

Regular hand washing is one of the basic rules of good hygiene at work. Do not rely on gloves to provide protection.

Use cleaning agents and sanitisers according to manufacturers' and/or workplace instructions.

You have a legal responsibility under the Health and Safety at Work Act 1974 not to endanger your own health and safety, nor that of other people who may be affected by the way you work: colleagues, customers, contractors and anyone else with reason to be on the premises.

Illness

Staff employed in the preparation and service of meals must report personal illness immediately.

Avon COUNTY COUNCIL FOR SERVICES YOU NEED

You will be excluded from work in connection with meals if you, or any member of your family, are suffering from any of the following:

- diarrhoea – including dysentery, enteritis, typhoid, food poisoning

- infective hepatitis

- septic wounds, septic spots or boils – applies to you only, not other members of family

- any other feverish condition.

This exclusion must continue until permission to return to work has been granted by a doctor or medical officer for environmental health.

Holidays or visits abroad

Before starting work after a trip abroad you will be asked to sign the foodhandlers' certificate of fitness, declaring that you are not suffering from boils, whitlows, a sore throat, running ears or an open sore and have not had an attack of diarrhoea and/or sickness in the previous 3 days.

NVQ **SVQ** **RANGE CHECKLIST**

LEVEL 1   LEVEL 2

G2.1 Maintain a professional and hygienic appearance

laid down procedures in all relevant

☐	health and safety legislation	☐
☐	food hygiene legislation	☐
☐	establishment procedures	☐

Introduction

The ability and confidence to handle all money transactions accurately gives you a firm foundation on which to develop your food and drink service skills.

Care and attention to detail is particularly important because mistakes with money lead to much ill-feeling. They may be put down to carelessness rather than dishonesty, but people do not easily forget errors.

The growth of non-cash transactions

The facility to pay by credit card, cheque or voucher is an important convenience for many customers. Anything which encourages customers to spend money is good for the business too, providing the transaction does not prove to be a fraudulent one. Your vigilance and attention to procedures will greatly reduce this risk.

Fun and money can mix! The counter staff of this school are dressed for a special Mexican day.

To customers who have enjoyed their meal, paying the bill gives a chance to thank the staff with a little extra.

Units and elements covered in this section

LEVEL 1 **LEVEL 2**

G4 Operate a payment point and process payments
– G4.1 Open, operate and close payment point
– G4.2 Handle and record payments

G5 Handle and record non-cash payments and refunds **LEVEL 2**
– G5.1 Handle and record cheque and credit/debit card payments
– G5.2 Handle and record refunds

Contents guide

Use of tills – standards checklist

1 Till checked before session starts:
   – till read
   – float checked
   – adequate change available
   – adequate receipts available.
2 Till input errors reported to person in charge.
3 Items added up correctly and customers told the price.
4 Correct change counted back to customer.
5 Dispute reported to person in charge.
6 Customer dealt with politely.
7 Till drawer closed after use.
8 Money in correct section.
9 Cheques and credit cards handled correctly.
10 All sales rung up.

Payment point procedures   `LEVELS 1 + 2`

You will get training and guidance on procedures that are specific to the type of operation you are working in and the equipment you are using.

General opening procedure

1 Is the float correct? This is usually a fixed amount, sufficient to give change to the first customers. However, it may be your responsibility to convert some or all of the float to change.

2 Is the cash drawer of the till properly organised, with notes and coins in the correct sections?

3 Are there adequate stocks of credit card vouchers, spare till rolls, and customer bills (if you use pre-printed ones)?

4 Do you have a pen available which you can lend to customers who want to write out a cheque or sign a voucher?

5 If you are responsible for products sold by the till, e.g. newspapers, road maps, gift items, confectionery, check that stocks are correct and everything is attractively displayed.

6 Give-away and promotional items handed to customers at the till should also be checked.

General procedure for operating a payment point

Your customers will have confidence in your ability when it is clear to them how much they are being asked to pay, how the calculation has been arrived at, and what change they are due.

The detailed steps for the various types of payment are described in the rest of this section.

1 Keep your cash drawer tidy, with the different coins in their correct sections; notes, cheques, vouchers and bags of spare change in their proper places. Notes should be put in the drawer so that they are lying flat, all facing in the same direction and the same way up.

2 Always keep the cash drawer shut when you are not actually putting money in, or taking money out. If you have to leave the till for some reason, lock it and take the key with you (unless there is a system for someone else to take over from you).

3 If you drop a coin on the floor, give the customer another coin from the till. Look for the lost coin when the cash drawer is safely shut, in a quiet moment.

4 Keep an eye on the change situation. Customers should not have to wait or be asked to produce the right amount because you have run out of change.

5 If there is a procedure for preventing the amount of cash in the till from building up too much during service (which would be a security risk), inform the relevant person in good time.

6 If you make an error in ringing up a transaction, the usual procedure is to start again, cancelling the incorrect one and informing your supervisor. Even if permissable, trying to adjust on a subsequent transaction can soon become impossibly complicated.

General closing procedure

The total value of cash, cheques, credit card vouchers, etc. in the till, less what you started with (the float), should agree with the till reading for total sales during the session. Too much or too little means you will have to spend time checking back to see where the error occurred. Of course, it will be too late to correct some errors, such as giving incorrect change.

If you are responsible for counting the money, it will help to divide notes and coins up into bundles or piles of a certain value, e.g. £100 for notes, £10 for £1 and 50p coins, £1 for 10p's, etc.

> **Tips procedure**
>
>
>
> All tips will go straight away to the supervisor's desk.
>
> At the end of the week the money will get distributed to everybody in equal shares compared to the working hours.
>
> Do not put tips into your pocket. You could be misunderstood.
>
> NEVER KEEP TIPS, even if the customer gave them to you personally.

In situations like the above, where the tips are pooled and then distributed on a structured basis, the employer is responsible for informing the Inland Revenue of what staff have earned from tips.

When staff keep their own tips, it is their responsibility to declare the amount received on their Tax Return.

> **Another approach to cash responsibility**
>
> In some restaurants, serving staff use the till only to record customer purchases, calculate and print the bill:
>
> - cash is kept by individuals (e.g. in a pouch held around the waist), not in the till
> - you are responsible for providing your own float (i.e. it is your own money)
> - when a new party of customers arrives, you 'open the table' on the till
> - as the meal progresses you key in items ordered
> - when the bill is requested you sub-total the bill, adding service where this applies
> - when payment is made, you close the bill and hand the receipt to the customer
> - at cashing-up time, you hand over cash and/or credit card vouchers/cheques for the total of the bills you have dealt with
> - if customers have left you cash tips, you should end up with more money in your pouch than you started with (tips added to credit cards are usually paid with wages)
> - if you have collected too little money from customers, you will personally suffer the loss

There should be no difference in the care you take, whether you are dealing with a customer direct, or with a work colleague who has collected the customer's money.

Handling and recording payments

LEVELS 1 + 2

Accuracy is all-important. Customers would much rather wait a few moments longer than find they have been charged £17.00 instead of £1.70.

Taking cash

Protect yourself against misunderstandings, genuine or otherwise: 'I gave you £20, this is change for £10':

- state clearly the value of the note handed over

- check the note for forgeries. Hold it up to the light: you should be able to see the water mark and the metal strip which runs through the note. Feel the quality of the paper for anything unusual

- place the note on the clip on the till, or clearly visible and separate from the other monies in the till

- check on the visual display that you have pressed the correct keys for the amount tendered

- count out the change in the least number of coins and notes possible. Count upwards from the amount due to the amount handed over

- count the change again in the same way, this time on to the counter/table top, plate or tray, or into the person's hand

- place the note in the till and close the drawer.

Handle only one transaction at a time.

Dealing with mistakes

If you realise you have made a mistake as you count the change into the customer's hand, apologise, stop counting at once and ask if you may take the money back again: 'I'm terribly sorry, I seem to have made a mistake. May I start again, please?'

Recount the change to yourself, correct it as necessary, then count into the customer's hand.

If you find yourself getting confused, either because you can't seem to get the total to agree, or the customer keeps interrupting, ask the manager to come to your assistance. On no account leave your till drawer open and unattended. Either use the phone, or ask a colleague to call the manager for you.

Customers may try and confuse you on purpose. A favourite trick is to hand over a £10 or £20 note, and just as you finish counting the change, proclaim that they meant to give you £5. The £5 will be thrust at you, with a request for the higher denomination note to be returned. Don't waste time trying to sort it out, call your manager.

Presenting the bill at table

1 Fold the bill in half so that the person who is paying will be the only one to see the total. Place on a plate, small tray or in a bill folder and take to the table.

2 Place the bill by the host, or if the host is not known, the person who:

- ordered the food and/or drinks

- asked for the bill

or place it in the centre of the table if it is a mixed party where everyone will be contributing.

3 Leave the customer to check the details and return when payment has been placed on the plate, or if the customer appears to have a query.

4 Collect the payment, check the amount handed over, count out any change required, receipt the bill, then place the receipt and any change on the plate and return this to the customer's table.

5 Do not hover as if expecting a tip. If a tip has been left, collect it after the customers have departed unless they specifically invite you to take it earlier.

You must be careful to give the correct change to every customer. If you give incorrect change, the customer will become annoyed and you will more likely lose that person's future business.

Non-cash transactions `LEVEL 2`

Payment by cheque

Only accept payment by cheque when the customer can produce a valid cheque guarantee card (see ACTION 10).

Because of the low limit that banks will guarantee with cheque cards (£50, sometimes £100), some businesses will accept cheques for larger amounts provided the customer produces a form of identification, e.g. current driver's licence, or a company security card with a photograph of the person. You may have to get a manager to verify the transaction. Customer's address details may have to be noted on the back of the cheque.

Payment by credit card

Check that the card is accepted by your workplace. If not, ask if the customer has ... and name a card which is accepted. Then examine the expiry date and whether the card has been reported lost or stolen.

Imprint the voucher with the card details (name of customer, account number, date of expiry) and payee details (your workplace). For:

> *electronic* machine, swipe the card through the slit so that the information encoded in the black band on the back of the card is read

> *hand* machine, place the credit card underneath the voucher, and run the imprinter over in both directions.

Check that the card details have been accepted properly/ imprinted clearly on the voucher. Key in or write the amount to be charged, the date and description of the goods sold, e.g. 'Food', 'Meal'. If service charge has been included on the bill, you should complete the total figure (many customers are irritated by the practice of leaving the total column open, in the expectation of a tip).

Ask the customer to sign the voucher. Keep the specimen signature on the card out of sight while this is done. This makes it more difficult for a dishonest person to copy the signature. Check that the signatures match.

Depending on the amount to be charged, you may need to telephone the credit card company to obtain authorisation. State your establishment reference number, the card number and the amount to be charged. You may be asked to indicate whether the customer is male or female. Record the authorisation code on the voucher. If using an electronic imprinter, the authorisation will take place automatically.

Return the card to the customer, with the appropriate copy of the voucher and receipted bill. Place the other copies in the till or other suitable place.

In view of the customer, tear up the carbons from the voucher – these carry the card holder's signature, etc.

The differences explained

A **cheque guarantee card** means that the bank will honour the cheque, even if the person writing the cheque has insufficient funds in his/her account. With some banks, credit or debit cards also act as cheque guarantee cards, e.g. Barclaycard and Connect.

A **credit card** – such as Access, Barclaycard or Visa – is issued by a bank or finance company that offers its customers credit up to an agreed limit. When the customer purchases a meal and charges it to the card, the voucher is paid in through a regular bank, and the money credited to the restaurant's account. The restaurant is charged a commission – for this reason not every catering establishment will accept such cards, others make a surcharge.

Each month the customer is sent a statement by the credit card company itemising the various charges and demanding a minimum payment. Interest is charged on outstanding amounts. The customer can avoid paying interest by clearing the account each month.

With a **charge card** – such as American Express or Diner's Club International – the customer is billed once a month for all the items charged during the month. This account must be cleared in full. There is no credit.

The restaurateur sends the vouchers to the company concerned for payment.

A **debit card** – such as Connect or Switch – acts like an electronic cheque. The amount is immediately debited against the customer's bank account.

You may also come across the term **affinity card**. With this, the bank gives a percentage of the card holder's usage to charity (e.g. Midland to the National Trust, Girobank to Oxfam).

Eurocheques are issued by banks for use in other countries. The traveller can issue cheques in specific currencies (e.g. £ sterling) approved in advance by the bank. Like ordinary bank and building society cheques, they should be accompanied by a cheque guarantee card, and the procedure for accepting them is the same.

Travellers' cheques are issued by banks and travel agents in the traveller's own country and are available in £ sterling, US $ and many other currencies. The cheque is signed once at the time of issue, and a second time when used to pay for something or to exchange for cash. The cheques come in various values and their value is guaranteed, provided the two signatures match.

Handling and recording refunds

Changes or reductions to a customer's bill should always be supported. For example:

- the manager's initialled signature against the cancellation of the main course item (following a complaint)
- a return docket, e.g. because the customer decided not to have the second bottle of wine
- complimentary docket, e.g. liqueurs at no charge for regular customers.

Payment by charge card or direct debit card

The procedure is similar to accepting payment by credit card, and authorisation must be sought from the issuing company for amounts over a pre-set limit.

Charging to an account

If the meal or drink is to be charged to a hotel guest's room number or charged to a company account:

- ask the customer to sign the bill or docket (sometimes called a check)
- confirm details of account/room number to be charged
- take or send the signed dockets to whoever is responsible for preparing the final bill, without delay.

Hotel guests may be asked to produce their key card before charging items to their bill, or you may be asked to telephone reception to confirm the person is staying in the hotel and it is acceptable for the bill to be signed.

Discount vouchers and sales incentive cards

Your company may take part in a national scheme, or have its own vouchers or cards designed to encourage repeat custom. Schemes vary: some give customers a certain amount off their bill, others award them points or tokens towards a range of products, air travel, holidays, etc. Check the correct procedure with your manager.

Travellers' cheques

When these are in £ sterling:

- the customer will select a cheque or cheques of the appropriate value
- ask the customer to date each cheque, make it payable to the restaurant/hotel, and sign it for a second time in the appropriate place
- check that the two signatures agree (you may also need to check against the customer's passport)
- where the value of the cheque(s) is higher than the amount due, give the required change (in £p). If not, ask the customer for the balance in £p.

Payment by cheque or credit card provides you with the name of the customer, which means you can give a more personal 'Thank you, Miss Sylvester'.

With this system details of everything the customers have ordered are automatically kept, itemised and printed on the bill.

These students use a special credit card issued by their college. A record is kept of every purchase and students are billed at the end of term. The card also doubles as an identification card for entrance to the library, etc. A similar system is used to keep a record of meals consumed by college staff. For convenience, their card is kept by the till.

Computers in the restaurant

Some restaurants use very advanced technology. Orders are punched into hand-held terminals. These can prompt the server, e.g. at 9.30 a.m. with the sales cue 'which Danish?', at 9.30 p.m. 'which liqueurs?', or for steaks 'well done, medium, rare?' and the order cannot proceed until one of these keys is entered. The equipment can also:

- calculate average spend per customer
- monitor sales performance of staff
- log who was on duty at any particular time
- if someone phones in sick, suggest the most suitable replacement, based on the history it has collected of staff members' performance.

Payment by voucher or token

Employees of some companies receive these as a contribution towards the cost of their meal and refreshments. There are a number of variations:

- company-specific, for a designated meal in the staff restaurant, e.g. lunch, when it is simply a matter of collecting one voucher or token per person
- company-specific, for a certain value, e.g. £1.50, one issued per meal, per duty, the customer paying cash for anything that costs more than this. There are no refunds for meals that cost less
- company-specific, for a rather higher value, e.g. £20 issued every month. These work like a Phonecard, every time they are used the value decreases. In the period between issue of new cards, the customer pays cash for meals
- issued by a national organisation such as Luncheon Vouchers, which can be exchanged for food in those restaurants (and supermarkets) which accept them. Purchases over the value of the voucher are paid for in cash. It is not in the customer's interests to purchase items less than the voucher's value, since you cannot give change. Check that the voucher has not expired.

Dealing with problems

In general:

- try to keep calm
- remain polite and respectful
- move out of earshot of others
- avoid direct eye contact where this will further embarrass, intimidate or anger the customer
- if you make a mistake, apologise sincerely and do whatever is necessary to correct the problem
- never attempt to apprehend customers yourself
- if you have any doubt at all about your ability to deal with the situation, call your manager.

Errors or voids Write 'cancelled' through incorrect bills and put aside for the manager. Incorrect credit card vouchers should be torn into small pieces (to reassure the customer).

Invalid cheques, cheque cards, etc. Explain why you cannot accept payment and suggest alternatives, e.g. 'I am afraid your cheque card has expired, Miss Cohn. Have you got the new one, or would you like to pay by credit card? We accept ...'

Customers attempt to depart without paying Assume they have forgotten, and tactfully remind them, out of earshot of other customers.

Customer departs without paying Inform the manager at once, giving as many details as you can remember of the customer.

Authorisation refused Explain tactfully, e.g. 'I'm very sorry, Mr Sperry, but authorisation has been refused. I'm sure that if you get in touch with your credit card company they will explain. In the meantime, would you like to use another method of payment?'

Suspected fraud If the card company asks you to retain the customer's card, suggest the customer contacts the company and speaks to them directly (offer a phone with some privacy). Do not give the card to the customer.

Disputed bill Check each item carefully, where necessary referring to the original order for the table and checking with copies retained by the kitchen, dispense bar, etc.

RANGE CHECKLIST

LEVEL 1 — **LEVEL 2**

G4.1 Open, operate and close payment point

open, operate and close tills or billing machines with cash drawers to deal with these methods of payment

- [ ] cash [ ]
- [ ] tokens [ ]
- [ ] vouchers [ ]

G4.2 Handle and record payments

use tills or billing machines with cash drawers to handle and record these methods of payment

- [ ] cash [ ]
- [ ] tokens [ ]
- [ ] vouchers [ ]

G5.1 Handle and record cheque and credit/debit card payments **LEVEL 2**

use tills or billing machines with cash drawers to handle and record these types of cheque

- [ ] bank or giro or building society cheques
- [ ] Eurocheques
- [ ] sterling travellers' cheques

and these credit/debit cards

- [ ] credit cards
- [ ] charge cards
- [ ] debit cards

and deal with these discrepancies

- [ ] errors or voids
- [ ] invalid cheques, cheque cards and credit/debit cards
- [ ] authorisation refused
- [ ] suspected fraud

G5.2 Handle and record refunds

handle and record refund of

- [ ] cash or credit

deal with these discrepancies

- [ ] authorisation refused
- [ ] discrepancies in refund documentation

ACTION 10

Compare the following procedure for accepting payment by cheque with that in your workplace. Then design a poster or checklist which would help you and your colleagues to remember the key points.

Payment by cheque

Make sure that:

- the date on the card has not expired
- the name on the card and the cheque are the same
- the cheque is from the same bank as the card
- the cheque is for not more than the card limit
- the signature on the cheque is the same as that on the card, and the signature on the card has not been obviously tampered with. If you are in any doubt, ask the customer to sign again on the back of the cheque.

Ensure that the cheque has been completed accurately:

- the date is the date of the transaction
- the details have been written in ink
- the amounts in words and figures agree
- the payee details are correct
- any amendments to the cheque (e.g. a correction to the date) have been initialled by the customer.

If satisfied with these checks, write the cheque card number on the back of the cheque, together with the expiry date of the card and your initials. If the customer has written the card number on the back of the cheque, make sure that it is correct.

You should only accept one cheque per transaction: if the bill comes to more than the card limit, ask the customer to pay the difference in cash or by credit card.

Preparing and clearing – table and tray

Introduction

There are two main aspects to preparation for service:

- getting ready the behind-the-scene areas and all the items that you are likely to require for service to run smoothly

- creating surroundings in which your customers can enjoy their food and drink.

Both require a methodical, planned approach. And even the straightforward routine that does not vary from day to day, relies on attention to detail and consistency. Problems will soon develop if, for example, the salt and peppers have not been filled. If these occur during the peak service period, you are likely to have to break off from what you should be doing to put matters right, and this will lead to further problems.

In establishments where a range of functions is taking place, some of the preparation tasks will be unique to a particular event. You may have special table arrangements and settings to prepare, or an entertainment stage to help set up. This requires good communications.

Responsibility for preparation activities may be shared between you and other service staff, perhaps on a rota basis, or operating as a team. There may be certain duties which you only carry out in an emergency, perhaps because a member of staff is away ill. Whatever the arrangement, you should develop the habit of checking that everything is exactly as it should be, *before* service starts.

Contents guide

A Directors' Dining Room set for lunch. The highly polished table, fine glassware and china, and self-service bar are typical of this style of catering where everything is expected to be of the best quality, with no expense spared.

The setting for a banquet. A well-set table should not look overloaded, nor sparse. There should be an overall symmetry to the final appearance – with chairs, napkins, glasses, menus, candles, etc. lined up.

 **Units and elements covered in this section**

1C1 Prepare and clear areas for table or tray service **LEVEL 1**

- 1C1.1 Prepare service areas and equipment for table or tray service
- 1C1.2 Prepare customer dining areas for table or tray service
- 1C1.3 Clear dining and service areas after service

2C1 Prepare and clear areas for table service

- 2C1.1 Prepare service equipment and areas for table service **LEVEL 2**
- 2C1.2 Prepare customer dining areas for table service
- 2C1.3 Clear dining and service areas after food service

Preparing service areas and equipment

LEVELS 1 + 2

The size of the service areas, the preparation tasks involved, and ones you personally carry out will depend on the style and size of your operation. In some places, ancillary staff will clean the silver, and return crockery, cutlery and glassware to storage after it has been washed.

Items which form part of the table setting

These include: crockery, cutlery, glassware, napkins and tablecloths, tablemats, ashtrays, vases, salt and peppers, etc.

Chipped or otherwise damaged items should be withdrawn from service. Check with your manager whether damaged items should be thrown away, or kept until the next stocktaking, so that loss from breakages can be worked out more accurately.

Some glasses are designed and made to be stacked.

Glasses should always be polished before use with a clean, lint-free cloth. If this is not done or the cloth is not absolutely clean, the glass will smell unpleasant, and spoil the drink. Glasses that have been stored upside down on shelves are particularly likely to pick up smells.

Caring for silverware

When using a proprietary silver cleaner, follow the instructions carefully. Wear protective gloves.

Rinse the silver in warm water before use and dry with a clean cloth. With decorated items it may be necessary to brush into all the grooves with a soft toothbrush.

Do not use polishes intended for brass, as they are likely to be abrasive and will scratch the silver.

To remove stains from the inside of silver-plated tea or coffee pots: pour boiling water into the pot and add a teaspoon of bicarbonate of soda. Leave for 10 minutes, then rinse well.

Special care is needed when cleaning knives with silver-plated handles and stainless steel blades – some silver cleaning agents will turn stainless steel black.

If stainless steel or silver-plated cutlery has smears because it was not washed and rinsed with care:

- dip the items in a jug of very hot water for a few moments
- polish with a clean, dry teacloth.

Caring for glassware

When washing:

- remove lemon slices, drink dregs, etc. before washing
- if hand-washing, wash one at a time to avoid breakages – it is very difficult to see clear glass under water. The water should be about 60°C
- use the correct amount of detergent – too much will leave traces on the glass surface and spoil the drink
- rinse in very hot water, about 80°C
- leave the rinsed glasses to dry.

When handling:

- avoid banging glasses against hard objects or each other – this eventually weakens them. Never use glasses as ice scoops, nor to hold cutlery
- don't subject the glass to sudden changes in temperature. Warm the glass first if you are going to fill it with a hot drink. If it has ice in, dump the ice and allow the glass to stand briefly before washing. Don't put cold drinks in glasses which are still warm from the washing.

To clean a stained decanter: put some rice (alternatively paper or tin foil rolled into balls) into the decanter. Add warm soapy water. Swill well. Rinse in fresh water and shake dry. Finish off the outside with a clean, dry cloth.

Accompaniments

These include: bread items, mustards, salad dressings, bottled sauces, pickles, etc.

Order new stocks in good time. You may have to complete an internal order form or *requisition*, and have this signed by a supervisor. New stock should be positioned so that stock is used on a first in, first out basis. Do not use beyond best-before or use-by dates. Keep stocks of slow-moving items to the minimum.

If any products have passed their use-by or sell-by date, inform your supervisor so that they are removed and destroyed after suitable account has been made. If they are retained, they must be separated from in-date stock and marked clearly 'Not fit for human consumption'. (Having out-of-date stock may contravene the food safety legislation and lead to prosecution – beverages are treated in the same way as solid food.)

Follow label or workplace instructions for storing sauces which have been opened. Some should be kept in the refrigerator. Wipe clean the outside of the bottle and around the lip.

Unless empty or with a lid, sugar basins, marmalade and jam jars should be kept, preferably covered with clingfilm, in a cupboard, when not in use.

Trays   `LEVEL 2`

Trays should be washed and sanitised regularly, not just wiped down. Allow to dry before stacking.

Other equipment used to serve food

Take particular care to clean trolleys well – not just the shelves and top, but also the legs and wheels.

Service dishes which have become stained with food should be polished before use.

Equipment to keep food and drinks refrigerated

Check that the operating temperature is correct. Both the interior, including shelves, and exterior should be kept spotless.

Rotate stocks. Discard (and record) items which have passed their storage life (with food this may be 12 hours or less).

Hot plates and plate warmers

If possible remove shelves and doors of hot cupboards to clean all crevices and channels thoroughly.

Turn equipment on so that the correct operating temperature is reached before service begins (and plates are warmed properly).

Caring for china

When washing:

- use a soft plastic or rubber scraper to clear off stubborn food debris, never a metal utensil
- do not use scouring pads or abrasive powders
- wash in water at about 60°C, with the correct concentration of detergent.

When stacking:

- use plastic-coated racks or baskets
- place the items for the dishwasher so they will not vibrate against each other, rattle or turn over during the wash
- avoid abrupt temperature changes (which can cause cracking) – never heat china over a flame
- never use china with gold, platinum or other metallic decorations in a microwave.

ACTION   11

Identify/state the use of each of the following items:

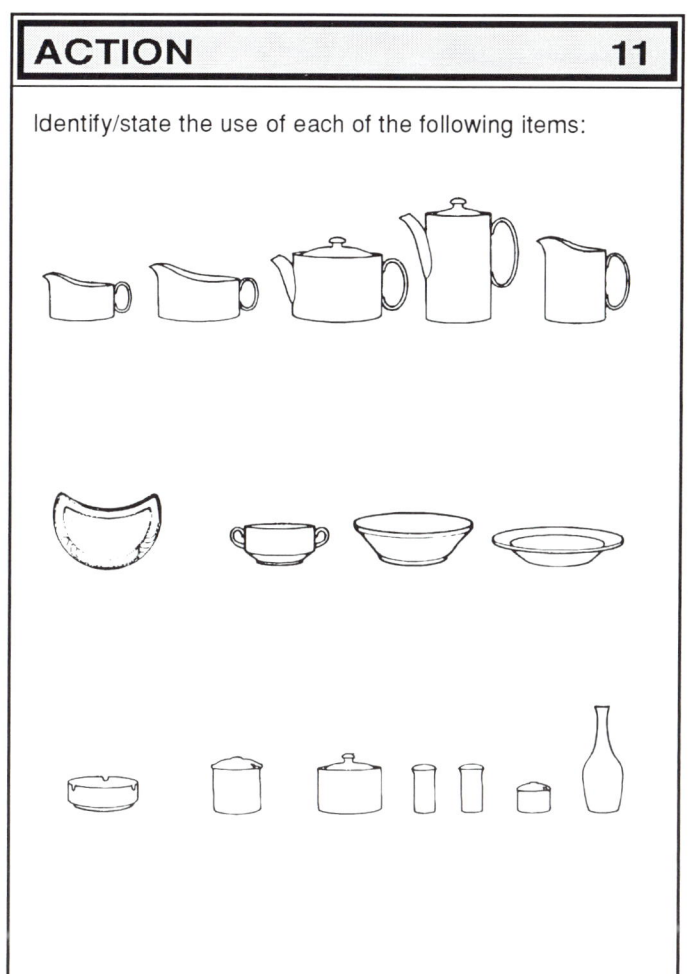

Clearing after service

LEVELS 1 + 2

If the dining area is in regular use, many of the preparation tasks for service will be done as part of the clearing-up routine. This may include:

- leaving the tablecloth (if used) on the table, and items which are used for every meal, e.g. salt and peppers, table numbers, flowers

- resetting the tables for the next meal, e.g. lunch after breakfast service has finished; or it may be the same meal, e.g. dinner the next day.

In other situations it is usual to strip the tables completely, wipe down all surfaces, and stack furniture so that the floor can be thoroughly cleaned.

General tasks include:

- removing rubbish

- sorting and counting used tablecloths, napkins, service cloths, etc. for laundering

- cleaning sideboards, guéridons and other preparation and service equipment

- returning food items to storage

- returning liqueurs, brandies and other drinks stocks to secure storage

- turning off equipment.

SAFETY

Clearing with a tray

1 Place the tray with half on the table, and hold the tray at the opposite end with the left hand.
2 Use the right hand to clear the table.
3 When carrying large, heavy trays, hold the tray with both hands, fingers gripped firmly underneath.
4 Go through fire and swing doors sideways or backwards, so that you push the door open with your body, not the tray. Make sure first that no one is approaching from the other side.

Remember:
- put heavier items at the centre of the tray
- stack plates of the same size together
- place cutlery together on the tray
- place rubbish away from the cutlery
- clear glasses on a separate journey, if possible.

NEVER:
- stack cups more than two high
- stack glasses
- use broken trays
- overload your tray.

 *Coppid Beech Hotel*

Cleaning rota

THE FOX & PHEASANT

Mon	All salt and peppers emptied, cleaned, thoroughly dried and refilled.
Tues, Sat	All vases cleaned and refilled with fresh flowers.
Wed, Sun	Coffee machines descaled and cleaned-up.
Thurs	All chairs washed, sanitised and polished.
Fri	Clean out the store room.

Restaurant close down

1 All tables washed, sanitised, polished and relaid.
2 Dessert trolley: put ice packs away in freezer. Clean down trolley with hot soapy water and sanitiser. Polish.
3 All desserts clingfilmed and put into main refrigerator.
4 Butters, milks and creams put away into the refrigerator.
5 Bread baskets cleaned out. Give old bread to chefs. Put serviettes in roll baskets and make ready for next session.
6 Biscuits tidied away into sections of tin they came out of.
7 Coffee cups laid up ready for the next session.
8 Coffee machines switched off after each session.
9 Check under tables for debris.
10 Remove all empty boxes and bin bags to the skip.
11 All windows closed.

Lunch pre-opening duties

 *Coppid Beech Hotel*

1 Polish glasses to set up for lunch: 150 each white wine, red wine, water.
2 Clear tables after breakfast.
3 Refill jam pots and sugars.
4 Prepare guéridons with: 5 each large forks, fish knives, dessert spoons, soup spoons, 1 tomato ketchup, 1 each English/French/German mustard, 1 tabasco sauce.
5 Prepare stations with: 50 each large knives, large forks, small forks, fish forks, dessert spoons, dessert forks, soup spoons, 5 ashtrays, 1 toothpick holder, 20 each red/white wine/water glasses, 10 waiter's cloths, 30 guest napkins.
6 Set up tables for lunch.
7 Clean coffee machine and get it ready for a new brew.
8 Clean all service areas.
9 Clean all rubbish bins and replace black bags.
10 Prepare 50 double liners for soup (dessert plates, napkins and soup saucer)
11 Polish all cloches (plate cover – shown in use on page 7).
12 Prepare all silver trays.
13 Prepare wine coolers and stands, and 2 red wine decanters.
14 Prepare buffet display.
15 Prepare Champagne and liqueurs trolleys.
16 Take dirty linen to laundry and bring clean linen.
17 Vacuum the restaurant.

Preparing dining areas for table service

LEVELS 1 + 2

Approach your own preparation tasks thoughtfully and do them in a logical order. For example, spend a few minutes counting on to a tray and polishing all the cutlery you will need. This will usually be quicker than returning several times because you have run out of spoons, or have too many knives.

General procedure

Before being placed on the table, all items should be checked to ensure they are spotlessly clean, and not chipped or damaged in any way.

Take special care when handling cutlery, crockery and glassware not to touch with your fingers any surface which will come into contact with food, drink or the customer's mouth.

1 Put the tables and chairs in the correct position. If large parties are expected this will mean finding out what special arrangements are required.

2 Check that tables and chairs are clean and polished. Inspect furniture for damage, and that tables do not wobble.

3 Lay the cloths (see overleaf) and/or position the tablemats. Tablemats should be carefully lined up, so that the straight surface (if any) is parallel to the edge of the table, and about 1.25 cm from the table edge. If the mat has a design or the name of the establishment, check that these details are facing where the customer will be sitting.

4 Put down the show plate (if used) in a central position in front of each customer's chair, about 1.25 cm from the table edge. The crest or establishment name should be facing the customer.

5 Lay the cutlery from the inside working outwards. Doing it in this order helps to get the positioning correct first time.

6 Place the side plate, and the side knife on the plate (if this is the style).

7 Place the glass(es).

8 Place the napkin.

9 Place the salt and peppers in the centre of the table (more than one set will be required for a large table).

10 Position table decorations (e.g. flowers), promotional cards, etc. Table numbers, if used, should face the entrance to the restaurant.

Certain items should not be put on the table until just before, or when the customers are seated. These include butter, jugs of milk and water which should be served chilled, and mustards, jams and other accompaniments if they are not in a container with a lid.

ACTION   **12**

In the boxes alongside each of these place settings, draw your own diagram to show the equivalent arrangement in your workplace.

1 Setting when customers have a choice of individually-priced dishes (à la carte menu).

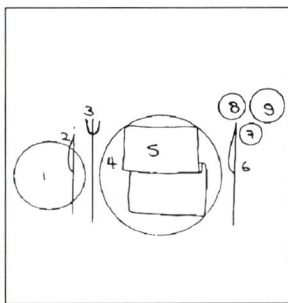

Key: (1) side plate, (2) small knife, (3) large fork, (4) show plate, (5) napkin, (6) large knife, (7) white wine glass, (8) red wine glass, (9) water glass.

2 Setting for a limited choice of dishes (table d'hôte or banquet, or function menu).

Menu: Stilton soup, Roulade of salmon lined with mousseline of halibut, Médaillons of pork fillet, Apple charlotte

3 Setting for a full breakfast. (Alternatively, draw the place setting for a different function menu from 2 above.)

Key: (1) side plate, (2) small knife, (3) small fork, (4) large fork, (5) napkin, (6) dessert spoon, (7) large knife, (8) small knife, (9) cup, saucer and teaspoon.

Clothing the table

Linen cloths have a smooth and a rough side. The smooth side looks best, so should be uppermost. The rough side will help grip on the table. A baize or felt undercloth will give the table a luxury feel, help to deaden the noise and cushion customers' wrists.

Select the right size cloth for the table. The table top should be covered adequately, with the points hanging equally over the table legs, but the cloth should not drag on the floor. An overlap of 30 to 45 cm is ideal.

Handle the cloth as little as possible to avoid creasing or marking it.

Ideally, tablecloths come from the laundry in screen folds (also called Z or accordion folds). You can recognise this, as one long side (the *open* edge) will contain a hem, a double fold and a hem. The other side will contain two double folds.

1 The open edge should be towards you. Take hold of the top hem between the thumbs and first fingers, and the double fold between the first and second fingers.

2 Drop the bottom flap over the far edge of the table.

3 Let the rest of the cloth lie on the table. Release the central fold and gently draw the top flap across the table until the whole cloth is opened out.

4 Smooth the cloth. Check it is central, the edges even and parallel to the floor. If possible the points of the cloth should be hanging over the legs of the table. Check that there are no stains or tears (if so, replace the cloth).

These steps can be adapted to change a tablecloth when customers are in the restaurant. As the fresh cloth is pulled over the table, the soiled cloth is pulled away from underneath. This (rather difficult) technique avoids noisy flapping of cloths and exposing the often unsightly tabletop to other diners.

The centre fold of the cloth should run straight down the middle of the table.

There is no need to flap tablecloths around as if you were hanging out laundry.

Slip cloths can add interest to the table setting, providing a contrast of colour. They also reduce laundry bills, as they protect the main cloth from soiling.

The main aim of checklists is to reduce the chance of forgetting something, and to help in the planning and allocation of work. For this reason the best checklists – like the one for The Old Orleans Restaurant reproduced below – are quite detailed.

Have a go at writing a similar checklist for preparing the dining/restaurant area in your workplace.

11 am checklist   **OLD ORLEANS**
                                            A TASTE OF THE DEEP SOUTH

1 Popcorn machine assembled and first batch made.

2 Relishes out (corn, onion and tomato and chili).

3 Mustards out (French, English and American).

4 Coffee machines on and first batch prepared.

5 Hot towel machine full of 'HOT' hot towels.

6 Dessert area stocked up, desserts portioned as appropriate.

7 Hot fudge 'hot' and ready to serve.

8 Music on at right volume. All lights working.

9 All tables set to Old Orleans standard:
  – all sugar containers clean and full (with individual portion packets)
  – salt and pepper never less than half full
  – all cutlery polished
  – table/table mats clean and fresh
  – never less than 15 white napkins
  – toothpick glass full
  – ashtrays and matches on every smokers' table.

10 Sideboards fully stocked.

Folding napkins

There are a large number of attractive ways of folding napkins. For the best results with the more elaborate folds, you need a good quality, linen napkin which has been starched so that it is stiff.

The more expensive paper napkins will produce good results with some folds, but not those that rely on great firmness. Experiment to see what works well.

Before you start folding, always make sure your hands and the surface you are using to fold the napkins are absolutely clean.

When considering what fold is best for a particular table set up, you should consider:

What will look best on the table – sometimes the napkin can add height to an otherwise rather flat table, but when the table has flowers, candles, and several glasses at each setting, the napkin may look best lying flat in a neat fold on the show plate.

Hygiene – folding involves touching the napkins.

Time – complex folds take a long time to make.

Attractively folded napkins can also add interest and style to the presentation of food and drink items, e.g. a bread roll in a rose.

ACTION 14

Assume a customer wants to hold a theme event in your workplace. Choose the theme yourself, e.g. a Caribbean evening or Valentine's dinner, and develop some ideas for decorating the tables, the room itself, and for clothes for the staff to wear. It may help to visit your local library to find out something about the chosen country or area of interest.

With the help of your supervisor or tutor, contact some suppliers of speciality tablewear to check what is available and the cost.

Rose or Water lily  Visa® Napery Fabrics

1 Fold all corners of open napkin to centre
2 Fold new corners to centre
3 Turn napkin over and fold all 4 corners to centre.
4 Holding centre firmly, reach under each corner and pull up flaps to form petals. Reach between petals and pull flaps from underneath.

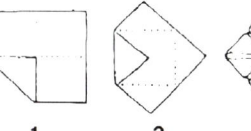 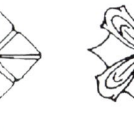

Goblet fan

1 Fold napkin in half.
2 Pleat from bottom to top.
3 Turn napkin back one-third of the way on right (folded) end and place into goblet.
4 Spread out pleats at top.

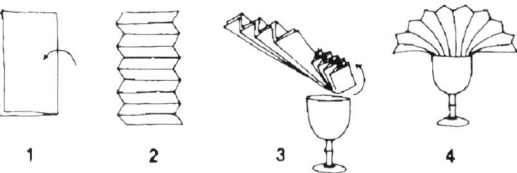

Clown's hat

1 Fold napkin in half bringing bottom to top.
2 Holding centre of bottom with finger, take lower right corner and loosely roll around centre, matching corners.
3 Complete the cone.
4 Turn napkin upside down, then turn up hem all around. Turn and stand on base.

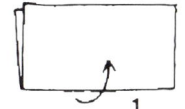 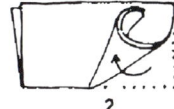  

Bishop's mitre

1 Fold napkin bringing top to bottom.
2 Fold corners to centre line.
3 Turn napkin over and rotate ¼ turn.
4 Fold bottom edge up to top edge and flip point out from under top fold.
5 Turn left end into pleat at left, forming a point on left side.
6 Turn napkin over and turn right end into pleat, forming a point on right side.
7 Open base and stand upright.

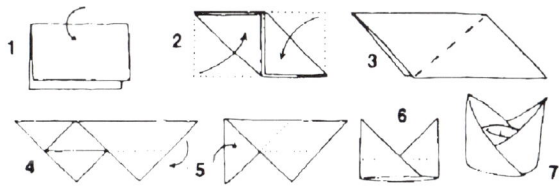

Glassware

Where a drink – and this can include water, as well as the full range of soft drinks, wines, beers, etc. – is going to be served with the meal, the table setting usually includes the appropriate glasses.

While the convenience of the customer is always important, another reason for placing an attractive glass on the table is to remind customers that they might enjoy a drink with their food. This boosts sales.

SAFETY ▲ ▲ ▲

Probably the safest way to carry the large number of glasses that are required for setting up the tables at a buffet or banquet is to use a dishwasher basket. If this is not practical, use a tray or carry them in your hand as shown below. Be very careful – the consequences of falling over are obvious.

Take care not to bang the glasses together. Even if there are no obvious signs of damage, the glass gets weakened internally.

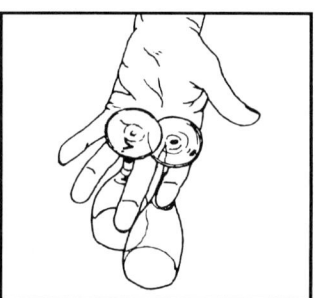 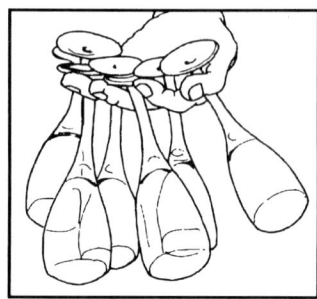

Note how the stems of the glasses are wedged under one another, to provide a firmer hold.

By loading the glasses in a logical sequence (left to right, then back again), and pushing them well back between your fingers, it is possible to carry 6 or 8 comfortably.

Wine glasses

Glasses should be large enough and the right shape — narrower at the lip than in the bowl — to concentrate the scent and aroma of the wine (known as the bouquet).

The glass should be clear, colourless and as thin as possible, and plain rather than cut-glass to allow the appearance of the wine to be appreciated.

The bowl should be relatively large. Where different glasses are used for white wine, the bowl is generally slimmer and more elegant than those for red.

The stem should be of moderate length, so that the temperature of the hand need not affect the temperature of the wine.

Wine glasses with long stems, sometimes used for Hocks and Mosels, look beautiful, but they are more easily tipped over or broken. Many establishments use one or two standard glasses which suit most types of wine, and even sherries and ports.

ACTION 15

You are asked to collect the glassware to set out for a small private party. The drink service requirements are:

- Martini cocktails on arrival
- white wine with the first course
- red wine with the main course
- Champagne with the sweet
- brandy with the coffee
- water to be available throughout the meal.

Assuming that your establishment uses the glasses illustrated on the right, which ones would you collect stocks of, and for what use?

Indicate the principal use of any remaining glasses.

No.	Use	No.	Use
1		6	
2		7	
3		8	
4		9	
5		10	

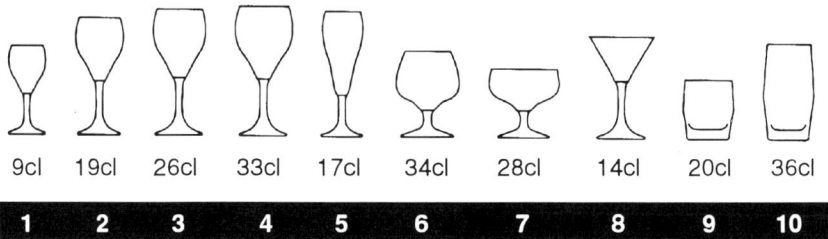

9cl	19cl	26cl	33cl	17cl	34cl	28cl	14cl	20cl	36cl
1	2	3	4	5	6	7	8	9	10

Preparing for tray service `LEVEL 1`

The surface of the tray acts as a miniature table setting. In most of the situations in which tray service is used, there is no opportunity for service staff to add the sweet cutlery later, or bring coffee cup, saucer, etc. from the sideboard. This means the tray should carry everything that the customer will require for the meal.

General procedure

1 Place a suitable size cloth on the tray or trolley. In some situations a paper or plastic tray liner is used. (As well as improving the presentation, the liner helps stop items sliding around the tray.)

2 Arrange the cutlery, crockery, glassware, napkin accompaniments, etc. on the tray, as if it were the place setting at a small table.

3 Where trays are prepared in advance, cups and glasses should be left upside down, as protection against dust. If possible, cover the trays with a suitable cloth. Cover sugars and jams with lids or clingfilm (or place on the tray until the last moment). If the trays are stored on a rack system, glasses and other tall items are laid on their side.

Room service trolleys

These are often the folding type. Fully opened, they provide a surface area equivalent to a table. Arrange everything on the centre part of the trolley. The place settings will be moved into position after the trolley has been taken to the room and the flaps opened out.

Room service trolleys and trays can be set up in advance when the requirements are fairly predictable. An example of this is a full English breakfast to be served to hotel guests in their rooms. Menu choice is unlikely to affect cutlery or crockery requirements.

 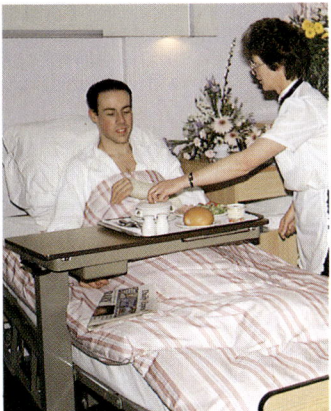

In some situations it is more practical to set the tray up once the order has been taken. An example of this is a luxury private hospital offering an extensive room service menu.

ACTION   16

A guest has placed this room service order. Draw a sketch showing how you would set up the tray.

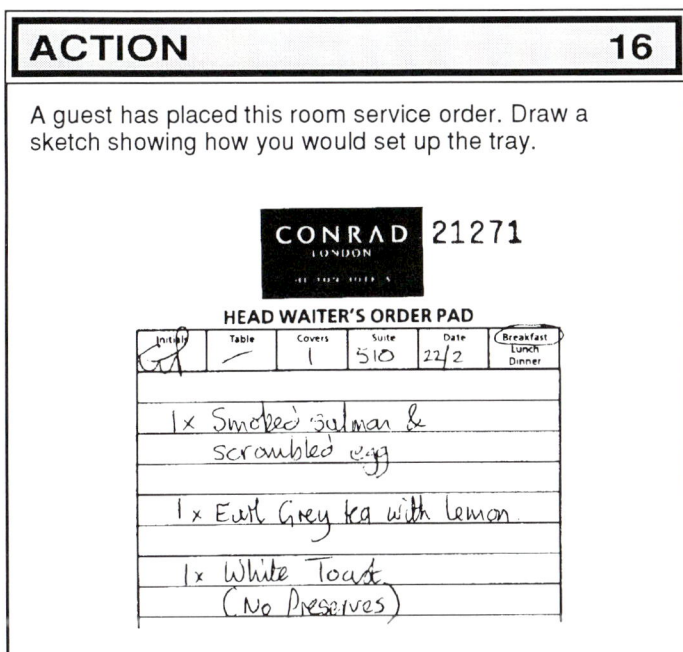

CONRAD 21271
LONDON

HEAD WAITER'S ORDER PAD

Initials	Table	Covers	Suite	Date	Breakfast / Lunch / Dinner
	/	1	510	22/2	

1 x Smoked salmon & scrambled egg

1 x Earl Grey tea with lemon

1 x White Toast (No Preserves)

In hospitals and similar establishments where tray service is used for a large number of meals, a conveyor belt system is operated, each member of staff being responsible for placing a different dish or group of items on to the trays as they move by.

1C1 Prepare and clear areas for table or tray service

2C1 Prepare and clear areas for table service

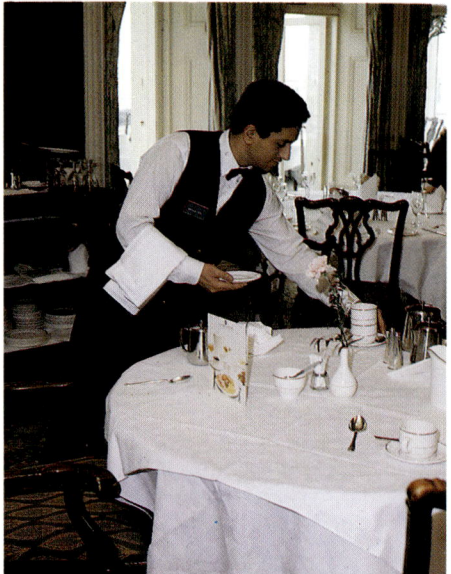

Clearing the table (here, after breakfast) is easier when there is a sideboard nearby (left of picture). The used items can be carried to the sideboard and there loaded on to a tray.

ACTION 17

Produce a short checklist of preparation activities for your own workplace. Use a direct writing style similar to the one used by the nightclub chain, Ritzy.

Refer as necessary to the other industry examples given in this section. Add illustrations or cartoons where they will help communicate the important messages.

Ritzy

FOYER

- surfaces will sparkle
- floors will be vacuumed, clean and free of fluff and bits
- windows will shine
- notices will be clear, legible and easy to see

MAIN HALL

- the dance floor will glow with polish and reflect the lights
- stairs will be free of obstructions
- furniture will be clean and comfortable
- bars will be dry and polished
- glasswork will shine
- chewing gum will be removed

NVQ SVQ RANGE CHECKLIST

LEVEL 1

1C1.1 Prepare service areas and equipment for table or tray service

involving these items

☐ trays ☐ crockery
☐ cutlery ☐ glassware
☐ linen or disposable linen
☐ hot and cold beverage dispensers
☐ refrigerated units
☐ service utensils ☐ trolleys
☐ seasonings
☐ sugars and sweeteners
☐ prepared sauces and dressings

1C1.2 Prepare customer dining areas for table or tray service

involving these

☐ crockery ☐ cutlery
☐ glassware ☐ ashtrays
☐ linen or disposable table coverings
☐ linen or disposable napkins
☐ condiments and accompaniments
☐ decorative items

1C1.3 Clear dining and service areas after service

for

☐ customer dining areas
☐ service preparation areas & trolleys

involving these

☐ trays ☐ crockery
☐ cutlery ☐ glassware
☐ ashtrays
☐ linen or disposable linen
☐ seasonings
☐ sugars and sweeteners
☐ prepared sauces and dressings
☐ hot and cold beverage dispensers
☐ refrigerated units

LEVEL 2

2C1.1 Prepare service equipment and areas for table service

restaurant table service or banquet service involving these

☐ service cutlery and silverware
☐ glassware ☐ trays/trolleys
☐ service dishes & flats
☐ hot plates & plate warmers
☐ refrigerated units
☐ hot and cold beverage dispensers
☐ dry seasonings and flavourings
☐ mustards, sauces, salad dressings
☐ prepared bread items

2C1.2 Prepare customer dining areas for table service

in restaurant table service or banquet service, full place settings for

☐ à la carte menu
☐ table d'hôte menu
☐ buffet functions

and these

☐ crockery
☐ cutlery and silverware
☐ glassware ☐ ashtrays
☐ napkins and table coverings
☐ table decorations
☐ condiments and accompaniments
☐ heating ☐ lighting
☐ music
☐ ventilation or air conditioning

2C1.3 Clear dining and service areas after food service

for restaurant table service and banquet service

☐ customer dining areas
☐ sideboards or sidetables or trolleys
☐ service preparation areas

involving these

☐ crockery
☐ cutlery and silverware
☐ glassware
☐ menus or menu holders
☐ table decorations
☐ ashtrays
☐ condiments and accompaniments
☐ hot plates and plate warmers
☐ refrigerated units
☐ hot and cold beverage dispensers
☐ heating ☐ lighting
☐ music
☐ ventilation or air conditioning

Greeting customers

LEVELS 1 + 2

The appropriate greeting from you will get your relationship with the customers off to a good start. In most cases this means a friendly, warm smile.

As they enter the restaurant

You may need to enquire if they have reserved a table:

Yes – ask for the name and check with the reservations record. For regular customers, or a special party, you are likely to know which table has been prepared and there will be no need to refer to the book.

No – confirm (tactfully if it is an individual) the size of the party (in case others are due to arrive), decide which is the best table to seat them at, and show them to it. If no tables are available, give an estimated waiting time. Provided this is not too long, the customers will usually welcome your suggestion that they should have a drink in the bar: 'I will bring you the menu and take your order after you have had a chance to study it'.

Help with coats and bags as required.

Keep in contact with customers waiting for a table: tell them of any change to the estimated delay, see that they are offered further drinks, and never let someone else get their table first.

At the table

The ideal arrangement is to meet the customers as they are brought to the table. You can help everyone get seated comfortably, pull out chairs, unfold napkins, hand out menus, etc.

If the customers are already seated and studying the menu by the time you arrive (and the sooner this happens the better), welcome them, e.g. 'Good evening'. In some restaurants, staff introduce themselves by name. You might then offer drinks, or take the food order.

 **Units and elements covered in this section**

1C2 Provide a table or tray service **LEVEL 1**
- 1C2.1 Greet customers and take orders
- 1C2.2 Serve customers' orders
- 1C2.3 Maintain dining and service areas

2C2 Provide a table service **LEVEL 2**
- 2C2.1 Greet customers and take orders
- 2C2.2 Serve customers' orders
- 2C2.3 Maintain dining and service areas

Contents guide

Reservation details

Whether the reservation details are kept in a book, diary, printed sheet or simple handwritten form, the minimum information required is:
- day/date
- time of arrival
- number in party
- smoking or non-smoking
- any special needs or requirements, e.g. vegetarian, disabled, children
- name of customer booking
- telephone number and/or address and/or company details.

Some places take the customer's credit card number in advance (to discourage those who make reservations and neither cancel nor turn up).

Cancelled reservations

If there is a cancellation the original reservation should be scored through neatly but clearly, with a note of the day and time when it was cancelled and by whom (and that person's telephone number if different from the details already recorded).

If some misunderstanding has occurred, and you have rubbed out the reservation, there will be no way of checking. Customers have been known to cancel and then turn up. That's great if you have got a table, and no further enquiries need be made. If the restaurant is full, the situation could become tricky – time to get the manager!

Taking orders   LEVELS 1 + 2

Systems vary, from hand-held computer terminals to relying entirely on your memory, but the aims are the same:

- to find out what the customers require to eat and drink

- to pass this information on to those responsible for preparing the food and drink

- to establish what has been, or will be, consumed so that payment can be made. This link may be rather indirect where guests have paid an inclusive price for accommodation and meals – but a check is nevertheless useful. It is not unknown for hungry guests to try to get two breakfasts, or for the generous of heart to try and sneak in friends for a free meal.

An efficient control system enables management to compare the amount of food purchased with the number of meals served, monitor popularity of different items, and reconcile or marry up customer orders with the amount of cash taken.

Taking the order provides an opportunity to promote sales.

General procedure for taking orders – table service

In some restaurants all orders are taken by the restaurant manager or head waiter or waitress. A variation is for waiting staff to take the orders for certain items: sweets, cheese, coffee/tea, etc. In some clubs the customers (members of the club) write the order down.

1 Record what food and drink items each customer at the table requires.

2 Note the table number.

3 Note the number of customers (or covers) at the table. This helps you to check that you have got everyone's order (3 main courses, but 4 covers?). And it gives a clearer picture to others involved in the preparation, service and payment (the drinks server knows to bring 3 glasses, for example).

4 In some situations, the date is required – not for those involved in preparation and service, who will know the order has been taken that day, but for control purposes.

5 If you make a mistake with an order, and have to start again with a fresh order form, do not throw away the incorrect one if it carries a serial number. Cancel the original and attach it to all the copies. Unaccounted for order forms may lead management or the auditors to suspect fraud (e.g. keeping the customer's payment for yourself).

Presenting the menu

Ensure that:

- the host of the party is always identified

- the menus are always presented open to the ladies first, leaving the host until last

- the menu content/layout is fully explained:
    - seasonal menu
    - regional dishes
    - fixed price menu
    - roast trolleys
    - vegetable selection.

Remember:

- the guest does not know the menu, you do

- take every opportunity to sell

- check with the chef prior to service for any items and replacements and always explain these when presenting the menu

Taking an order

Ensure that:

- the guest is not left for a long period of time reading the menu (5 minutes is usually ample time)

- a pink triplicate order pad with the guest identification grid is used to record all food orders

- a well presented ballpoint pen is always used

- writing is clear and easily legible

- each guest is identified by clothing, never by removable items (e.g. glasses) or personal features.

Some variations

Pre-printed order forms and numbered menu items – the time taken to write orders is much reduced where the order form is preprinted with dish/item names. A code or item numbering system can also save time, e.g. 15 = Spanish Omelette. If customers ask for a Spanish Omelette, it's up to you to remember or check the menu to find out what number to write down. It will irritate customers if you expect them to do this for you: 'What number is the dish?'

Hand-held computer terminals – press the key or code allocated to the dish. Some terminals will prompt you with selling opportunities 'Ice cream?' (with apple pie) or reminders 'How done?' (for steak).

The time the order was taken – recorded in those operations where there is a general emphasis on speed. A promise may be given about the service time, e.g. 'We guarantee to serve your meal and present your bill within 30 minutes, or we will tear up the bill' (Harry Ramsden's, the chain of fish restaurants).

Memory aids

A plan of the table may help you to remember which customer ordered which dish. Alternatively put a note by each item, e.g. 'Dark suit'. Customers do not appreciate being asked who is having the soup when not a few minutes before they told you.

Shortcuts

Write only the key details, 'Soup' when there is only one soup on the menu, 'Wild mushrooms' or 'Rissotto' rather than 'Rissotto of wild mushrooms and saffron'. There should be no risk of ambiguity. 'Mushrooms' might mean a special vegetable requirement. 'Rissotto' would only do if there was no other rissotto available.

Many establishments have standard abbreviations which everyone uses. If this is not the case and you develop your own shorthand, check that the kitchen staff and the person making up the bill understand it.

Being accurate, helpful and clear with the order

Always note clearly how many people require each dish.

It will help the kitchen if you keep all the starters together, and all the main courses together, perhaps with a line between the two. When the shout is given 'Starters away, table 6', the chef at the hotplate can quickly check that everything is ready, and not have to scrutinise each word on your jumbled-up order.

Do make a careful note of any special requirements: 'Fried eggs, well cooked', 'Mixed salad NO onion'.

If you are in any doubt – and that includes concern that the customers are clear about what they have ordered – read back the order.

Know your customers: religious and cultural dietary needs

Roman Catholics

May eat any foods they choose, except on Days of Obligation (Ash Wednesday and Good Friday) when no flesh food should be offered.

Egg and cheese dishes are suitable for these occasions.

Jews

Dietary laws prohibit the eating of pork or bacon. A strict Jewish diet uses only Kosher food.

The Local Authority does not provide Kosher food but does expect to supply a full range of dairy and vegetable products which will be suitable.

Muslims

Do not eat meat, offal or animal fat unless it is halal meat.

The Local Authority does not intend to supply halal meat but a choice menu will offer egg, fish, cheese or vegetarian dishes every day. Muslims can eat deep fried food which is cooked in vegetable oil.

Sikhs

Do not eat beef or pork. Devout Sikhs will keep to a vegan diet. Non-vegetarian Sikhs may eat fish, mutton, cheese and eggs. Sikhs never eat halal meat.

Hindus

Do not eat beef and rarely pork. May eat cheese, milk or vegetarian dishes. Some keep to a vegetarian diet eating no meat, fish or eggs.

Different types of vegetarianism

Semi or **demi vegetarians** – exclude red meat or all meat, but fish and other animal products are still eaten. Some also exclude poultry.

Lacto-ovo-vegetarians – exclude all meat, fish and poultry. Milk, milk products and eggs are still consumed.

Lacto-vegetarians – exclude all meat, fish, poultry and eggs. Milk and milk products are still consumed.

Vegans – consume no foods of animal origin. Diets comprise vegetables, vegetable oils, cereals, nuts, fruit and seeds.

Fruitarian – an extreme form of veganism, which excludes all foods of animal origin and also pulses and cereals. Diets comprise mainly raw and dried fruit, nuts, honey and olive oil.

 National Dairy Council.

Customer skills when taking orders

If the customers are not ready to order, offer to return to the table. An enquiring pause at this stage may produce the useful response 'We'll be ready in about 5 minutes', or 'We are just trying to make up our mind about the Surprise Menu' (giving you a sales opportunity).

Face the customers as they make their choice. Look at them when they speak.

Show respect for the customers and try to project your wish to help them enjoy their meal. This may mean a strictly upright posture and 'Thank you, ma'am', or sitting at the table with a customer dining alone, or kneeling on the floor beside a group of customers. It may mean being jovial and chatty, or quiet and respectful.

Judge whose order you should take first. The protocol can be complicated (see page 44). Fortunately, customers will often sort themselves out on whose turn it is to order, or one will act as the spokesperson.

Be patient when customers are indecisive or change their minds. Offer some suggestions, or try and gently guide them to a decision.

Prompt for further requirements. 'Would you like a side order of onion rings?' 'Our avocado with crab and mayonnaise would make a good starter with your lamb cutlets, sir'. Done well, this will boost sales and increase customer satisfaction.

Hospitality and selling standards checklist

Customer acknowledged by smile/eye contact/welcome.

Customers served in turn.

New customers made to feel welcome.

Customers attended to quickly.

Advice on products offered where appropriate.

Effective observation skills demonstrated.

Complaints handled politely and dealt with in appropriate manner.

Selling opportunities exploited, e.g. suggesting a drink to accompany a meal.

New lines/products offered.

On selling

At the end of the main course, rather than saying 'Would you like anything else?', offer customers the choice of TWO items. They are more likely to order something if they have the choice between dessert and coffee or between coffee and liqueur.

ACTION   18

Experience in serving customers will tell you that no matter how many questions you think you have the answer for, you still get surprised by what people don't know, or want to know, or get wrong.

Form a small discussion group with some of your colleagues, and for each of the following examples come up with one or two of your own.

Don't know – and you had assumed they would know: 'Say, how exactly is the cannelloni made?'

Don't know – because they have not eaten in your style of restaurant before: 'Oh dear, do I need to order the main course as well now?'

Want to know – and the need for such information had never occurred to you: 'Is the soup thickened with flour?' (vital information to someone with an allergy to flour).

Want to know – in spite of the detailed menu description: 'This "Fillet of haddock on spinach with light curry sauce", how is the fish cooked, and is the sauce mild?'

Want to know – because they are unfamiliar with traditional – and **get wrong** – French menu terminology: 'The "Choux-fleurs polonaise", that's a way of doing Brussels sprouts?' (No, it's a way of doing cauliflower.)

Want to know – because they are showing off to their colleagues: 'I expect in a place like this you only serve **wild** salmon?'

Want confirmation of – but you can't give it: 'Do you get the breast or leg with the Bombay Duck?' (Bombay Duck is actually dried fish, served as an accompaniment to curry.)

Get wrong – and because you didn't check carefully enough when the order was taken, put you in an embarrassing situation: 'This Gazpacho is cold' (it should be); 'But I ordered Claret and this is red' (all Claret is red); 'This Steak Tartare has not been cooked' (it is meant to be served raw).

Menu knowledge

Basic information you should be ready to give includes:

- any items not available
- specialities of the day and special promotion on specific items, as briefed by management
- for each dish the main ingredients and summary of how it is made
- items that take a particularly long time to prepare, and those suitable for someone in a hurry
- dishes suitable for vegetarians
- what variations to dishes are possible, e.g. baked potato, not chips, with any main course
- price of dishes.

Don't promise what can't be delivered: 'That should be fine, but I'll just have a word with the chef.'

By taking a real interest in the menu, and what people like to eat and drink, you will enjoy the challenge of anticipating and answering the many questions you will receive.

ACTION	19

Get together with a few colleagues. Work through the following list of dishes, taking it in turn to describe the next dish on the list to the other members of the group (playing the role of customers).

The aim of describing each dish (details must include at least the main ingredient and cooking method) is to be informative and accurate, and to create interest.

The Brasserie Restaurant *Birmingham College of Food* *Tourism & Creative Studies*		*The Grand Union Restaurant* *Ealing Hospital*	
Salade Niçoise	☐	Lamb Médaillon Marsala	☐
Pasta Carbonara	☐	Quorn & Spinach Lasagne	☐
Club Sandwich	☐	Potatoes au Gratin	☐
Grilled Salmon Steak with Hollandaise Sauce	☐	Dutch Apple Tart and Custard	☐

5th February 1993

LUNCH

Cream of chicken soup

* * *

Fillet of haddock on a spinach bed
with light curry sauce
or
Smoked cold meat platter

Buttered new potatoes
Sweetcorn fritters

* * *

Hot sweet waffles with redcurrants

* * *

More on menus

Menus tell customers what foods they will be eating, or, if there is a choice, the range they can select from.

Menus usually rely on words to explain what each dish is and how it is prepared, so it is important that they are accurate and clear. Although some establishments still use the traditional language for menus – French – a short explanation of each dish is usually given in English.

When set or limited choice menus are offered, consideration has to be given to balance, colours, texture, flavours, interest and nutritional balance.

Adjusting the table setting

Once you have taken the order and passed on the details to the kitchen, you may need to give thought to what cutlery the customers require:

- supplying an extra knife and fork when you bring the main course, as in a pizza restaurant (where all the knives and forks are likely to be the same size and design and are used for fish as well as meat)

- bringing an extra fish knife and fork with the fish to the customer who used the wrong cutlery for an earlier course in a banquet/set menu situation

- adjusting the basic table lay-up (e.g. table knife and fork) to suit the dishes ordered.

If the table is set for more customers than required, remove the extra place settings. Use the show plate, if there is one, or a clean plate or small tray:

- if the napkin is folded in such a way that it will act as a base, place it on the plate

- pick up each item of cutlery one at a time, and place it on the napkin/plate

- also collect the side plate and the glass(es).

Changing the place setting so that each customer has the right knives, forks, spoons, etc. for the dishes which he or she has ordered.

There are three reasons for removing surplus cutlery after you have taken the order:

- customers don't want their table cluttered up with cutlery they won't be using

- cutting down washing up – if left on the table, the extra cutlery will probably have to be washed

- as a memory prompt to you of what customers have ordered.

By not putting a lot of cutlery on the table in the first place, you help the business cut down on its overheads.

ACTION 20

A colleague has collected the cutlery required for a party of 4 customers. You are given the plate with the cutlery and a copy of the order (below).

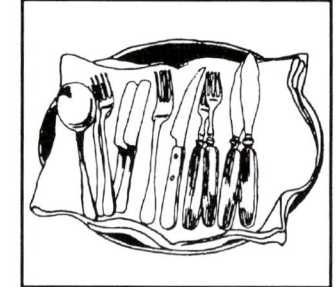

On the order the four customers are identified as 'Host', 'Pearls' (the host's wife is wearing a pearl necklace), 'Bow tie' (which the gentleman guest is wearing), and 'Silk' (referring to the lady guest's blouse). There are, of course, other ways of reminding yourself who has ordered what, e.g. 'Window' is someone in the window seat, or 'A', 'B', 'C', etc. with a mini-plan on the order to indicate which is 'A'.

This is how the table is set now.

Do your own illustration to show how each place setting will look once you have delivered the cutlery. Decide for yourself, and note where each guest is sitting.

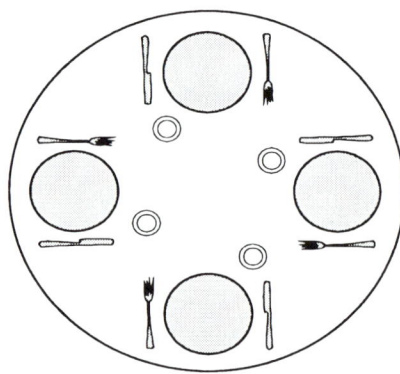

TABLE No. 1   COUVERTS 4

Bow Tie Leek + Potato Soup	Swordfish
Silk Grilled Tuna + Avocado	Spiced Cabbage
Host Wild Mushrooms	Grilled Sirloin Rare
Pearls Grilled Italian Vegetables	Chicken

DATE .... INITIALS cl

3 | 21

ACTION 21

1 For each of these dishes – from the menu of *The Brasserie* restaurant – indicate the cutlery which the customer who ordered that dish would require (by ticking under the appropriate symbol).

2 Indicate the dishes you would recommend to a vegetarian (in the column on the extreme right).

Birmingham COLLEGE OF FOOD · TOURISM · CREATIVE STUDIES

Dish	Cutlery symbols	Vegetarian
French onion soup	☐ ☐ ☐ ☐ ☐ ☐ ☐ ☐ ☐ ☐ ☐ ☐	☐☐
Deep fried brie with cranberry sauce	☐ ☐ ☐ ☐ ☐ ☐ ☐ ☐ ☐ ☐ ☐ ☐	☐☐
Sauté of wild mushrooms	☐ ☐ ☐ ☐ ☐ ☐ ☐ ☐ ☐ ☐ ☐ ☐	☐☐
Country pâté	☐ ☐ ☐ ☐ ☐ ☐ ☐ ☐ ☐ ☐ ☐ ☐	☐☐
Tapenade – black olives, tuna, capers and anchovy pâté served with French bread	☐ ☐ ☐ ☐ ☐ ☐ ☐ ☐ ☐ ☐ ☐ ☐	☐☐
Parma ham with melon	☐ ☐ ☐ ☐ ☐ ☐ ☐ ☐ ☐ ☐ ☐ ☐	☐☐
Smoked Scotch salmon	☐ ☐ ☐ ☐ ☐ ☐ ☐ ☐ ☐ ☐ ☐ ☐	☐☐
Warm salad of goat's cheese, smoked bacon and hazelnuts	☐ ☐ ☐ ☐ ☐ ☐ ☐ ☐ ☐ ☐ ☐ ☐	☐☐
Two eggs en cocotte à la crème	☐ ☐ ☐ ☐ ☐ ☐ ☐ ☐ ☐ ☐ ☐ ☐	☐☐
Two shirred eggs with bacon	☐ ☐ ☐ ☐ ☐ ☐ ☐ ☐ ☐ ☐ ☐ ☐	☐☐
Omelette of your choice	☐ ☐ ☐ ☐ ☐ ☐ ☐ ☐ ☐ ☐ ☐ ☐	☐☐
Pasta piccante	☐ ☐ ☐ ☐ ☐ ☐ ☐ ☐ ☐ ☐ ☐ ☐	☐☐
Pizza napoletana	☐ ☐ ☐ ☐ ☐ ☐ ☐ ☐ ☐ ☐ ☐ ☐	☐☐
Braised tofu with sun-dried tomatoes and wild mushrooms with a hoisin sauce	☐ ☐ ☐ ☐ ☐ ☐ ☐ ☐ ☐ ☐ ☐ ☐	☐☐
King prawns with garlic and herbs	☐ ☐ ☐ ☐ ☐ ☐ ☐ ☐ ☐ ☐ ☐ ☐	☐☐
Char grilled fresh tuna with bruschetta	☐ ☐ ☐ ☐ ☐ ☐ ☐ ☐ ☐ ☐ ☐ ☐	☐☐
Poached salmon with hollandaise sauce	☐ ☐ ☐ ☐ ☐ ☐ ☐ ☐ ☐ ☐ ☐ ☐	☐☐
Char grilled lamb cutlet with ratatouille	☐ ☐ ☐ ☐ ☐ ☐ ☐ ☐ ☐ ☐ ☐ ☐	☐☐
Pork médaillon with calvados & cherry apples	☐ ☐ ☐ ☐ ☐ ☐ ☐ ☐ ☐ ☐ ☐ ☐	☐☐
Bookmaker sandwich	☐ ☐ ☐ ☐ ☐ ☐ ☐ ☐ ☐ ☐ ☐ ☐	☐☐
Ploughman's lunch	☐ ☐ ☐ ☐ ☐ ☐ ☐ ☐ ☐ ☐ ☐ ☐	☐☐

Serving at table

LEVELS 1 + 2

The best decisions in the many different situations you face will develop not from learning a set of rules, but out of a good understanding of the issues involved:

- what order to serve customers in
- which side of the customers to serve from
- what accompaniments to offer with particular dishes
- the sequence of different meals and special events such as banquets

backed by the skills to:

- serve food and drink
- clear between courses.

Order to serve customers in

A formal event is one occasion when you will be given clear rules to follow (an example is given in the activity opposite). In other situations you should try and respond to the customers you are serving. For example:

- if the men in the party have helped the women to the table, and are behaving with what you might think of as old-fashioned courtesy, follow the convention of women before men, the host last
- if the host is a woman who declines your offer to pull her chair out, she would probably expect her male guest to be served first
- if a party of men and women seem to be treating each other as equals and there is no obvious host, serve in whatever order comes naturally and is most efficient, e.g. clockwise.

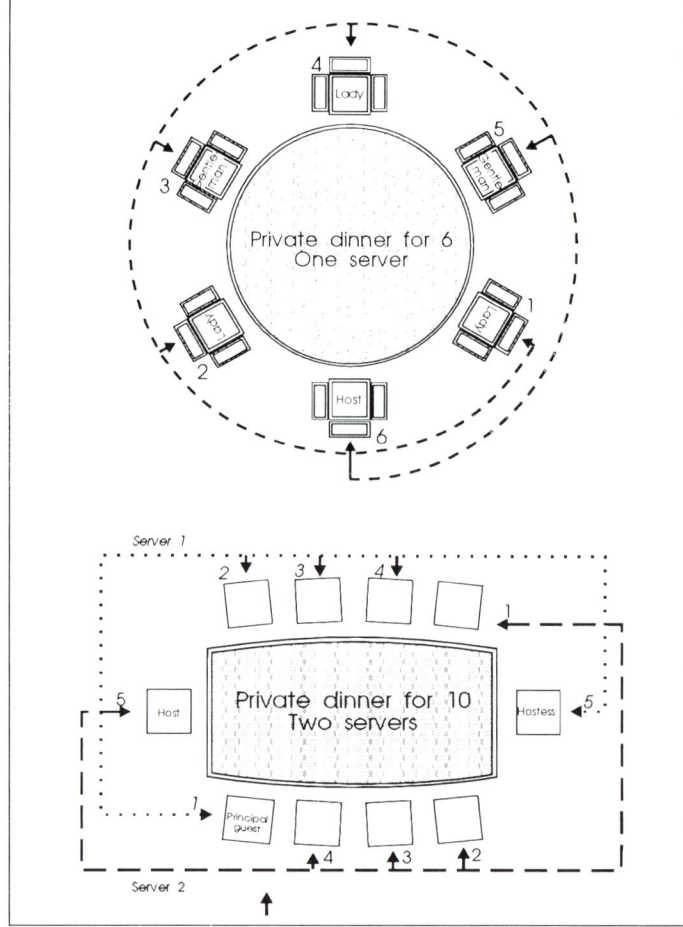

There are various opinions on which order to serve a party of guests. The traditional rules are: women before men; the host last; old before young; children after ladies.

In some restaurants children will be served first, as they tend to get impatient quickly.

A priority with hot food is to get it to the customers as quickly as possible. These illustrations show two ways in which tradition and efficiency can be combined.

Side to serve customers from

You should avoid:

- stretching in front of customers

- needlessly interrupting conversations

- surprising customers – this might happen if you serve one item from the left, the next two from the right, then switch back to the left, all without apparent reason. There could be an accident if the customer suddenly turns in the direction you approach from

- giving the impression of chaos. The symmetry of a banquet is ruined if the serving staff are moving in different directions from each other. The service flow will also be interrupted, and you will be in danger of bumping into colleagues.

Views on which side to serve from generally deal with three categories:

Drinks – most customers use their right hand to hold a glass or cup they are drinking from. Glasses and cups are therefore placed on the right and you should serve anything that goes into the glass or cup from the right. Make an exception for those left-handed customers who prefer to drink with the left hand and rearrange the table setting accordingly.

Placing of clean plates (on to which the food will be served) – some prefer the right, others the left.

Offering or serving of food – generally the left.

Accompaniments

These are offered because they:

- improve the flavour of certain foods, e.g. finely ground, dried ginger with melon

- provide contrast of texture, e.g. toast with pâté

- help counteract richness of food, e.g. apple sauce with pork

- have become traditional, e.g. gravy with roast meat.

Timing will be important if you are responsible for preparing some of these, e.g. freshly-made English mustard, fresh hot toast, buttered brown bread.

With others it is mainly a matter of remembering to collect the item from the service area, your sideboard or the kitchen.

Pay some attention to how the accompaniment is presented, e.g. sauceboat on doily-covered salver, crusts of toast removed.

ACTION 22

The sides of service which might be followed in a traditional/luxury restaurant are shown in the left hand columns below, e.g. present the menu from the *left*, offer/pour water from the *right*.

Use the two workplace columns to indicate what side of service you are expected to use, e.g. present menu from the *left*. Where there is no preference put a **?** in the left and right columns.

From the left			From the right	
Tradit-ional/ luxury	Your work-place		Tradit-ional/ luxury	Your work-place
✓	□	present the menu		□
✓	□	offer bread rolls		□
	□	offer/pour water	✓	□
✓	□	remove fish fork		□
	□	remove fish knife	✓	□
	□	serve soup	✓	□
	□	remove soup spoon	✓	□
✓	□	serve fish		□
	□	pick up crockery and cutlery from first course	✓	□
	□	position main course plate	✓	□
✓	□	serve main course		□
	□	bring down sweet spoon	✓	□
	□	pick up crockery and cutlery from main course	✓	□
✓	□	bring down sweet fork		□
✓	□	place side plate and small knife for cheese		□
✓	□	serve cheese		□
✓	□	offer biscuits, celery for cheese		□

ACTION 23

Many restaurants have standard accompaniments for different types of dish, e.g. a relish tray which is offered with all burgers. In others the accompaniments form part of the presentation of the dish and are prepared by kitchen staff, e.g. thin slices of toast arranged on the plate of pâté.

In those restaurants serving traditional dishes, it is often the responsibility of serving staff to make sure the appropriate accompaniment is offered to the customer. Test your knowledge of these by completing the following quiz.

Tick the 'correct' (i.e. traditionally accepted) accompaniments. There may be more than one. Keep in mind that some customers may request accompaniments other than those listed. They should, of course, be given what they ask for, or, if it is not available, offered alternatives.

For the accompaniments you have not ticked, name one dish that the accompaniment should be offered with.

Tomato juice
- ☐ Lemon slice ....
- ☐ Cheese straw ....
- ☐ Worcestershire sauce ....
- ☐ Tabasco sauce ....

Fresh grapefruit
- ☐ Ginger ....
- ☐ Brown sugar ....
- ☐ Caster sugar ....
- ☐ White pepper ....

Smoked salmon
- ☐ Cayenne pepper ....
- ☐ Lemon wedge ....
- ☐ Buttered brown bread ....
- ☐ Hot toast ....

Prawn cocktail
- ☐ Buttered brown bread ....
- ☐ Toast ....
- ☐ Tomato sauce ....
- ☐ Freshly milled white pepper ....

Spaghetti
- ☐ Rye bread ....
- ☐ Cheese straws ....
- ☐ Parmesan cheese ....
- ☐ Freshly milled black pepper ....

Smoked trout
- ☐ Lemon wedge ....
- ☐ Cayenne pepper ....
- ☐ Horseradish ....
- ☐ Buttered brown bread ....

Melon boats/sliced melon
- ☐ Brioche ....
- ☐ Lemon segment ....
- ☐ Caster sugar ....
- ☐ Ground ginger ....

Minestrone soup
- ☐ Poppadums ....
- ☐ Parmesan cheese ....
- ☐ Melba toast ....

Fish fried in batter/bread crumbs
- ☐ Tomato sauce ....
- ☐ Lemon wedge ....
- ☐ Mayonnaise ....
- ☐ Tartar sauce ....

Poached fish in a sauce
- ☐ Croissants ....
- ☐ Pitta bread ....
- ☐ Croûtons ....
- ☐ Worcestershire sauce ....

Sorbet
- ☐ Hot chocolate sauce ....
- ☐ Water biscuit ....
- ☐ Raspberry sauce ....
- ☐ Wafer ....

Green or mixed salad
- ☐ Mayonnaise ....
- ☐ Olive oil ....
- ☐ Vinegar ....
- ☐ Vinaigrette ....

Roast beef
- ☐ Brown sauce ....
- ☐ Gravy ....
- ☐ Mint sauce ....
- ☐ Dijon mustard ....

Roast lamb
- ☐ Freshly milled pepper ....
- ☐ Cranberry sauce ....
- ☐ Redcurrant jelly ....
- ☐ Mint sauce ....

Roast pork
- ☐ Horseradish ....
- ☐ Gravy ....
- ☐ Apple sauce ....
- ☐ English mustard ....

Roast turkey
- ☐ Gravy ....
- ☐ Soy sauce ....
- ☐ Cranberry sauce ....
- ☐ Bread sauce ....

Grilled steak (beef)
- ☐ Chutney ....
- ☐ Béarnaise sauce ....
- ☐ Parsley butter ....
- ☐ French or English mustard ....

Curry
- ☐ Nan bread ....
- ☐ Sliced beetroot ....
- ☐ Parmesan cheese ....
- ☐ Grated coconut ....
- ☐ Orange segments ....

Chateaubriand
- ☐ Bombay duck ....
- ☐ Béarnaise sauce ....
- ☐ German mustard ....
- ☐ Gravy ....

Pasta dish
- ☐ Ketchup ....
- ☐ Grated Parmesan ....
- ☐ Freshly milled black pepper ....
- ☐ Tomato relish ....

Cheese
- ☐ Butter ....
- ☐ Apple ....
- ☐ Sliced banana ....
- ☐ Rolls or biscuits ....

Sequence of different meals and special events

Customers generally expect certain items to be offered at particular stages of the meal. In many cases this is a combination of tradition and the way in which the palate reacts to different flavours and textures. At breakfast, for example, fruit juice at the beginning of the meal sharpens the palate. Drunk after a strong beverage like coffee, the juice tastes unpleasant.

The menu is usually built around the accepted order of dishes, moving from the light and delicate to the more substantial. The dessert or sweet course will be designed to finish off the meal. But because customers' appetite will depend on what they have eaten before, the sweet order is not taken until the preceding course has been eaten. This would not apply where there is a set menu and no choice, but careful menu planning will have taken account of likely preferences.

As in so many other aspects of food and drink service, traditions and tastes are changing. This is partly the influence of visitors to Britain. Many Americans like to drink coffee throughout their meals, and also insist on iced water. The French take cheese before their dessert.

Serving guests checklist

1 Prepare all areas for service.

2 Carry out tea and coffee jugs in the correct manner, i.e. one in each hand.

3 Bring soup out in soup jug and carry in hand.

4 Use plate rack to carry out main meals.

5 Fill plate rack to capacity and use spare hand to carry salads only.

6 Collect salads first.

7 Serve sweets using rack system.

8 Take out cheese and biscuits in large basket and offer to customer. These should not be left on table.

9 Use rack to take empty plates/bowls away.

10 Maintain a smiling and helpful attitude with customers at all times.

Chef and Brewer, owners of Old Orleans restaurants, are rightly proud of the 26-point Order of Service.

All service staff are trained in the service of food and drinks, and move between bar and restaurant duties regularly.

The kitchen staff are trained in seating and greeting techniques, and from time to time are given these duties in the restaurant. The pressures they experience in the kitchen can then be related to what is happening 'front of house' during different stages of the meal service.

ORDER OF SERVICE

1 Introduce yourself by your first name as soon as possible (3 minutes maximum).

2 Offer popcorn.

3 Suggest drinks as customers read menu.

4 Ring drinks into till.

5 Serve drinks.

6 Take order, suggest side orders and drinks, ask how burgers and steaks should be cooked.

7 Always suggest wine with main courses.

8 Ring order into till.

9 Deliver starters.

10 Clear starters, empty glasses etc. and check what will be required to accompany main courses (e.g. bibs and side plates), and give hot towels after Buffalo Wings.

11 Let the kitchen know you've cleared the starters.

12 Take out bibs and side plates, steak knives.

13 Deliver main courses, inform customers about hot towels, napkins on table and offer relishes and mustards.

14 Before leaving ask customers if there is anything else they require and say: 'Enjoy your meal'.

15 Check back within 2 minutes:
   – Are you having fun?
   – Is the food good?
   – Do you need anything else?

16 Give hot towels when people are finished with main courses.

17 Clear all the finished plates, empty glasses, napkins and hot towels.

18 Return with menu and suggest desserts.

19 Suggest coffee with dessert order and ask when it is required – if nothing else required, give bill.

20 Ring desserts and coffee into till.

21 Clear dessert plates and coffee cups.

22 Ask if customers 'require anything else'. No customer should have to ask for the bill.

23 Present bill in a Thank You card on a side plate with 4 complimentary sweets per person and a comment card.

24 When presenting the bill say: 'Pay me when you are ready'.

25 Take payment and return change promptly with the receipt.

26 As the customers leave, thank them and say 'We look forward to seeing you again'.

NB It is not Old Orleans style to script our waiting staff, so please feel free to find your own way of giving the same message as in the order or service.

Banquets

Every aspect has to be carefully coordinated. You will usually be briefed before the event on:

- *the menu, the service requirements and accompaniments for each dish* – with plate service each member of staff might carry 3 or 4 dishes. If there are sidetables in the room, 6 or 8 dishes might be taken on trays to the sidetable, and then in 2s to the table. With silver service, each person can serve up to 10 or 12 customers from the same serving dish

- *what drinks will be served and when* – if wine is to be offered to all guests, for example, there may be a limit on the amount per guest. If it is up to guests to order and pay for their own drinks, there may be time to take drink orders before everyone sits down. In this situation, bottles of wine will be opened and left on the tables so that guests can help themselves

- *what signals will be given to indicate different stages of the meal* – usually clearing after each course will not start until the last guest has finished, and the head waiter/waitress has given a signal.

- *special requirements* – if there are to be speeches, serving staff will have to work very quietly, or, more usually, they will be expected to serve the coffee, brandy, etc. quickly, then leave the room. Sometimes guests will retire for a time from the banquet room, while the tables are completely cleared, possibly re-arranged and a dance floor put down.

Difficulties experienced by those with visual disabilities

Certain styles of food service present problems: food served silently; meat or poultry served on the bone; and banquet-style meals, where there is no individual order or Braille menu. In situations like that, I can feel hungry and frustrated because I don't know if the food is there or, if it is, what it is, and I am denied the essential elements of anticipation and savouring.

 Joseph Pardini, who has been visually impaired since childhood, in Personally Speaking, 26 November 1992

St John's College Fellows' Dinner

1 Soup/starter served. Soups are dished up at the hotplate, other starters silver served.

2 Wine served. Draught beer and Guinness are available as alternatives. Collect from the buttery bar at about 7.25 p.m. Some Fellows drink only white wine, and are served from the buttery bar supply when other Fellows have red wine.

3 Bread offered. Toast is placed on the tables beforehand.

4 Soup/starter cleared.

5 Vegetable dishes placed on table.

6 Main course silver served. If the Master or President is residing, vegetables are served to him and his two neighbours; other Fellows help themselves from the dishes on the table.

7 Second round of wine/beer served.

8 Main course cleared.

9 Sweet served. Usual choice is between specified sweet/savoury (silver served), fruit pie (dished up at hotplate), or cheese (choice of cheese board or Stilton) and biscuits.

10 Sweet cleared.

11 When presider is ready, hand-bell rung for Grace.

Between steps 6 and 8, the Butler clears away the sherry from the Green Room and lights the candles ready for coffee service. Coffee is set out between steps 9 and 10.

Order of service: formal dinner

Waiter/waitress on station 1 starts serving with the President and proceeds to the right. Station 2 starts to the left of the President. As soon as station 1 has started, other stations begin serving.

Intermediate clearance

This takes place on the completion of the last course. The only items left on the tables are: table decorations including candelabra and flowers, and a port glass in front of each diner.

Loyal toast

The port and Madeira are placed in front of the President and Vice Presidents who pass the decanters in a clockwise direction. Staff follow the decanters round the table to offer water to any diner who declines port or Madeira. All staff then leave the dining room before the President gives the toast.

Coffee

Coffee is served after the Loyal Toast and a team of three is normally allocated to each station. Cigars, cigarettes and liqueurs are offered, then all staff leave the dining room.

 Adapted with permission, Royal Air Force School of Catering

Because banquets are generally for large groups of people (around 20 to 500 or more), their success depends on good teamwork and timing.

Serving food and drink

Your aim is to get the food to the customers in the best possible state:

- well presented, so that it looks attractive
- at the right temperature, so it is enjoyable to eat
- hygienically, so that it is safe to eat.

The rules are mostly to do with timing:

- serve drinks before food
- collect the food when it is needed
- collect plates before or with the food
- collect and serve cold food before hot food
- serve the main item of any course first, e.g. meat before vegetables.

If you have to ask a colleague to take over a table you are serving, pass on any information which will help to give quality service, e.g. that the guest does not want to be offered any more wine.

LEVEL 2

Carrying plated food

1 Use the right hand to pick up plates 1 and 2, and to pick up and carry plate 3.
2 Use the left hand to carry plates 1 and 2.
3 Hold plate 1 with the first two fingers (on the underside of the plate), and the thumb (on top of the plate).
4 Make a platform with the third and fourth fingers and the base of the thumb to hold plate 2.

If left handed, you may prefer to switch this routine.

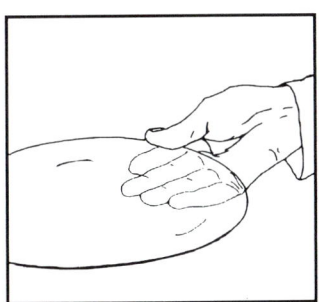

Picking up a (glass) plate. Note the position of the fingers (to provide a safe grip) and the thumb (well clear of the eating surface).

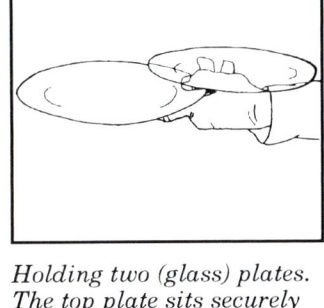

Holding two (glass) plates. The top plate sits securely on the platform provided by the base of the thumb, and the tips of the third and fourth fingers.

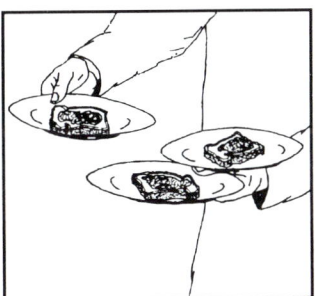

Carrying all three plates (this time with food).

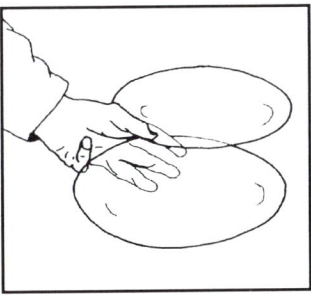

With practice it is possible to carry three plates in one hand. Plate 1 (lower of the two) is supported underneath by the second and third fingers, and on top by the first finger. Plate 2 is held between the thumb and first finger.

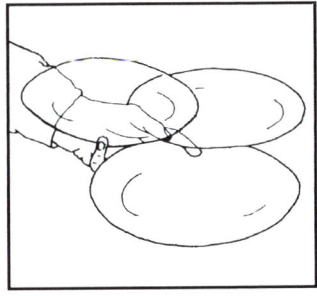

Plate 3 then sits on the platform formed by the base of the thumb, the base of the hand and the tip of the little finger (crooked upwards).

General points to note when serving food and drink

The plates should be at the correct temperature. Hot food must be served on hot plates (but not so hot they cannot be handled), cold food on cold plates.

Use a serving cloth to hold hot plates. Warn customers when plates are very hot.

Take care that sauce or gravy is not spilt on the table as you put the dish down.

Carry filled soup plates very carefully to avoid the soup swirling on to the rim of the plate, which will leave an unsightly 'tide mark'.

If the plate rim has had gravy or sauce spilt on it, wipe with a clean serving cloth or paper napkin before taking to the table.

If you drop cutlery or crockery on the floor, return it for washing. Discard dropped food. Pick up the dropped item as soon as you can but avoid unnecessary interruptions to the service.

The correct way of serving is determined by what your customers expect, and your workplace procedures.

Serving cheese

Waiting staff are sometimes responsible for preparing the cheese board, as well as its service.

1 Bring out cheese from refrigerator about one hour before use.

2 Arrange the cheeses so that there is a variety of shapes, colours and flavours. Decorate with celery, grapes, apples, radishes, etc., but don't swamp the cheese.

3 Use a large surface so each cheese can keep its flavour and crumbs apart from the other.

4 Use a separate knife for blue cheeses. (Some restaurants provide a different knife for each cheese.) A fork will be useful to help pick up cheeses.

5 When cutting a whole cheese, a horizontal slice should be taken, leaving the top surface as even as possible. Scooping is wasteful.

6 Wedges should be cut lengthways from nose to crust. Never cut across the nose of a wedge.

7 Remove pieces of cheese that have become so small they look unappealing.

8 Provide the customer with a clean side plate, side knife (and sometimes fork) and a fresh dish of butter. Cruets should be available. Biscuits, bread, celery, radishes and fruit may be offered or left on the table.

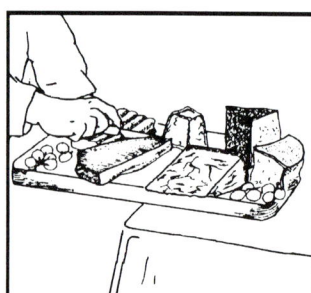

The cheeseboard can be heavy, and some cheeses are hard to cut. Rest the edge of the board on the table to get firm support.

✎ *Courtesy Milk Marketing Board and Caterer & Hotelkeeper*

ACTION 24

The ticked items in the left column below indicate the typical sequence of events for the service of a Continental breakfast. The list also includes steps which relate to the service of breakfast for those who want a more substantial meal. Tick the steps which might apply to:

• traditional full English breakfast (as offered in your workplace or in a hotel which you know)
• the speciality breakfast of a hotel popular with tourists from Europe and America.

Cont'al		Eng-lish	Spec-iality
	Present menu	☐	☐
☑	Take order for fruit juice & beverage	☐	☐
	Take order	☐	☐
	Pour iced water	☐	☐
	Serve hot porridge/cereals	☐	☐
	Clear starter	☐	☐
☑	Serve hot beverage	☐	☐
☑	Serve hot roll/croissant and/or toast	☐	☐
	Serve main course	☐	☐
	Offer maple syrup (for waffles)	☐	☐
	Offer cold meat platter	☐	☐
	Offer cheese platter	☐	☐
	Offer fresh fruit basket	☐	☐
	Clear main course	☐	☐
☑	Offer more beverages & toast	☐	☐
☑	Check table for butter, marmalade, milk, etc.	☐	☐

Clearing between courses

Clearing plates one or two at a time, and stacking them on the sideboard or out of the room, has the advantage of quietness. Generally it is more practical to stack them in your hand, as you move around the table.

Trays can also make clearing easier. They are particularly useful after customers have left the table and there are a lot of items to remove.

Start clearing when all customers have finished. Leave a slight pause so customers do not feel hurried.

'Crumbing down', if part of the routine, is usually done after the main course. Use a folded napkin (or special brush made for this purpose) to brush the crumbs from the table surface on to a plate.

If customers are smoking, change the ashtray regularly. Take care when lifting the ashtray off the table – ash is light and may blow or fall out of the ashtray. With some ashtray designs, you can invert a clean ashtray over the full one, then remove both, the clean ashtray acting as a lid. Once you have got the full ashtray safely to your tray, place the clean one down on the table.

General procedure for clearing plates   LEVEL 2

Plates are normally removed with the right hand, from the right hand side of the customer.

Picking up the 1st plate

1 Move back away from the customer and transfer the plate to the left hand for stacking.

2 Standing behind the customer, gently scrape any remaining food into a pile with a fork.

3 Arrange the knife and fork at right angles, with the knife blade under the bridge of the fork.

Picking up the other plates

4 Remove the next customer's plate. Transfer it to the platform you have formed (see illustration).

5 Remove the knife from this plate and slip it under the fork on the lower plate.

6 With the fork, scrape remaining food on to the lower plate. Place the fork with the rest on the lower plate.

7 Continue to clear plates until the table is cleared, or no more plates can be carried safely. Eight is normally the maximum, but if there is a lot of debris, it is easier to clear a few plates at a time, and remove to the sideboard or the wash-up area.

When clearing side plates which are small (e.g. after the cheese course) it may be helpful to take a clean dinner plate to the table. This can act as the first plate and it will be much easier to stack cutlery and scrape debris on to this larger plate.

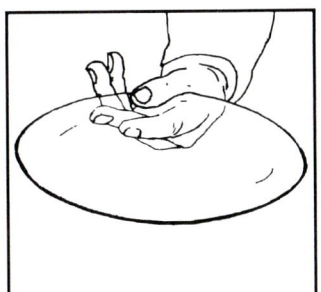

The first plate is gripped securely by the thumb (on top), with the first and second fingers underneath. The tips of the third and fourth fingers form a platform (with the base of the wrist) for the second plates (and those stacked on top of it).

Cutlery can be prevented from sliding around the stacking plate by positioning the first fork so that the thumb can hold it against the plate.

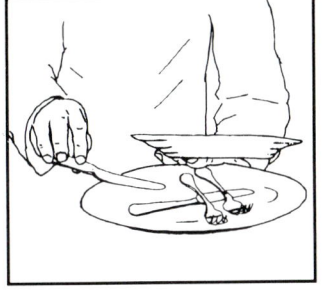

The knife blade is placed under the fork to reduce the risk of cutlery falling off. Knives and forks should be angled so that if any fall off the plate, it will be on to the floor, not the customer.

With experience, you can transfer the cutlery and any debris to the lower plate as you move between customers.

Crumb down when you need to. Customers may see it as an unnecessary interruption of their conversation if you insist on trying to brush away crumbs that aren't there.

ACTION   25

What is wrong about the way these plates are being cleared? Comment against the illustration and/or in the space below.

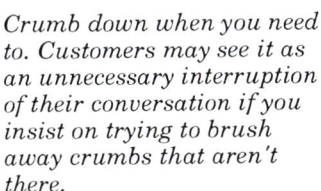

Tray service

LEVEL 1

With tray service you will not usually be face-to-face with customers to collect their orders.

In hotels a special room service order form provides a convenient way of informing guests what is available for breakfast/morning tea, together with the cost. The same form is used to place the order, and is designed so that it can be hung on the outer door handle of the bedroom or suite.

1 Collect the orders during the night – the night porter may be responsible for doing this.

2 Prepare the trays as far as possible in advance (see page 35).

3 Add the last minute items (hot beverage, toast, cooked breakfast, etc.) and set off for the room so that you arrive at the requested time. Punctuality is obviously always important, but for business guests who have appointments to keep, planes to catch, etc., even a few minutes delay could be disastrous.

4 Pass on details needed to make up the guest's bill without delay.

Taking room service orders by telephone

1 Answer the phone with an appropriate greeting, e.g. 'Good evening/morning, room service, Aden speaking, how may I help you?'

2 Write down the order on the check pad, offering advice as appropriate on the menu.

3 Ask for the name of the guest and the room number.

4 Repeat the order, the guest's name and room number to confirm the details.

5 Thank the guest and give an estimate of when the order will be delivered (or confirm that it will be delivered at the time the guest has requested).

The final check

When checking a tray, imagine you are about to eat the meal and go through in your mind all the stages. For an English breakfast this might be:

- a knife and fork for the egg and bacon
- cup and saucer for the beverage
- teaspoon to stir the beverage
- butter and marmalade or jam for the toast
- small knife for cutting and buttering the toast
- side plate for the toast
- napkin to keep crumbs off the bedding and for wiping the mouth
- salt and pepper to season the food
- sugar (white/brown) or saccharin to sweeten the beverage.

Sequence of service for breakfast

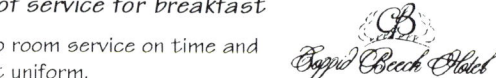

1 Report to room service on time and in correct uniform.

2 Check you have enough mis en place. If not prepare more. Check that we have fresh coffee. If not make fresh.

3 Arrange door knob orders in correct time order, i.e. the earliest first and the latest last.

4 Pick up orders to be delivered and arrange tray/trolley.

5 Deliver the order as follows:
  - each order must leave room service 3 to 5 minutes before order should arrive
  - use only service lift
  - before entering guest room, knock firmly 3 times and announce 'Room service, good morning'
  - when guest answers the door, greet warmly using his/her name, i.e. 'Good morning Mr Jones, your breakfast, sir.'
  - if you are using a trolley make sure to set it up properly for the guest putting the first course in front of the guest
  - when serving hot dishes remove from hot box and place above fork
  - ask if guest would like chairs placed around the trolley
  - when using tray place on table or desk, make sure the guest has plenty of elbow room
  - offer to pour coffee/tea, open curtains, turn on light, etc. Be sure to ask first
  - present check to guest for signing, offering hotel pen
  - enquire if everything is satisfactory and depart by saying 'Thank you Mr Jones, I hope you have a nice day'.

6 Return to room service straight away collecting any dirty trays/trolleys along the way.

ACTION 26

From the example room service procedures given here and your own knowledge, prepare a checklist which could be used by the catering staff responsible for preparing and delivering meal trays to the offices of directors and senior management.

Patient meal service

The Clementine Churchill Hospital

1 Check board for any dietary or other specific room serving instructions, e.g. requested serving time is different from normal, food needs cutting up, nurse must be told when/before meal is served.

2 Check that ALL items ordered on the menu are presented on the tray, and that the tray is properly set up.

3 BEFORE knocking on the door, look at the name on the door. If there is a DO NOT ENTER display, return to the room service pantry and check with the nursing staff when the patient's meal can be served. Follow procedure for disposal of patient's food.

4 Knock on the door and wait for a response. If no reply, knock once more, pause for several seconds before slowly entering the room.

5 Greet the patient: 'Good morning/afternoon/evening Mr/Mrs/Ms...' If you cannot pronounce the surname, or no name is apparent on the door, simply address the patient using Sir or Madam.

6 Introduce yourself at this point if you are meeting the patient for the first time. Never ask the patient about his/her reason for admission.

7 Place the tray on the over-bed table such that the patient can eat/drink comfortably.

8 Do not leave the room before asking the patient if the tray is positioned to his/her satisfaction. Point out that the metal lid over hot food items is extremely hot and offer to remove it.

9 If the menu does not indicate a post-meal beverage, check that the patient has not simply overlooked this item.

10 When you return to collect the tray, ask the patient if he/she enjoyed the meal.

11 If the patient has not finished when you return, ask if he/she is enjoying the meal/beverage and, if necessary, reassure the patient that there is no need to hurry.

12 Any significant patient comments you receive during your visits to a room, must be passed on to the duty supervisor at the earliest convenient moment.

Maintaining dining and service areas

LEVELS 1 + 2

Cluttered tables and an untidy room reflect badly on all the serving staff and the standards of your workplace in general. Problems occur when things are really busy, and you can just about cope with the customers who are already at your tables, and the new arrivals.

There is no easy solution. Try and remain calm, continue to work methodically, and make the most of each journey to or from the service area. It will only take a few moments longer if you clear some things from an adjacent table, before you go off to collect the next course for a group of customers.

Clearing should be carried out as quietly as possible. Handle the cutlery gently but firmly. Do not bang the plates when scraping or piling them, even if there are no customers present.

You mustn't leave the kitchen empty handed. Please collect cutlery, crockery, etc. which has been washed and return it to the restaurant. This eliminates congestion in the kitchen.

THE FOX & PHEASANT

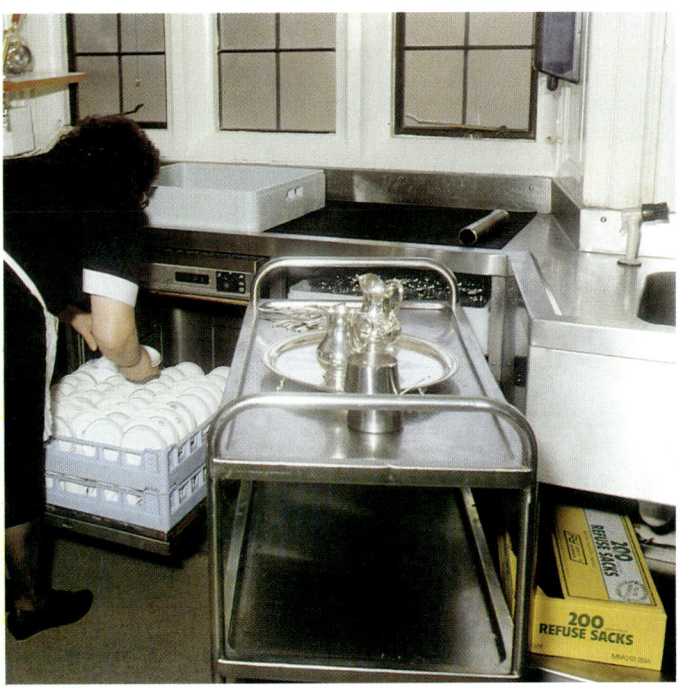

If you are responsible for doing the washing up yourself, you will realise how helpful it is when colleagues stack used crockery, cutlery, glassware, etc. neatly, put rubbish in the bin, and empty bottles in the proper place.

Good timing and good teamwork are the keys to good service.

RANGE CHECKLIST
NVQ SVQ

LEVEL 1

1C2.1 Greet customers and take orders

in table service or tray service, with these customers

- [ ] adults
- [ ] children
- [ ] large parties
- [ ] those with mobility difficulties
- [ ] those with communication difficulties

and provide information on these

- [ ] items available
- [ ] dish composition
- [ ] prices, special offers and promotions

1C2.2 Serve customers' orders

in table service or tray service, serving these

- [ ] soup
- [ ] hot drinks
- [ ] cold soft drinks
- [ ] hot plated items
- [ ] cold plated items

and these

- [ ] seasonings
- [ ] sugars and sweeteners
- [ ] prepared sauces and dressings

1C2.3 Maintain dining and service areas

in table service or tray service, involving these

- [ ] crockery
- [ ] cutlery
- [ ] glassware
- [ ] ashtrays
- [ ] condiments and accompaniments

LEVEL 2

2C2.1 Greet customers and take orders

in restaurant table service or banquet service, with these customers

- [ ] children
- [ ] large parties
- [ ] customers with bookings
- [ ] customers without bookings
- [ ] those with mobility difficulties
- [ ] those with communication difficulties

providing information on these

- [ ] dishes available
- [ ] prices
- [ ] dish composition and method of cooking

2C2.2 Serve customers' orders

with plated or silver served items, using these

- [ ] dishes, liners or flats
- [ ] trays or trolleys
- [ ] service cutlery and silverware
- [ ] service cloths or linen
- [ ] cutlery and crockery
- [ ] condiments and accompaniments

2C2.3 Maintain dining and service areas

involving these

- [ ] crockery
- [ ] glassware
- [ ] cutlery and silverware
- [ ] ashtrays
- [ ] table coverings
- [ ] napkins
- [ ] dry seasonings and flavourings
- [ ] mustards, sauces and dressings
- [ ] prepared bread items

ACTION 27

Using a format similar to the table below (used in the room service department at the Coppid Beech Hotel), produce a selling recommendation checklist which would be helpful in your workplace – for table service or tray service, or a more appropriate situation.

You may find it helpful to refer back to the ideas you developed in ACTION 3 on page 7.

| Guest order | Selling recommendations | | | |
	No. 1	No. 2	No. 3	No. 4
Soup	Sherry	Salad	Beverage	
Soup and salad	Wine	Beverage	Dessert	Coffee/cognac
Main course	Soup/salad	Dessert	Coffee/cognac	Wine
Champagne	Strawberries	Canapés		
Wine	Mineral water	Canapés		
Snack	Soft drink	Salad		
Coffee	Snack	Beverage		

Carvery and buffet service

Introduction

In both carvery and buffet service, customers leave their table to choose from the dishes and roast joints of meat on display. With some types of buffet there may be only informal seating, the majority of people choosing to stand.

Carveries

Carvery service can offer customers good value for money – particularly if there is no restriction on portion size. They give customers the opportunity to choose their favourite types of roast meat, while enjoying seeing the joints being carved.

In restaurants where carvery service is offered, the first course and sweets are usually brought to the customers at their table by the serving staff. If the customers have selected a roast joint for their main course they leave the table, choose which meat they would like at the carvery counter and either carve for themselves or, more usually, indicate their requirements to the chef who will be standing by.

Often three or four meats will be on offer (e.g. pork, beef, lamb and turkey) accompanied by gravy and the appropriate sauces (apple, horseradish, mint, cranberry, etc.). Dishes of vegetables and potatoes are also available, sometimes for customers to serve themselves.

Buffet service

Some establishments offer nothing but a buffet service. Others offer buffet service for certain meals such as lunch, or for specific occasions such as a dinner dance or conference lunch. Sometimes buffet service is combined with table service, for example, at breakfast when customers help themselves to cereals and fruit from a buffet table and serving staff bring the toast, hot dishes and beverages to the table.

Often the customers only serve themselves to the food. The tables are already set with the cutlery and glasses that will be required. Serving staff supply wine, other drinks and beverages and clear the tables during and after the meal.

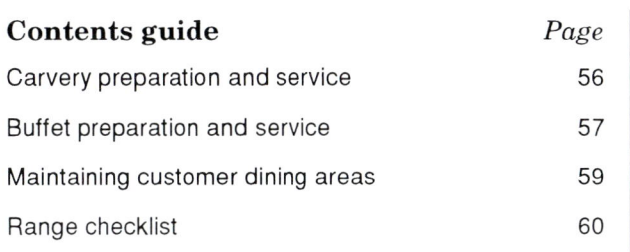

Carveries and buffets give an opportunity for impressive displays of food. They can give customers a wide choice of dishes, and provide a fairly fast, efficient means of service suited to many different sorts of occasion.

The arrangements for paying for the buffet may have been agreed in advance between the organiser and the management, in which case the guests and serving staff are not involved in any cash transactions. Alternatively, a fixed price buffet may be offered, including as much as the customer chooses to eat or a specific limit of a starter, main course, sweet and coffee, for example. In some buffets, customers will pay only for what they have chosen.

Buffets may be completely self-service – for example, for small business meetings serving staff may set up the buffet on a table in an adjacent room, with everything that is required including cutlery, napkins, crockery, wine and other drinks, coffee and liqueurs. The serving staff will not enter the room until the customers have returned to their meeting.

Usually, however, serving staff are present during the buffet service, clearing after courses, removing serving dishes as they become empty, replenishing as necessary.

Serving staff may also be stationed behind the buffet table to serve some or all of the dishes to customers. This helps preserve the presentation of the food and control portion sizes. It also speeds up service.

 **Units and elements covered in this section**

LEVEL 2

2C4 Provide a carvery or buffet service
- 2C4.1 Prepare and maintain a carvery or buffet display
- 2C4.2 Serve customers at the carvery or buffet
- 2C4.3 Maintain customer dining areas

Carvery preparation and service

Generally chefs will be responsible for bringing out the joints of meat and for carving. You need to know what roasts are available, so that you can advise customers.

Preparing the dining area

The general procedures are similar to the preparation of dining areas for table service (see section 5).

1 Wipe down and polish tables and chairs. Position them according to the standard layout for the restaurant and the special requirements of any large groups of customers who have booked in advance.

2 Lay tablecloths and/or placemats. What cutlery is put on the table will depend on the menu choice and your restaurant's policy. For example, it may consist of a large knife (on the right of the setting), a large fork (on the left of the setting) and a small knife on or by the side plate. Other cutlery is added once customers have ordered. Napkins will usually be folded and placed by each setting. A wine glass may complete the setting.

3 Check that each table has salt and pepper pots, mustards and sauces (unless these are available at the carvery or brought to the table when customers have chosen their food). Promotional material, menus, no-smoking signs, flowers, table numbers, etc. should be in position. Ensure menus and promotional material are in good condition.

Preparing the carvery counter

1 Restock the carvery counter with plates, having checked that each one is clean and not chipped or cracked. Turn the plate warmer or hot cupboard on in time for the plates to warm before service starts.

2 Ensure that all surfaces of the counter are clean, with no smears. Promotional displays must look attractive if they are to be effective. Menus should be accurate, e.g. with correct details for the roast of the day. If you write up the menu board, use plain, clear lettering. Plan the layout carefully so that you do not have to squash up words at the end of the line. Ask someone to check your spelling.

3 Place sauces and accompaniments on the counter.

4 Put out sufficient service utensils for the vegetables, spoons and ladles for the sauces.

5 As plates will probably be very hot when customers collect their meat, many restaurants have a supply of paper napkins at the counter.

6 If this is your responsibility, collect vegetables, salads, gravies, hot sauces, Yorkshire puddings, etc. from the kitchen and position on the counter just before service begins.

ACTION 28

Some customers find carveries and buffets intimidating. Breakfast buffets can be a particular problem when it is not clear what dishes customers are meant to help themselves to, and which are served.

Note briefly below what you could do to help in each of the situations described. Ask some colleagues and friends to do the same. Discuss how your approaches compare. What other situations can they think of, where your attentiveness as a server would really help the customer?

1 A child is too short to see the extent of the buffet display.

2 A guest has put some of the dessert (not having recognised what it is) as well as main course items on the same plate.

3 A guest is in a wheelchair.

4 A group of children keep running back to the buffet table, and darting in and out between customers.

5 A guest has difficulty walking.

6 A guest's hand is very shaky and you are worried the food might spill off the plate.

7 A guest has severely impaired vision.

8 A breakfast customer has gone straight to a table, and is looking around the room impatiently. (Everything is available on the self-service buffet, except for tea/coffee. Your colleague who should be serving that table is very busy with a large group of customers.)

Buffet preparation and service

There are three types of buffet:

Table buffet – customers sit at tables to enjoy the food which they have chosen and collected from the buffet.

Fork buffet – usually a stand-up affair, although some seating may be provided, this would not be at a laid-up table. Customers collect their food, a napkin and fork from the buffet table. Staff circulate throughout the room collecting plates which have been finished with, refilling drink glasses, etc. You might also be offering second helpings in this way, or new dishes.

Finger buffet – no cutlery is provided. The food is a size which can be easily popped into the mouth in one go. Customers help themselves to food from a buffet table, or staff circulate with dishes, or both methods may be in operation. Some chairs may be provided for customers who find it uncomfortable to stand for long periods.

An advantage of fork and finger buffets is that those attending can circulate freely among the other guests.

Preparing the buffet table

If this is your responsibility, you will be given instructions and perhaps a plan showing the general organisation of the room.

Clothing the buffet table

The traditional buffet table covering is a white tablecloth, which falls almost to the floor at the front, and is pinned around to cover or 'box in' the sides of the table.

Special buffet cloths provide a quick way of 'dressing the front and sides of the table. These come in various designs and colours, some with very decorative frills.

Banquet rolls are also available. These are in effect a very long disposable tablecloth. The required length is simply cut off, so that most lengths of table can be covered with just one cloth.

Slip cloths placed over the top of the buffet can provide attractive colour contrast, and check-patterned cloths give a touch of bright informality.

Any overlap of cloths on a table should face away from the direction that customers will first see the table. The overlap will be less noticeable, and so a better first impression is created.

If a number of cloths have to be used to cover a long table, the overlaps should all be in the same direction, preferably away from the main approach to the table. Do check that the cloths are level at the bottom.

Plates and cutlery

Plates can be arranged on the buffet table itself (at one end of the table, or in piles along the table), or on a smaller table nearby. Customers should not find themselves selecting food without a plate on which to put it.

Dessert plates should be near the desserts, hot plates near hot food. Where customers might choose a combination of hot and cold food, it may not be appropriate to have hot plates.

If staff are responsible for serving all the dishes, it makes better use of space on the buffet table and is more convenient for everyone if plates are kept at the back of the table, where the serving staff stand.

Where buffets are a regular feature, the food is often displayed on a purpose-built counter, with one area for chilled dishes and another for hot dishes.

Buffet table arrangements

Round, hollow circle, long and straight, shallow V and U shape are the main options. What shape is best depends on the size and shape of the room, number of customers to be served, quantity of food to be displayed on the buffet and, in a meal with two or more courses, how many courses are placed on the buffet at one time. Maintaining a smooth flow of customers is the priority.

The buffet table itself should:

- be large enough to hold all the food without over-crowding, and to allow for the customers to make their choice in comfort
- allow space for staff to serve in comfort, and to move around as necessary to replace dishes of food
- be positioned so that customers can readily reach it from their tables, move along the table to make their selection and return safely with their plates of food. If a queue is likely to form, people returning to their tables should not have to excuse their way through those still queuing for food.

Around 75 customers is the maximum that one buffet line can serve. For more than that, or faster service, two or more buffet lines are usually provided.

Arranging the food on the buffet table

If you are helping to arrange the display of serving dishes, consider:

Colour – variety and contrast of colours can add interest to the display, but overdone will create a messy effect. If you are using flowers or ornaments, their colours should not clash with the surrounding food.

Height – flat arrangements tend to look dull and lifeless. If it is practicable, mix the shape and height of serving dishes. A variation in height can also be achieved by using tiered tables, placing some dishes on stands, blocks or even upturned saucers. If you do this, make sure the dish is stable.

Shape – introduce variety with the position of different shaped serving dishes. For example, place a square dish of stuffed eggs among the round bowls of mixed salad.

Focal point – the eye is drawn to this, and then out to the surrounding display. The focal point could be the main dish, e.g. decorated ham on a stand, or a flower display, basket of fruit, candelabra, or even a statue (at elaborate buffets these are carved out of ice or butter).

Simplicity – remember the objective of the display is to make the food look appetising. Over-elaborate arrangements will distract attention from the food.

Clarity – avoid over-crowding the display, so that customers can appreciate the choice.

Ease of service – put dishes which are difficult to serve where the server/customers can most easily gain access, e.g. individual fruit tartlets which are firm and fairly easy to pick up, beyond the blueberry meringue pavlova, which is rather crumbly.

Palatability of food – place hot foods at the end of the buffet service line. Otherwise the food will cool off while customers make further selections of cold foods. Place sauces and dressings next to the items they are intended to accompany. In this way customers will be helped to match them to the right foods.

Menu order – if the arrangement includes starters, main course items and sweets, cluster the various dishes making up each course together.

Portion control – expensive items, e.g. smoked salmon, are sometimes placed where access is more restricted, or at the point of the display where customers have already filled their plates.

Preparing the dining area

For fork and finger buffets, preparation includes:

- positioning occasional tables, covering these with tablecloths
- arranging informal seating
- placing ashtrays and perhaps supplies of napkins.

Table buffets

Fully laid-up tables, with cutlery, side plate, glasses, etc. are the most convenient arrangement for customers. Other combinations include:

- table knife and fork, napkin and cruets. Customers collect other items as required from the buffet table, e.g. dessert spoons. But a second journey is required if customers forget cutlery
- tablecloth and cruets only. Customers collect cutlery from the buffet (often wrapped in a napkin). This is ideal when a number of customers may eat at each table during the course of the meal, or in informal settings (e.g. a buffet lunch by the swimming pool, or in the lounge or garden of a pub) where customers can take the food to their seats.

If the buffet is part of a large function, and there is a table plan so that guests sit at specific seats, the table numbers should be easy to see as guests enter the room. Familiarise yourself with the room layout, so that you can help guests who have trouble finding their table.

General points to remember when serving behind the buffet table

Establish with colleagues who are helping, what range of dishes each person will serve. A sensible arrangement will avoid getting in each other's way, without being so restrictive that the customers have to wait because the person in charge of the rice is serving another dish, even though you personally are doing nothing at that moment.

Use separate serving equipment for each dish.

Serve the correct portions. There are three main ways of controlling portion sizes when this is required and when staff are serving particular items:

- specifying quantity, e.g. two slices of meat per person, or each flan or pie to be cut into six

- using particular size serving equipment, e.g. two tablespoons of peas per person

- arranging the garnishes to indicate each portion, e.g. eight slices of lemon on a paella for eight.

The plate size provides another method of portion control – a small plate will be filled sooner than a large one.

Use a serving cloth to hold hot plates, and warn customers when plates are very hot.

Do not over-fill customers' plates. Position items so that the food looks as attractive on the plate as it did on the serving dish – with variety of colour, height, etc.

Ask before giving customers gravy, sauce, cream, etc. If you spill any on the rim of the plate, wipe it off with a clean serving cloth.

Replace or remove serving dishes regularly. This may be done as soon as the dish is half empty, or left until there is less than an average serving left. You shouldn't have to chase around a huge dish to find enough peas. On the other hand, the gâteau dish is best removed once the last portion has been served.

If you are serving a hot food, e.g. braised rice, from a dish with a lid, replace the lid during quiet periods to keep the food hot.

Lift lids from hot dishes carefully, so that any condensation which has formed is caught in the lid, rather than falling on to the food or buffet cloth.

If you are responsible for replenishing dishes, follow a strict routine of *first in, first out*. Dishes prepared first should be used first.

If separate tables are used to display different courses, the tables can be cleared once the customers have finished eating that course.

Flower arrangements and other decorative items are normally left until the meal is completed.

In between periods of service, tables have to be reset and the restaurant kept tidy.

Maintaining customer dining areas

Customers generally have more control over the timing of their meal in buffet and carvery service. When they wish, they will leave their table to collect food from the buffet. You have to be aware of what is happening, so that you have cleared plates and cutlery from the previous course by the time your customers return to the table.

Sometimes you will need to invite customers to go and make their choice of food. In a breakfast buffet arrangement, some customers may not realise that they should serve themselves to fruit juice etc.

On other occasions you may have to exercise some modest 'crowd control', so that long queues do not form at the buffet. This can simply be a matter of reassuring a party of customers that you will invite them to go to the buffet table in a few moments.

ACTION 29

You have been asked to help arrange the food at a buffet for a group of 20 delegates at a conference. Number each dish on the menu and use these numbers (e.g. 3 – Leg of lamb) to indicate where you would place the food on the buffet table below.

Mid-Wales Electrical Components Ltd

Luncheon

Thursday, 21 July

Menu

Avocado vinaigrette

Fillets of plaice with watercress, leek and vermouth

• • • • • •

Leg of lamb pot roast

Carrot and coriander quiche

• • • • • •

Potato and feta cheese salad

Mixed bean salad

Tomato and cucumber salad

• • • • • •

Summer pudding

Pears with butterscotch sauce

• • • • • •

Selection of Welsh cheeses

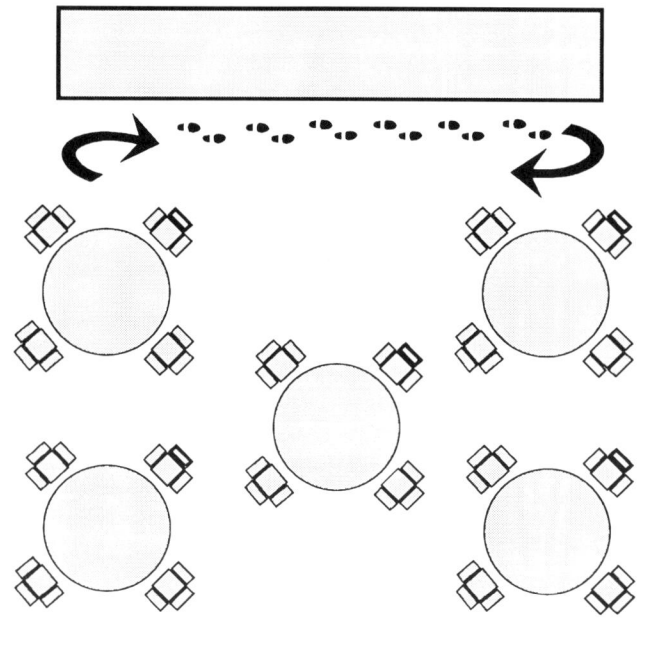

NVQ SVQ RANGE CHECKLIST

LEVEL 2

2C4.1 Prepare and maintain a carvery or buffet display

in buffets or carveries where food is served to the customer, use these

- [ ] dishes or flats
- [ ] service cloths or linen
- [ ] glassware
- [ ] table coverings
- [ ] flowers
- [ ] hot dishes
- [ ] accompaniments
- [ ] service cutlery/ silverware
- [ ] crockery
- [ ] cutlery and silverware
- [ ] napkins
- [ ] decorative items
- [ ] cold dishes

2C4.2 Serve customers at the carvery or buffet

at buffets or carveries where food is served to the customer, use these

- [ ] dishes or flats
- [ ] service cloths or linen
- [ ] service cutlery/silverware

to serve these

- [ ] hot dishes
- [ ] accompaniments
- [ ] cold dishes

2C4.3 Maintain customer dining areas

in buffets or carveries where food is served to the customer, involving these

- [ ] crockery
- [ ] glassware
- [ ] table decorations
- [ ] napkins
- [ ] cutlery/silverware
- [ ] ashtrays
- [ ] table coverings

ACTION 30

Prepare some notes for a short talk which you could give to your colleagues on the safety aspects of carvery and buffet service. Give careful thought to how you can get across the important points in a memorable, effective way, e.g. with diagrams or illustrations. Here are some safety points to start you thinking.

◇ **Do not overload buffet tables. If using trestle tables, make sure the structure is secure before loading.**

◇ **Position cables for hotplates so they do not trail across floors. Do not overload electrical sockets.**

◇ **Do not leave lighted candles unattended.**

◇ **If using carved ice displays, make sure there is no danger of the melted ice dripping on to electrical fittings (e.g. spotlights), or on to the floor.**

Silver service

Introduction

Here your technical skills come into their own. Silver service done well adds great style to the occasion. Your customers can enjoy the ceremony of transferring the beautifully presented food from service dish to plate.

Silver service skills

There are many names for the different styles of service, and in different parts of the world the same names have a different meaning (see Glossary). Fortunately most people agree on what is meant by 'silver service':

> food transferred from serving dish to customer's plate by the waiter or waitress using a serving spoon and table fork – or more appropriate cutlery, e.g. spoon only, two forks.

This section, like the NVQ/SVQ unit, deals with silver service in the restaurant, and buffets or carveries.

In the restaurant, the serving dish is taken to the customer. The customer's plate is either:

- on the table, in front of the customer, and you hold the serving dish nearby

or

- on a trolley (or guéridon) positioned by the customer's table, where the serving dish is also placed, giving you two hands free to hold the spoon and fork.

Sometimes the serving dish is presented to the customer then placed on the sideboard, perhaps on a dish warmer, and the food served on to the plate there.

In a buffet, the customer comes to the food. If it is quite a long buffet arrangement, the customer will hold the plate and move down the table, choosing dishes which you serve using a spoon and fork or more appropriate equipment. The main difference from silver service in the restaurant is that you will often have two hands free to hold the serving equipment.

In a carvery, the customer also comes to the food. The chef will carve the meat on to the plate, then hand it over to the customer.

Units and elements covered in this section

LEVEL 2

2C5 Provide a silver service
- 2C5.1 Silver serve food
- 2C5.2 Clear finished courses

Contents guide

Silver service is used in a wide variety of contexts, but less frequently now for service of main course dishes in luxury hotels and restaurants (where once nothing but silver service was used).

Importance of timing

In restaurant silver service you may have to serve up to 6 or 8 customers from the same dish. In banqueting you could be serving 10 or 12. Customers don't want to have to wait a long time while you move from one person to another. And of course hot food will be losing heat from the moment it leaves the kitchen hotplate.

Importance of presentation

The presentation of the food on the customer's plate relies on your skills. With care, masterpieces created in the kitchen will look as impressive after you have transferred the food to the customer's plate.

Silver service in the restaurant

The basic sequence of service is:

1 collect clean plates (hot for hot food, cold for cold food)
2 assemble plates on the sideboard, or take direct to the table
3 position a plate in front of each customer
4 collect and serve the food.

With a small party, you will usually be able to bring everything from the kitchen in one journey: plates, serving dishes of food, sauces, etc. Hotplates are useful for keeping serving dishes of hot food warm while you position the plates.

If using a trolley or guéridon, put the plates in front of customers after you have served each plate of food.

Posture

This assumes you are serving from the left.

Stand slightly behind and to the left of the customer to be served, back straight, feet together, serving dish just above waist level.

Step forward with your left foot, into the space between the customers. As you do this:

• lower the serving dish between the customers

• bend forward so that the dish just overlaps the edge of the customer's plate

• keep the serving dish at a height of 25 mm above the level of the customer's plate

• keep the serving dish absolutely horizontal.

Depending on how tall you are, you may need to bend your back to get the serving dish to the right height. Some people prefer to bend at the knees, keeping the back straight.

When you have served the food:

• rise as you gently pull back out from between the customers

• lift the serving dish out between the customers' shoulders (not over their heads)

• shift the weight of your body on to your right foot

• withdraw your left foot and the serving dish into the aisle space, keeping the spoon and fork over the dish to avoid drips.

Form a small group with some of your colleagues, and discuss the changing skills of serving staff. To get the debate going read the extract from *Caterer & Hotel-keeper*, below. Here are some other suggestions:

• what are the advantages and disadvantages of silver service from the point of view of the: (1) customers, (2) chefs, and (3) food servers?

• what restaurants/catering establishments in your area still use silver service, and why do you think this is?

• what places have replaced silver service with another form of service, and how successful do you feel the change has been?

• how do the prices of silver service establishments compare with other restaurants of similar standard?

On the changing skills of serving staff   **CATERER** *& Hotelkeeper*

Gerry Iver, 25, is head waiter at London's Hotel Meridien. There, he explained to Eve Jones, 'Everything is plated except soups, which are served and garnished at the table. And at lunchtime roasts are carved from the trolley, and items such as salmon and sea bass may be filleted at the table.'

Explaining his reaction to the fact that many of the traditional serving skills are not required by this style of service, Iver added: 'One part of our skills may have been taken away, but it has been replaced by greater awareness of what the guest is actually eating. A good waiter knows exactly how each dish has been prepared, and will have tasted it so he can describe it properly. He should know which produce is in season, which sauces blend best with each dish and why certain rules have changed.

'There is no room for nostalgia. You have to be receptive to what is happening now, not just sit back and regret the passing of some skills.'

In many restaurants which have changed to plated service for most dishes, soup is still served at the table.

Placing the plates

Hold the pile of plates resting on the palm of the left hand, which should be covered with one end of a serving cloth, the cloth wrapped around and over the top of the pile.

On approaching the appropriate side of the customer, pick up the plate by the rim with the tips of the thumb and fingers of the right hand.

Keep the plate horizontal.

Lean forward slightly and gently slide the plate on to the centre of the place setting in front of the customer.

Presenting the food

At the sidetable, remove the dish cover (if there is one). Lift carefully, tilting the cover as you do so. Any condensation will be caught in the lid, rather than dripping on to the tablecloth or the food.

Present the serving dish to the customers before any is served, so that everyone at the table may admire the dish in its entirety.

There is no need to make a separate step of presenting a dish which is for one person.

Portioning

Be clear before you start serving what the portion size is per customer. This may be:

- common sense, e.g. when there are 3 pieces of stuffed courgette for 3 customers
- clear from the arrangement and/or decoration of the food on the dish, e.g. meat grouped in layers of 3 slices, each with a parsley decoration
- a matter of judgement: a dish of peas and 4 customers to serve.

If you are going to be serving a large party with a dish like peas, where there is no easy way of measuring each portion, try and get some practice first using a similar item (e.g. dried peas). Otherwise you may find yourself having to decrease the serving size as you move around the table.

Order of service

The main item should be served first. This would be the meat, fish or vegetarian special in the main course, followed by the potatoes and other vegetables.

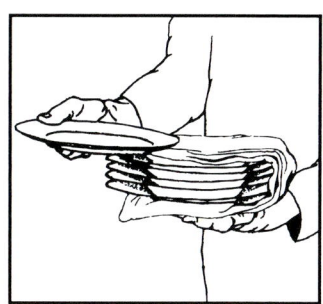

Placing clean plates in front of customers. Note how the thumb is kept well clear of the centre of the plate, from which food will be eaten.

HYGIENE

When not in use, carry your service cloth neatly folded over the forearm. Never place it under your armpit or over your shoulder.

Your posture and appearance contribute to the presentation of the food you are serving.

Service procedure: vegetables

1. Collect the vegetable and potato selection along with the sauceboat of sauce when collecting the main course.

2. Place the two entrée dishes, sauceboat and ladle on a 300 mm flan plate lined with a lace mat.

3. Position the tray on the folding guéridon.

4. When all the main courses have been served, remove the lids from the dishes and place on the folding guéridon.

5. Offer the vegetable and potato selection along with the sauce accompaniment to each guest, serving from the left, placing the vegetables between 2 o'clock and 6 o'clock.

6. Check guest satisfaction before leaving the table.

Service equipment

It looks neater if you use a carefully folded service cloth underneath the serving dish. The cloth helps prevent the serving dish from slipping, and for a hot dish it provides essential protection against the heat. For a large dish, the cloth should be folded so it lies up the lower portion of your arm, where the dish will be resting.

If the serving dish is of a shape or size which makes it difficult to carry, place it on a larger, flat serving dish, preferably lined with a doily or dish paper.

Use a clean serving spoon and fork (or equivalent) for each dish you take to the table. When you are serving two or more vegetables from the same serving dish, you may need extra serving equipment to avoid spoiling the appearance and flavour of the different items.

For practical reasons, soup is usually served at the trolley or sidetable. This avoids having to carry a heavy tureen around the table. When the soup plate is resting on a liner, it can be carried more easily, with less danger of your finger coming into contact with the soup.

Using a serving spoon and fork

The curve of the fork should lie in the bowl of the spoon.

Hold the two together so that the palm of the hand and all the fingers are over both handles. Make sure that both are comfortably balanced.

Insert the first finger midway between the spoon and fork handles. This acts as a lever so that the fork prongs and spoon bowl may be opened and closed to hold the items securely.

To serve a stuffed tomato, or a similar shaped, rather delicate food, you may find it easier to turn the fork the other way around, so that it curves around the food.

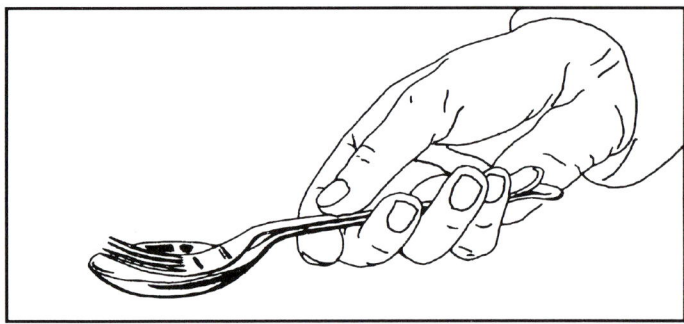

Holding a spoon and fork. The curve of the fork lies in the bowl of the spoon.

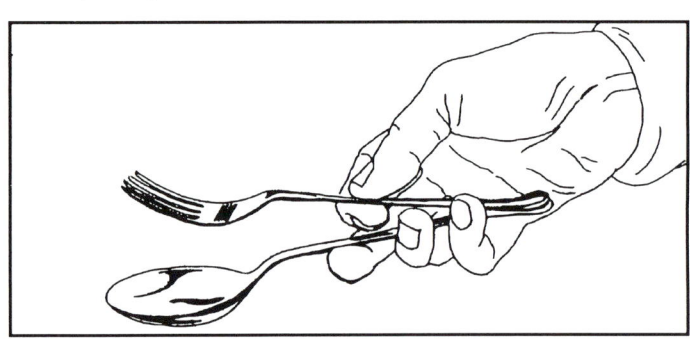

The first finger acts as a lever, to help open and close the spoon and fork.

Another way of opening the cutlery out is to press the ends of the spoon and fork together, with the tip of the small finger.

You may find it easier to lift a rather long, delicate piece of food using two forks, splayed out slightly.

Alternatively, use a spoon and fork, splayed out, or two fish knives.

Positioning the food on the plate

Generally meat or fish is put on the customer's plate, lower centre, with vegetables on one side and potatoes on the other. Gravy, sauce and/or accompaniments go at the top right-hand side.

When serving dishes with a pastry crust, portion the pastry, place to one side, spoon the filling on to the plate, then add the portion of crust.

Although it should not happen, if you find a portion of food (e.g. fillets of fish) too large to lift elegantly with a spoon and fork, you may find it easier first to cut the food across the middle with the spoon. Never drag the food off the serving dish on to the plate.

Place portions of sweet or savoury flans which are triangular in shape with the point towards the customer.

For sauce, gravy or cream, ask whether the customer would like it beside or poured over the food.

Clearing finished courses

The procedure for plates is described on page 51.

For soup plates with liners, you will find it easier to collect only two plates at a time and take them to the sideboard for stacking.

At a large table this may not be practicable, and you will have to stack them as you move around the table. This is complicated and noisy as you have to keep moving the soup spoons:

- use the upper position on your hand (see illustrations on page 51) to stack the liners, and the lower position to stack the soup bowls and spoons

- each time you clear a soup plate and its liner, place them in the upper position on your hand

- move the soup spoons up from the lower pile to the soup bowl you have just cleared (in the top pile)

- move the soup bowls and spoons back to the lower pile.

If any customers have left some soup in the bowl, return to the table to collect them one or two at a time.

ACTION	32

Gather a small collection of objects with which to practise your silver service skills. Ask two or three friends to play the role of customers and judges. Here are some ideas for suitable objects to serve your friends:

- new potatoes
- sprouts
- slices of very fresh bread
- peas
- slices of old toast
- rice
- absorbent rubber wiping cloth cut to size of a slice of meat
- damp sponge (about the size of a bread roll)
- sauce boat with custard (or other liquid of similar consistency)

Spend time first planning how your skills should be assessed. For example, you might agree that points should be awarded for:

☐ Speed (time taken to serve everyone)

☐ Dexterity (how well the spoon and fork are used to handle the object)

☐ Posture (how well you stand when serving)

☐ Position (how well the serving dish is held)

☐ Presentation on the plate (how well the objects are arranged on the plate)

Silver service from the buffet or carvery

In this form of service, the emphasis is on:

- providing a personal service, with the chance to explain the various dishes available, and serve the customer's choice expertly

- assisting with portion control, since most customers will accept what you give them as the right amount. Left to serve themselves, they might have several slices of smoked salmon, for example

- helping to keep the presentation of the dishes looking attractive.

Whether you hold the spoon and fork in one hand, just a spoon, or use some other cutlery such as a gâteau slice, will depend on the food you are serving. If there are no particular guidelines in your workplace, choose whatever will both hold the food most effectively and that you are comfortable with.

ACTION 33

Indicate what serving equipment and, where appropriate, how many sets you would need for serving the following:

	Serving fork	Serving spoon	Fish fork	Fish knife	Fish serving knife	Fish serving fork	Pie server	Cake lifter
bread rolls at a banquet	☐	☐	☐	☐	☐	☐	☐	☐
sliced smoked salmon at a buffet	☐	☐	☐	☐	☐	☐	☐	☐
truite meunière to 1 customer at the table	☐	☐	☐	☐	☐	☐	☐	☐
truite meunière at a buffet/sidetable/guéridon	☐	☐	☐	☐	☐	☐	☐	☐
individual steak and kidney pies at a buffet	☐	☐	☐	☐	☐	☐	☐	☐
curry presented in a circle of braised rice: to 1 customer at table	☐	☐	☐	☐	☐	☐	☐	☐
to 3 customers at table	☐	☐	☐	☐	☐	☐	☐	☐
whole decorated poached salmon on buffet	☐	☐	☐	☐	☐	☐	☐	☐
creamed potato, red cabbage and Brussels sprouts (in a 3-division vegetable dish) to 3 customers at the table	☐	☐	☐	☐	☐	☐	☐	☐
roast potatoes, peas, grilled tomatoes (in a 3-division dish) to 2 customers at table	☐	☐	☐	☐	☐	☐	☐	☐
fruit salad from a sweet trolley	☐	☐	☐	☐	☐	☐	☐	☐
gâteaux at a buffet	☐	☐	☐	☐	☐	☐	☐	☐

2C5.1 Silver serve food

in
- ☐ restaurant silver service
- ☐ buffet or carvery silver service

using these
- ☐ dishes, liners or flats
- ☐ service cutlery and silverware
- ☐ service cloths or linen

to silver serve these
- ☐ soups
- ☐ gravies or sauces
- ☐ bread rolls, potatoes or other solid items
- ☐ sliced meat or poultry
- ☐ rice, vegetables or other small or chopped items
- ☐ pies, tarts, flans or gâteaux
- ☐ puddings or spooned desserts
- ☐ cheese

2C5.2 Clear finished courses

in
- ☐ restaurant silver service
- ☐ buffet or carvery silver service

clear these
- ☐ crockery and cutlery
- ☐ ashtrays
- ☐ glassware
- ☐ condiments and accompaniments
- ☐ table decorations
- ☐ starter or dessert
- ☐ main courses

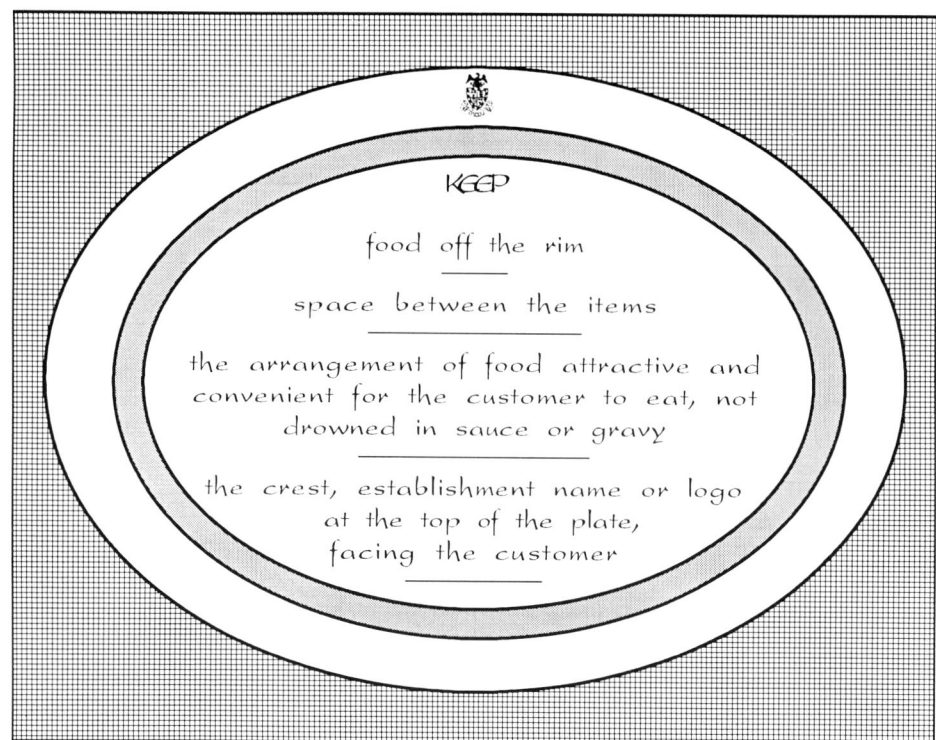

KEEP

food off the rim

space between the items

the arrangement of food attractive and convenient for the customer to eat, not drowned in sauce or gravy

the crest, establishment name or logo at the top of the plate, facing the customer

ACTION 34

On the left is one way to summarise the key points regarding the presentation of food on the customer's plate. Develop your own diagram or checklist which is suited to your workplace.

Test it out on some colleagues. While humour and a clever illustration can be most effective, it can be surprisingly difficult to come up with an idea which everyone likes.

Introduction

Drink sales have become much more important in all types and style of restaurant and catering operation. Powerful advertising, experiences gained on holiday abroad – these are just some of the influences behind the demand for a wider choice of drinks, and for more interesting ways of serving such all-time favourites as tea and coffee.

Knowing what you have to offer

Drink requirements cannot be taken for granted. What one customer enjoys, another does not. Popular ways of serving particular drinks give a good starting point. But even with these it is better to check than make assumptions:

- 'Would you prefer sparkling or still mineral water and would you like a slice of lemon, lime or orange in it?'

- 'Would you like ice and lemon with your gin and tonic, sir?'

Promoting drink sales

Clarifying what customers want also provides a sales opportunity:

- 'Straight whisky, madam, or with a mixer? We have dry ginger, lemonade.... I could also recommend some delicious whisky-based cocktails.'

- 'There is the house blend, sir, or we have a range of Indian and China teas. And, ideal for a lovely day like today, there is iced tea.'

The tone of your voice will say much about how interested you are in what your customers want – often more than the words you use. By being knowledgeable and enthusiastic about the range of drinks and food you can offer customers, and which drinks go well with which food, you will contribute positively to their satisfaction.

Satisfied customers are the ones who return and recommend your establishment to their friends.

Units and elements covered in this section

1C9 Provide a drinks service for non-licensed premises **LEVEL 1**
- 1C9.1 Prepare and serve non-alcoholic drinks
- 1C9.2 Maintain service areas during service

2C3 Provide a table drink service **LEVEL 2**
- 2C3.1 Provide a table drink service

By asking: 'What would you like as an aperitif?', 'May I recommend a wine with your meal?', 'Would you like a cappuccino?' at the appropriate points before, during and after a meal, you will almost always get a response of a firm order. If the question is not asked, the chance of a sale is lost.

With a little encouragement from you, many customers will enjoy trying a new drink, or treating themselves to something a bit special.

Preparing & serving non-alcoholic drinks

LEVEL 1

Tea and coffee are among the most profitable items sold by caterers. The food cost is quite low and the selling price can be relatively high.

General procedure

1 Serve drinks at the correct temperature. Serve tea and coffee freshly-made. Pots, when used for hot drinks, should be pre-warmed. Don't pour iced drinks into a glass still warm from the dishwasher.

2 Do not overfill pots – they are difficult to pour without spilling. An overfilled cup or glass can be difficult to drink from if the liquid is thin and very hot like tea.

3 Most customers (including many, but not all those who are left-handed) hold the glass or cup with their right hand. Put drinks down to the right of the customer, or directly in front if the customer is not having food. A handle should be turned to the right.

4 If a customer would like a fresh cup of coffee and the first, only half drunk, has gone cold, offer a clean cup.

5 When placing jugs or pots of liquids on the table, the handles should point towards the customer. Put sugar bowls, milk, cream, etc. within easy reach.

6 When a customer requests water, ask the others at the table whether they would also like some.

7 On serving bottled waters, pour some in each glass at the table, then place the bottle on the table with the label facing the person who ordered it. Serve bottled water chilled, but without ice, because ice cubes are made from different water. Serve ice cubes if requested.

8 If a customer at the end of a meal produces his or her own tea bag and requests a pot of hot water, oblige with a smile. There may be health reasons why the customer has to stick to a certain tea (e.g. herbal or decaffeinated).

A tray is generally the safest, easiest and most elegant way of carrying drinks to the customer's table.

ACTION 35

Discuss with some colleagues and your supervisor, trainer or tutor what went wrong in this case study, and what should have been done by the waitress.

I recently overheard two middle-aged women becoming bewildered by the extensive choice of coffees on the menu. Having established that espresso was the cheapest of the specialities, they asked for 'two white espressos'.

The waitress explained that espresso was black and suggested they might like to try cappuccino, with frothed milk. But, no, the ladies said they wanted 'just ordinary white coffee'. As cups of coffee were not on the menu, the waitress suggested individual cafetière pots, priced around 80% more than an espresso.

Two individual pots were delivered to the table, with the filter plungers only partly pushed down. Neither customer knew what to do with the plungers, with the result that they spilt their coffee while pouring it. They then realised that there was plenty in the pots for a second cup each – which neither of them wanted – and they were being forced into paying for four cups when they only wanted two.

 Carmen Konopka, 28 May 1992

Mineral waters have enjoyed an enormous increase in popularity.

Service of coffee at the table

1 The coffee cover, consisting of coffee cups, saucers, small side plates and coffee spoon, is placed to the right of the diner (at the position where the blade of the large knife rested) with the cup handle pointing to 5 o'clock.

2 Offer the sugar from the diner's left.

3 Enquire of the diner how he/she will take coffee: 'Would sir/madam like milk/cream?'. Never say: 'Would you like black or white coffee?'.

4 The coffee and milk or cream (on a tray) is served from the right-hand side. The coffee is poured first followed by the milk, the cup being filled only to within 10 to 15 mm from the top.

Making tea

1 Use freshly drawn water.

2 Preheat the pot with very hot water.

3 When the pot is hot, empty away the water and add the correct amount of tea. The general rule is: one teaspoon or bag per person and one for the pot. If your establishment serves speciality teas, get to know the correct quantities.

4 When the water is boiling, pour immediately into the heated pot. Bring the pot to the kettle, not the kettle to the pot, so the water has less time to go off the boil.

5 If you are pouring the tea for the customer, let the tea infuse for 3 to 5 minutes, stir the pot with a spoon and serve.

Making coffee

1 Use the correct coffee for the chosen method, in the correct quantity – follow workplace or packet instructions.

2 Once opened, ground coffee should be used quickly – within 24 hours is the recommendation.

3 Once made, keep hot at a temperature of about 85°C – 'coffee boiled is coffee spoiled'.

4 Ideally coffee should be served within 30 minutes of being made. Avoid keeping for longer than an hour. Stale coffee becomes bitter in taste.

5 Never pour brewed coffee back through spent grounds to strengthen. Never re-use grounds.

Methods of making fresh coffee

Espresso – check temperature and pressure of machine. Discard old grounds and rinse coffee holder well. Re-pack tightly with coffee. Wipe rim before inserting in machine (to ensure a good seal). Warm the cup before filling with coffee.

Vacuum pot or Cona – fill the lower bowl with cold water and put over heat. Place glass rod (or other filter mechanism) into top bowl (on its stand at this stage) and add coffee. When water has boiled, insert top bowl into lower bowl, twisting to ensure a good seal. When the water has all risen into the top bowl, lower the heat, stirring gently once or twice. Allow the coffee to infuse for 1 to 2 minutes. Remove from the heat. When coffee has filtered back into the lower container, put top bowl aside.

Filter method (with machine) – check machine is on. Place fresh filter paper in the holder. Add the coffee (usually a pre-portioned pack). Pour cold water into the top part of the machine. Place clean pot under filter. Do not remove pot until coffee has stopped dripping through the filter (or quickly place a fresh pot in its place). Do not leave almost empty pots on the hotplate – they are likely to boil dry and then the glass will crack.

Filter method (with funnel) – place fresh filter paper in the funnel. Add coffee. Place funnel over pot, then pour over not-quite boiling water. Use a circular motion, so you moisten all the coffee. Do not add too much water at once, otherwise it will overflow and take coffee grounds down into the pot.

Plunger (cafetière) method – place coffee in the bottom of the jug. Pour on not-quite boiling water and insert the plunger. Allow the coffee to infuse for 4 minutes or so, then push the plunger firmly down.

Maintaining service areas `LEVEL 1`

Keep storage and preparation areas spotless. Pay particular attention to the interiors of refrigerators and chillers (see section 3).

Regularly check the temperatures of refrigerators (below 5°C) and freezers (below –18°C). There will probably be a system for logging these.

Fresh cream and milk, and fresh fruit juices should be stored in the refrigerator for not more than two or three days, nor beyond the use-by date. Keep covered and well away from strong smells. Leftovers from pots served to customers with tea and coffee should be disposed of.

Rotate stocks, on a *first in, first out* basis. Do not order too much at one time from stores. Pay attention to use-by dates.

Key features of a good cuppa

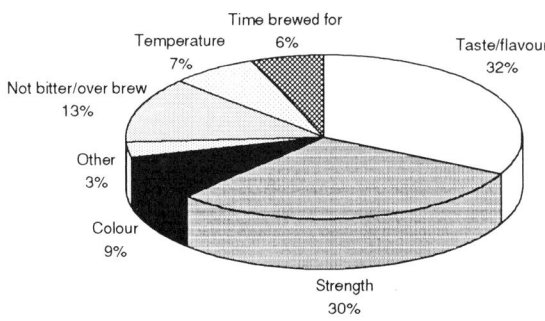

A survey for The Tea Council found that what made the 'perfect cuppa' was the colour, strength, taste/flavour and not bitter/overbrewed. You can help get these right by taking care to use the right quantity of tea, and to let it infuse properly. If you are serving tea by the pot, never let it stand around, but get it to the customer within 3 minutes if possible – after that the tea may be over-infused for some customers' taste.

Providing a table drink service LEVEL 2

Your restaurant could be held to blame if a customer leaves the premises under the influence of alcohol and causes an accident.

As the person serving customers alcohol, you are in the best position to anticipate possible problems, and by warning your manager in good time, prevent matters getting out of hand.

Laws on the sale of alcohol

Any establishment selling alcohol must have a licence. There are various types, each with certain restrictions. The three you are likely to encounter are:

On-licence – permits the sale of alcohol for consumption on the premises during certain hours. Pubs operate under this sort of licence. Restricted versions of the licence permit the sale of wine only, for example.

Restaurant licence – permits the sale of alcohol at any time with a substantial meal.

Residential and restaurant licence – permits the sale of alcohol at any time to residents or guests of the hotel or guesthouse. Guests may purchase alcohol for their friends (but not vice versa). Alcohol can be sold with a substantial meal to non-residents.

In unlicensed premises, customers may bring their own alcohol to drink with the meal. Some licensed restaurants also permit customers to bring their own wines, for example, but they will usually charge a fixed amount per bottle (corkage) as compensation for loss of revenue from sales of their own stock.

ACTION 36

Customers who are becoming intoxicated generally go through three stages. On the list below tick the signs which would merit calling your manager to say that there is a problem. Discuss your decisions with your manager.

Green level
- [ ] talkative
- [ ] relaxed, comfortable, happy

Yellow level
- [ ] louder or more talkative
- [ ] quieter
- [ ] over friendly
- [ ] curses at your slow service
- [ ] complains drinks are getting weaker

Red level
- [ ] spills a drink
- [ ] sways when walking
- [ ] slurred speech
- [ ] asks for a double
- [ ] unable to pick up change
- [ ] becomes tearful or drowsy
- [ ] has difficulty focusing
- [ ] falls or stumbles
- [ ] annoys or argues with other customers

National Restaurant Association, Washington, DC

Who can and cannot be sold alcohol

The licensee has the right to refuse to serve any person. No reason need be given.

In a licensed bar, under 18s may not buy or drink alcohol. A bar is defined as any place exclusively or mainly used for the sale and consumption of alcohol.

In premises which have a restaurant or area set aside for the service of meals (provided it is not also a bar), and when those concerned are eating a meal, then:

- over 16s may buy and drink beer and cider (and, in Scotland, wine)
- under 16s may, at the licensee's discretion, drink alcohol of any type provided it is purchased by an accompanying adult.

You are committing an offence if you serve alcohol to anyone who is under-age, or drunk, or who has been declared a habitual drinker by the courts. Inform your manager immediately if you suspect customers are drunk, or if they are disorderly or behaving violently. Such behaviour is illegal on licensed premises.

Quality and quantity of drinks

You must serve the correct measure of the correct drink:

- if a customer orders an Armagnac brandy you cannot serve a cognac unless you have first explained that no Armagnac is available, and offered an alternative which the customer has accepted
- if wine is sold by the glass it must be clear to the customer how much the glass contains. The wine list or menu will state the amount, e.g. 125 or 175 ml (these will be the only legal quantities from 1995). It is up to you to serve it in the correct measure
- whisky, gin, rum and vodka may only be served in multiples of 25 ml, unless they are part of a mixed drink, e.g. a cocktail. (Until 1995 the imperial measures can be used, e.g. ¼ gill.)
- beer and cider, unless sold by the bottle or can, may only be sold in multiples of ½ pt (the one-third pint measure is not much used).

Strength of alcoholic drinks

The label of pre-packaged drinks (e.g. bottles of wine) has to state the alcohol content by volume (e.g. 12%). This information must also be provided for a representative sample of dispensed drinks, e.g. draught cider or beer.

The most convenient place for stating the alcoholic content of drinks is the drinks list. As the amount of alcohol between one drink and another varies substantially, you will show a concern for the well-being of customers by being able to give accurate information when asked.

Serving drinks at table

If your customers have not finished their drinks at the bar when the table is ready, offer to carry the glasses for them.

If a second round of drinks is ordered, serve them in fresh glasses.

Place drinks on the right-hand side of the customer. If the glass has a handle it should also be on the right so that the customer can pick up the glass more easily.

1 Whisky, gin, vodka and other spirits are normally poured into the glass away from the table (e.g. in the dispense bar), and then brought to the customer on a small tray or salver, often lined with a doily or napkin to stop the glasses slipping around the tray.

2 When a mixer has been ordered with the spirit, take the mixer bottle to the customer so that you can add the desired amount. If any mixer remains in the bottle, leave it on the table so the customer can add more later.

3 Bottled (or canned) beers, lagers, soft drinks, mineral waters, etc. are usually taken in the bottle to the customer's table where all or some is poured into the glass. This option is obviously not available for dispensed drinks (e.g. draught beer, mixers).

4 In some restaurants, after dinner liqueurs and brandies are served from a trolley. The trolley with the selection of available drinks and a stock of clean liqueur and brandy glasses is wheeled to the customers' table, and the drinks poured as the customers make their selection. The quantity of drink served is measured in a thimble measure, or with liqueurs by filling the liqueur glass up to a particular level.

Drinks service procedure

Baggid Beech Hotel

1	Approach table. Ask if ready to order	
2	When taking an order always offer an alternative	'Would you like Gordons or Bombay Gin Sir/Madam?'
3	Offer appropriate accompaniment	e.g. ice and lemon
4	Repeat the order to guest	Order must be repeated to confirm that you have taken it correctly
5	Leave the table	Don't forget to thank the guest first
6	Print guest bill on computer	Check all items are correct before printing
7	Collect drinks from dispense bar	Use a tray
8	Serve drinks from the right	Ladies first
9	Leave the table	Say 'Here is your gin and tonic, Sir/Madam'

Liqueurs trolley

1	Replace dirty napkins on the trolley with clean ones	Napkins should be changed on a daily basis
2	Wipe off all the liqueur bottles before putting them on the trolley	Bottles pick up dust from the air
3	Fill up the trolley with enough glasses	Liqueur glasses, brandy glasses, port glasses
4	Place bottles in the same category next to each other	Cognac, Armagnac, brandy and liqueurs
5	Make sure you have got a measure and some small plates with napkins	Always use a measure when pouring a liqueur. Always serve the liqueurs with an underliner

Cocktail trolley

1	Ensure that you have all the spirits you need for the cocktails you are making	Nicely presented and facing the customer
2	Ensure that you have all the equipment you need	Cocktail shaker – mixing glass – strainer – cocktail spoon – stirrer
3	Ensure you have got all the cocktail garnish that you will need	Lemon slices – orange slices pineapple slices, cherries
4	Ensure that you have a bucket of ice	Always refill the ice and don't wait until you run out

ACTION   37

For each of the following situations, indicate against the drink suggestions those you would:

★ definitely recommend

☑ possibly recommend

☒ persuade the customer(s) against choosing.

Then, in the space provided under the last suggestion, write down a suitable drink from the range offered in your own workplace.

Young, romantic couple pre-celebration dinner drink
- ☐ Kir Royale: champagne and crème de cassis
- ☐ Love on the Rocks: vodka, peach schnapps and cranberry juice topped with orange juice
- ☐ San Francisco: pineapple and orange juices with dash of lemon and lime
- ☐ Virgin Colada: pineapple juice and cream of coconut blended with cream

Party of business executives before a working lunch
- ☐ Tio Pepe
- ☐ Purdey's Health Elixir with ginseng extract
- ☐ White wine spritzer
- ☐ Glass of red wine

Middle-aged couple at end of dinner, man worried about driving home
- ☐ Formosa Gunpowder: green leaf tea
- ☐ Decaffeinated coffee
- ☐ Manhattan: rye whiskey, Italian Vermouth, bitters
- ☐ Chocolate Monkey: chocolate fudge sauce and Ovaltine blended with cream and garnished with crumbled chocolate flake

Two rather prim ladies out for a shopping afternoon
- ☐ Rosehip tea: a pale tisane which aids the digestion, fruity and aromatic
- ☐ Freshly squeezed lime juice and ginger beer
- ☐ Earl Grey
- ☐ Gin fizz: London dry gin with lemon juice and sugar syrup, topped up with soda water

Two long-distance lorry drivers having their evening meal. They don't want wine and seem rather ill at ease in the restaurant – their favourite café is closed
- ☐ Tea or coffee
- ☐ Draught beer
- ☐ Soft drink
- ☐ Irish coffee (with whiskey)

All-male party out for a good evening: pre-dinner drinks
- ☐ Grolsch
- ☐ Rob Roy: Scotch whisky, Italian Vermouth, bitters
- ☐ Peach Crush: peach schnapps with cranberry and citrus juices
- ☐ Slow Comfortable Screw: sloe gin, Southern Comfort and orange juice

All-female party out for a good evening: post-dinner drinks
- ☐ Bloody Mary: vodka, tomato juice, lemon juice, Worcestershire sauce
- ☐ Crème de Menthe Frappé
- ☐ Brandy Alexander: brandy and dark crème de cacao with vanilla ice cream
- ☐ Coke Floater

Parents on shopping trip with difficult teenage daughter (drink for her)
- ☐ Sao Rica: Brazilian herbal fruit drink
- ☐ André the Peachlifter: apples, lime juice and coconut cream with peaches
- ☐ Peppermint Tea: refreshing, relieves headaches and nervous complaints
- ☐ Berro Caipirinha: the classic Brazilian cocktail made with Berro D'agua, fresh lime juice, crushed ice and sugar

Business person with client, has already ordered an expensive wine for lunch
- ☐ Champagne
- ☐ Dim Sim: vodka, cointreau, red wine
- ☐ Dry Martini
- ☐ Holsten Pils

Elderly, jolly couple having a snack before the early evening performance at the cinema
- ☐ Lemon Verbena: distinctive, powerful tea, said to ease rheumatic pain
- ☐ Bloody Caesar: spicy version of the Bloody Mary, with clamato juice
- ☐ Bucks Fizz
- ☐ Caribbean coffee (with dark rum)

Drink ideas courtesy Hudson's, Old Orleans, Coppid Beech Hotel and TGI Friday's

NVQ SVQ RANGE CHECKLIST

LEVEL 1

1C9.1 Prepare and serve non-alcoholic drinks

for drink service at the counter or at the table, serve these
- ☐ bottled or canned soft drinks
- ☐ machine dispensed soft drinks
- ☐ hot machine dispensed drinks
- ☐ hot beverages ☐ cordials

and provide information on
- ☐ price, promotions and special offers
- ☐ suitable alternatives

1C9.2 Maintain service areas during service

involving these
- ☐ bottled or canned soft drinks
- ☐ hot drink ingredients
- ☐ cold drink ingredients

and these
- ☐ crockery and cutlery
- ☐ all electrical equipment for beverage service
- ☐ trays ☐ glassware

LEVEL 2

2C3.1 Provide a table drink service

provide these drinks
- ☐ beer ☐ wine
- ☐ spirits or cocktails
- ☐ cold soft drinks ☐ hot drinks

using these
- ☐ glassware ☐ trays
- ☐ service linen

and deal with these customer groups
- ☐ those who comply with licensing legislation
- ☐ those acting in a drunken manner or violent or disorderly manner
- ☐ those under age requesting service or those under an exclusion order or those requesting service outside licensing hours

and provide information on these
- ☐ prices ☐ ingredients
- ☐ relative strength
- ☐ suitable alternatives

Introduction

There is a wider choice of wines in the UK than virtually anywhere else in the world.

Types of wine

Wines can be classified into red, white and rosé. Red wines are normally dry, but white and rosé wines can be dry, medium, sweet, medium dry and medium sweet. They can be still, or sparkling like Champagne (in glass on right of photograph below).

Fortified wines have had clear grape spirit (brandy) added to halt the fermentation. This raises the alcohol content to about twice that of natural wines. The best known examples are sherry, port, Madeira and marsala.

A good wine can only be made from a grape variety which suits the soil and climate of the region. But because the climate varies from year to year, no two wines are exactly the same, even if they come from the same type of grape, region and wine-maker.

Contents guide

Traditional methods are still used to make many of the finest wines. On the left, wicker baskets in use in the Douro valley of Portugal, centre of the port region. On the right, the traditional Spanish method of making quality sherries – the solera system. Old wines are refreshed by the addition of younger wines which then acquire the characteristics of the old wine.

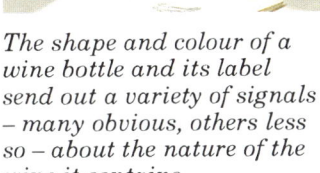

The shape and colour of a wine bottle and its label send out a variety of signals – many obvious, others less so – about the nature of the wine it contains.

Classic bottle shapes. From left to right: Alsace flûte, German, Champagne, Burgundy, Bordeaux.

 **Units and elements covered in this section**

LEVEL 2

2C6 Prepare and serve bottled wines
– 2C6.1 Prepare and serve bottled wines

Over 85 million bottles of wine are drunk in restaurants, hotels, pubs and clubs in the UK in a single year.

The label

Wine bottle labels might appear rather confusing, but the basic formula provides the key to understanding virtually any label you will see.

By law, every wine label must carry the following information:

- country where the wine was made
- alcoholic strength in percentage by volume (% vol)
- contents in litres, cl or ml – still wines of the standard size sold within the European Community must contain 75 cl (750 ml). Some bottles which pre-date this regulation (1988) contain 70 cl
- name and address of the responsible bottler or brand owner
- (for EC wines) the quality of the wine (see box).

Most labels also give a lot of other information:

- year the grapes were harvested, called the vintage
- region or area where the wine was made
- grape variety
- where the wine was bottled
- quality testing number (on many German wines)
- style of wine
- serving suggestions
- with white wines, the 9-point dry/sweet scale of the Wine Development Board: 1 is the driest, e.g. Chablis; 9 the sweetest, e.g. Trockenbeerenauslese
- with red wines, the 5-point scale of the Wine Development Board, to indicate the total taste experience: A indicates light and equally enjoyable with or without food, e.g. Beaujolais; E the bigger and more concentrated styles with a greater sensation of depth and fullness, e.g. Barolo.

The language of colour and wine style

UK	France	Germany	Italy	Spain
Red	Rouge	Rotwein	Rosso/ Tinto	Tinto
Light red		Rotling	Chiaretto	Clarete
White	Blanc	Weiss	Bianco	Blanco
Dry	Sec/Brut	Trocken	Secco	Seco
Medium	Demi Sec/ Demi Doux	Halbtrocken	Amabile/ Abboccato	Abocado
Sweet	Doux	Suss	Dolce	Dulce

The language of quality

UK	France	Germany	Italy	Spain
Table wine	Vin de Table	Deutscher Tafelwein	Vino da Tavola	Vino de Mesa
Table wine from a designated region	Vin de Pays VDQS (Vin Délimité de Qualité Supérieure	Landwein	Vino Tipico	Vino de la Tierra
Quality wine	AO or AOC Appellation d'Origine Contrôlée	QbA Qualitätswein bestimmter Anbaugebiete	DOC Denominazione di Origine Controllata	DO Denominacion de Origen
Top quality wine	AO	QmP Qualitätswein mit Prädikat*	DOCG Denominazione di Origine Controllata e Garantita	DOC Denominacion de Origen Calificada

* described in ascending order as Kabinett, Spätlese, Auslese, Beerenauslese, Eiswein (very rare), Trockenbeerenauslese (the best)

Source: Wine Promotion Board – descriptions of quality status vary from country to country and do not always relate precisely to each other.

ACTION   38

Design a wine label which could be used for your house wine. Choose an appropriate country, quality and style from the information in the two boxes above.

Name of your establishment and illustration or design ——————

Vintage (if appropriate) ——————

Quality classification of wine ——————

Style of wine ——————

Country of origin ——————

Contents of bottle ——————

Alcohol content ——————

Name and address of bottler ——————

Grape varieties

The most successful wine-producing countries have moderate, fairly sunny climates with no extreme weather conditions. However, new varieties of grapes, and advances in vine-growing and wine-producing techniques have made it possible to produce good quality wines in countries where the climate is less suitable – England, for example.

The choice of grape depends mainly on the climate of the region where the vines are grown. The type of soil also has a bearing, and in many regions the varieties are controlled by law.

White wines from the Mâconnais (shown here), a district of the Bourgogne (Burgundy), are examples of Old World wines known by the place where the vines grow, rather than the grape variety (Chardonnay).

Germany is known for its fruity white wines. The two main wine-making areas are Mosel-Saar-Ruwer and the Rhine (Rhein) Valley, which produces two distinct styles of wine, Mosel and Rhine.

Sémillon being harvested at Château d'Yquem, in Sauternes (famous for its luscious, sweet white wines). Only the grapes which are shrivelled with age and affected by Noble Rot (a type of fungus) are picked.

Why the grape variety has become more important — CATERER & Hotelkeeper

Traditionally, the Old World growing areas of France, Germany, Spain and Italy named wines after the place the vines grew. This system works well if you know exactly what sort of taste to expect from that area.

For New World producers, putting a place name on the label conveys nothing – especially if they produce a whole range of wines from the same area.

All this has led to the introduction of varietal labels – labels whose main purpose is to detail which grape variety is responsible for the majority of the flavour in the bottle.

 Brian Jordan, 7 February 1991

The main white grape varieties

Chardonnay	Chardonnay is the main grape of the Burgundy and Champagne regions. It makes dry wines, some light and crisp, some smooth, full and buttery. It is very successful in New Zealand, Australia, California, Spain, Italy, Central Europe, South Africa, Israel and Chile.
Chenin Blanc	Grown in the Loire in France and also in California, Australia and South Africa. The wines range from dry to very sweet.
Gewürztraminer	Speciality of Alsace in France, but also grown in Germany, California, Australia, Italy, Central and Eastern Europe. Makes aromatic, flowery wines.
Muscadet	Grown predominantly in the Loire, France. Makes dry, crisp wines when young.
Muscat	Grown in France, Australia and in Italy (Moscato), it makes mainly sweet wines.
Müller Thurgau	One of the popular German varieties, also grown in England. Makes flowery, soft wines, from sweet to dry.
Pinot Blanc	A near relation to Chardonnay, grown in Alsace, Burgundy and Champagne, where it is mainly used for sparkling wines, and in Austria and Italy as Pinot Bianco.
Riesling	Riesling is Germany's classic grape variety. It is also grown in France, Austria (called Rhine), Australia (Rhine), California (Johannisberg) and Italy (Renano). It makes high quality wines from sweet to dry, flowery when young and maturing well.
Sauvignon Blanc	One of the principal white grape varieties of Bordeaux. Also important in the Loire valley, in Italy, Chile, California, Australia, Bulgaria, South Africa and New Zealand. On its own it makes interesting, and distinctive, clean dry wines.
Sémillon	One of the varieties used to make Sauternes. Also grown in Australia and New Zealand to make single or blended wines, sweet or dry in style.
Sylvaner	Grown widely in Germany, also in Alsace and in England, California, New Zealand and Switzerland. Also called Silvaner.

How wine is made

The wine-making process falls into four basic stages:

Pressing – the grapes are crushed or squashed to release the juice.

Fermentation – the conversion of natural sugars in the grape into alcohol takes place through the action of yeast. (Cultured yeast is normally used, although some yeast occurs naturally on the grape skin.)

Racking – after the wine has fermented, it is allowed to settle for 4 to 6 weeks, then transferred by pump or siphon to fresh casks or containers. Great care is taken to leave the 'lees' or sediment undisturbed, and to avoid excess exposure of the wine to air.

Maturation – the wine is left to develop. This can be for several years with a very fine wine, and around six months for table wines.

The time to pick is when there is the correct balance of acidity and sugar in the grapes for the style of wine. The grapes being harvested here are Gamay.

The fermentation stage, when the grape juice becomes alcohol, takes place in large glass-lined or stainless steel containers. Wooden casks are still used by some traditional wine-makers.

The main red grape varieties

Cabernet Franc	Blended in the Bordeaux region to make claret. Also grown in the Loire, and in north-east Italy to make red and rosé wines.
Cabernet Sauvignon	Main red claret grape of Bordeaux, with Merlot and Cabernet Franc. Also grown in Bulgaria, Australia, Chile, California, Israel, New Zealand, South Africa and Italy. Ages well.
Gamay	The Beaujolais grape which makes light, fresh wines normally drunk young. Also grown in the Loire and in Switzerland.
Grenache	Grown in Southern France, Spain and California, it makes fruity wines, generally pale in colour.
Merlot	Grown in Bordeaux, Italy, California, Australia and Eastern Europe, particularly ex-Yugoslavia. Softer than Cabernet Sauvignon and faster maturing.
Nebbiolo	One of Italy's noble varieties making big wines of great longevity such as Barolo and Barbaresco.
Pinot Noir	The single variety of the famed Côte d'Or in Burgundy. Contributes the greater part to the better Champagnes. Also grown in Australia, California, Switzerland, Hungary, New Zealand, Romania and as Spätburgunder in Germany.
Sangiovese	The principal red grape of Tuscany, used to make Chianti, and grown in much of central Italy.
Syrah	The best red grape of the Rhône, making dark robust wine which can mature superbly. Being experimented with in California and Italy and grown widely in Australia as Shiraz.
Tempranillo	The aristocrat of Spanish grape varieties associated particularly with Rioja.

*Red and white grape varieties from **Living with Wine**, published by the Wine Promotion Board, Five Kings House, 1 Queen Street Place, London EC4R 1QS*

During maturation fine wines are racked, often twice a year. This separates out the sediment and gives the wine a chance to breathe so that maturation continues. Here the candle is being used to ensure that all the lees or sediment is left in the barrel (Château Langoa, St Julien).

After racking, the barrels have to be topped up. The photograph shows this at Mouton-Rothschild, in Bordeaux.

How sparkling wine is made

In the traditional method, a second fermentation takes place in the bottle. The bubbles of carbon dioxide produced by the action of the yeast are trapped in the wine.

A mixture of yeast and sugar is added to the wine. The bottles are sealed and laid on their sides for a minimum of one year for non-vintage Champagne, three years for vintage Champagne and seven years or more for top quality Champagne.

The next stage is called *remuage*. The bottles are placed on special racks and over several months twisted and moved a little nearer to their final position, upside down. In this way the sediment gradually gathers towards the neck of the bottle.

The neck of the bottle is dipped into a freezing solution to solidify the sediment, which is then expelled.

This method was first developed in the Champagne region (hence the name *méthode champenoise*) and is imitated by producers of quality sparkling wines all over the world. From 1995 these producers will have to use other words to describe the method by which their sparkling wines are made, e.g. *Traditional method*, if they are to be sold in EC countries.

There are other less labour-intensive methods. The principal one is *méthode charmat*, also called *cuve close* or *closed tank method*. Secondary fermentation takes place in a large tank under pressure. The wine is then filtered and bottled. Asti Spumante is made in this way. The bubbles are larger and do not last as long in the glass as those in Champagne.

Pink or rosé champagne has become fashionable in recent years. Here the bottles are about mid-way through the remuage process. The special racks are called pupitres.

These bottles, in the cellars of Champagne Perrier-Jouet, Epernay, will make Belle Epoque, the vintage Champagne in the distinctively decorated bottle.

By the end of the remuage process, all the sediment has collected in the neck of the bottle. It is then put in a freezing solution before being expelled (dégorgement).

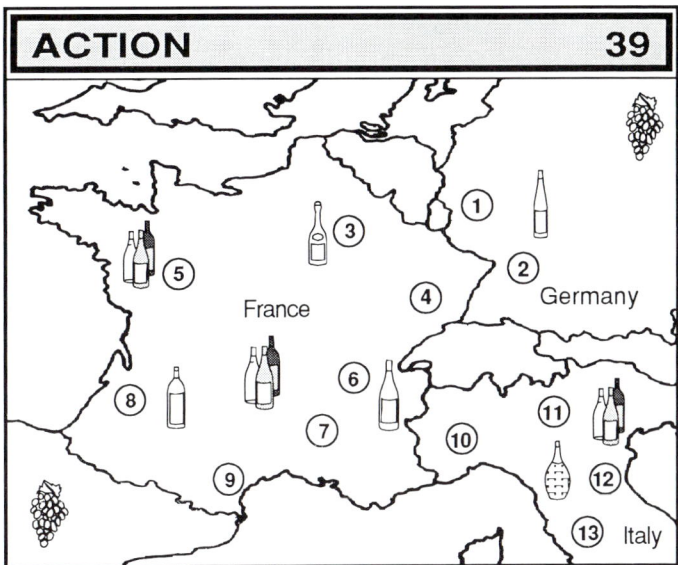

The list below includes the main wine-growing regions of France, Germany and Italy. For each region write the number in the box alongside to identify its location on the map, e.g. Burgundy 6.

If you would like a more challenging exercise, identify from among the well-known wines of that region, the deliberate mistake and write the number of the correct region. For example, in the Burgundy list, Château Latour is in fact from Bordeaux (8).

If you are unsure of any of your answers, have a look through restaurant and wine merchants wine lists (some of which have good maps of wine growing regions).

☐ Burgundy
  Beaujolais, Château Latour, Chablis, Puligny-Montrachet, Volnay
☐ Veneto
  Soave, Bardolino, Valpolicella, Réserve de la Comtesse
☐ Rhône
  Muscat de Beaumes de Venise, Meursault Charmes, Gigondas, Crôzes-Hermitage, Tavel Rosé
☐ Piedmont (Piemonte)
  Crémant de Bourgogne, Asti Spumante, Barolo
☐ Rhine (Rhein) Valley
  Entre-Deux-Mers, Hock, Liebfraumilch, Rheingau Riesling, Niersteiner Gutes Domtal
☐ Loire
  Rosé d'Anjou, Muscadet de Sèvre-et-Maine, Pouilly-Fuissé, Sancerre
☐ Tuscany and Umbria
  Médoc, Chianti, Orvieto
☐ Mosel-Saar-Ruwer
  Piesporter Michelsberg, Pouilly Fumé, Bernkastel Green Label
☐ Languedoc and Roussillon
  Corbières, Vouvray, Minervois
☐ Champagne
  Krug, Châteauneuf-du-Pape, Moët et Chandon, Bollinger
☐ Emilia-Romagna and The Marches
  Lambrusco, Pinot Blanc, Trebbiano, Verdicchio
☐ Bordeaux
  Graves, Barsac, Nuits St-Georges, St Emilion, Château Talbot
☐ Alsace
  Gewürztraminer, Fitou, Pinot Gris, Riesling

The fortified wines

Sherry and **port** are perhaps the best known fortified wines. Their name is protected by law (see box below). They both come in a wide range of styles (the main ones are explained below) and rely on traditional methods of blending developed centuries ago.

Three main grape varieties are used in sherry: Palomino, Pedro Ximénes (Pedro X) and Moscatel. About ten grape varieties account for the majority of port produced, and of these no single variety makes the best port.

Sherry is a versatile drink. As an aperitif (drink before a meal) it can be enjoyed on its own at room temperature or chilled, or on the rocks (with ice).

Port is usually served after a meal, at room temperature if red, and as an aperitif, chilled, if white.

Like sherry, **Madeira** ranges in style. *Sercial*, the driest, and *Verdelho*, with a fuller character and darker colour, are enjoyed before the meal as an aperitif. *Bual*, which is rich and full, dark amber to reddish brown, and *Malmsey* or *Malvasia*, which is rich and sweet, dark mahogany in colour, are usually drunk after a meal.

The drier **vermouths** are usually called French and the sweeter, Italian, although both are made in both France and Italy. Italian vermouths come in two colours, bianco (white) and rosso (red). Red is always sweet, whereas white vermouth can be dry or sweet. There is also rosé vermouth, which is medium dry.

Marsala is made in Sicily. Sweet marsala is used in cooking and as a dessert wine. Dry marsala, also white, is suitable as an aperitif.

Muscat and **muscatel** are made from the Muscat grape. Most are sweet and raisin-like with a strong bouquet. A well-known example is Muscat de Beaumes de Venise, from the Côtes du Rhône village of that name. The addition of grape spirit halts fermentation while some of the natural sugar remains in the wine. It is drunk young.

The finest sherries, the pale dry finos and amontillados, are made from the Palomino grape which thrives on the chalky albariza soil.

A bodega full of Manzanilla. This dry and crispy fino comes only from Sanlucar de Barrameda, a coastal town – hence the sherry's distinctive, slightly salty tang.

Behind the names

The name sherry is a corruption of 'Jerez' (pronounced Here-eth). The town Jerez de la Frontera is the main centre of the sherry-making district on the south-west coast of Spain.

Sherry-type wines produced in South Africa, Cyprus, California, etc. must show the country of origin on the bottle label in letters of at least the same size as those used for the word 'sherry'.

Port only comes from the Douro region of northern Portugal.

Madeira is a mountainous island in the Atlantic Ocean. It is a Portuguese territory.

Vermouths are flavoured with various herbs and spices, the main one being wormwood ('vermuth' in German).

Sherry styles

Fino	pale, straw-coloured, light and very dry
Amontillado	softer, darker and less dry than fino
Oloroso	dark gold or amber colour, soft and mellow, naturally dry but often sweetened
Cream	based on Oloroso, sweet and dark
Pale cream	based on Fino, light in colour and sweet

Port styles

Blended	wines of various years and vineyards blended to maintain the characteristics of a given brand, e.g. *ruby* – fairly young, ruby colour, full of vigour; *tawny* – matured long in vats or casks, has shed its red colour
Vintage character	blend of good quality ports of more than one year, matured in the wood
Vintage	port from one year of exceptional quality. Very full red colour with fine bouquet and taste. Vintage declarations are made in year 3 when the port is bottled and left to mature for 10 to 15 years and may continue to improve for up to 40
Late-bottled vintage	port of a single year, bottled after it has been in the cask for 5 years or more, ready to drink sooner than vintage port
Crusted	blended, bottled young and aged in the bottle, hence the crust

Appreciating wine

Getting the most out of wine is an art which needs to be practised.

1 Study the appearance of the wine. The wine glass should be no more than one-quarter full (the photograph shows the ideal type of glass). Hold it by the stem and tilt it slightly against a white background (e.g. a sheet of paper). Note the colour and the viscosity (how thin/thick) of the wine.

2 Take in the bouquet, aroma or 'nose'. Still holding the glass by its stem, swirl the wine vigorously to aerate it. Then smell the wine. Do not leave the nose in the glass but return as often as necessary, noting your impressions each time.

If necessary, hold one hand around the bowl of the glass to warm the wine slightly, and cover the top of the glass with the other hand. After a few moments, release your hand from the top and quickly breathe in the aroma which has built up.

3 Taste it by rolling the wine backwards and forwards over the tongue. After 'chewing' the wine in this way, suck in a little air to see how the wine develops.

After swallowing the wine (not recommended if you are tasting many wines!), notice what flavour lingers on your palate and throat, and how long it lasts.

Three senses are involved in the appreciation of wine: sight, smell and taste, in that order.

On removing the cork to let the wine breathe

CATERER
& Hotelkeeper

It is a widely held misconception that removing the cork lets the wine breathe. In fact it has no perceptible effect at all, with only the small amount of wine at the top of the neck likely to benefit. This has been conclusively proved in tests on both sides of the Atlantic.

The best method of aerating a wine is to pour it into a suitable receptacle (e.g. a decanter). With big red wines from the New World, where sedimentation is minimal, the wine benefits from being poured from one decanter or jug to another two or three times. Pour the wine with the maximum bubbling, not down the side as you would a lager.

Brian Jordan, 17 January 1991 (adapted with permission)

ACTION   40

A key factor in the appreciation of wine is the glass in which it is served. Name the glasses shown here, state their main uses and why they are considered particularly suitable (or not particularly suitable).

1
Copita. Traditionally used in Spain for sherry, increasingly popular elsewhere as its shape is ideal for concentrating the bouquet. But easily broken and difficult to clean.

2, 3, 4

5, 6   9, 10

7, 8   11

Preparing and serving wine `LEVEL 2`

The choice of wines in any one establishment varies according to the kind of customers it wishes to attract. Some offer a long wine list, while others may simply provide two or three house wines.

Whatever the type of restaurant or bar you work in, you need, at the very least, to know about the wines available at your particular establishment and their prices, so that you can assist customers in making a choice.

Wine with food

At places where food is served, staff need to know what is on the menu in order to be able to recommend a suitable wine for the dish chosen. Some restaurants change their menus regularly, or have dishes of the day which need special promotion. So keeping up-to-date with the food menu, whether on a daily or weekly basis, is important.

The following general guidelines will help you advise customers on suitable wines to complement the food they have ordered. But remember that the only hard and fast rule is never to show disapproval of a customer's choice. The choice of wine is up to the customer, not you.

1 Dry wines before sweet wines – if sweet wines are drunk first they tend to overwhelm the taste of the medium or dry white wines.

2 White wines before red wines.

3 Generally white wines go better with light dishes such as salads, and with fish and most white meat.

4 Red wines with red meat, game and other strongly flavoured dishes, and cheeses. Heavy stews, casseroles and mild curries in particular need a good solid red wine to do them and the wine justice. Some people prefer beer with hotter curries.

5 Sweeter wines are better drunk on their own, and the really sweet wines are delicious with desserts.

6 Avoid wines with food which contain acid such as grapefruit and salads with vinaigrette.

Who may not be served wine

In a licensed restaurant in Scotland, over 16s may buy wine with a meal. Elsewhere in the UK the minimum age is 18.

There is no age restriction on drinking alcohol with a table meal, provided it is purchased by a parent or other responsible guardian.

See page 70.

There are five aims in recommending a wine: to take the customers' tastes into consideration, not your own; to select a wine which complements the dish chosen, so that neither taste dominates the other; to satisfy the customer; to match or enhance the occasion; to increase wine sales.

ACTION   41

For each of the following situations, complete the two sentences, as you might to a customer in your workplace who had asked you to recommend a wine:

A If you are looking for something interesting and special, but not too expensive, I suggest ...

B In the lower price range, we also have ...

---

to accompany the first course, a light fish dish

A

B

---

to enjoy with the roast joint of the day

A

B

---

with vegetarian dish of the day

A

B

---

with the dessert

A

B

The right temperature

Wines generally taste best when served at the following temperatures – but, of course, this does not prevent individual customers from having different preferences:

medium and full-bodied reds – around 20°C

light reds, Beaujolais Nouveau – slightly cooler, around 17°C

whites and rosés – chilled, about 10°C

sparkling wines and Champagnes – well chilled, about 7°C.

The ideal temperature for storing wine is 10 to 12°C. Outside this range it will deteriorate after as little as three weeks. Furthermore, wine does not respond well to rapid changes of temperature. For these reasons a small stock is best kept at serving temperature in a chilling cabinet, refrigerator or a suitably warm room:

- most red wines should be stored at around 20°C for at least 4 hours before serving

- white and rosé wines should be chilled in a refrigerator or cooler for at least an hour

- sparkling wines and Champagnes should be placed in the refrigerator for 1½ hours.

If a customer orders a bottle which needs:

chilling – put in a bucket of ice and water for 15 to 20 minutes (if you add salt and move the bottle from time to time, 5 minutes may be sufficient)

warming – warm a decanter or carafe for a few minutes in a hot cupboard, then transfer the wine to this. Alternatively, wrap around the decanter a clean cloth soaked in hot water and well rung out.

Presenting and serving wine

Show (present) the bottle before opening to the person who ordered it.

If the wine is already cooling in a bucket, bring both to the table. Take the bottle carefully out of the bucket, wipe dry with a clean napkin or service cloth, and then present it.

Hold the bottle so that the label can be clearly read.

Once you have approval, open the bottle – how to do this is explained in detail on the next page.

If you return the wine to an ice bucket, be sure to leave the napkin hanging over the top of the bottle, or on the handle of the ice bucket. It will then be handy to wipe the bottle when you or the customer wants to refill the glasses.

Presenting the wine gives the customer the opportunity to check that it is the one ordered.

On the serving temperature of wine **CATERER** *& Hotelkeeper*

If a bottle of, say, an oakey Chardonnay is brought to the table in an ice bucket in which it has been immersed to reach the correct temperature, the first couple of glasses will be perfect.

However, if the bottle is then returned to the bucket, the rate of chilling increases as there is less volume to work on. Then, if after 10 minutes, another two glasses are poured, they will be too cold – but they will be nothing like as cold as the last two glasses, which will have almost lost their taste completely by the time they are drunk.

I have frequently rescued a bottle from the ice bucket when the temperature is right, but have to watch out for wine waiters anxious to restore the bottle to the bucket 'where it belongs'.

 *Brian Jordan, 24 January 1991 (adapted)*

SAFETY ▲▲▲

Red wine should not be warmed in a microwave. It is highly dangerous:

- placing narrow necked containers (i.e. wine bottles) in microwave ovens can cause the contents to boil suddenly and without warning, erupting violently

- the vapours given off by the alcohol as it is heated can cause an explosion.

 Merrychef Limited

General procedure for serving wine

1 Where possible, open the bottle in view of the customers. This is what most customers expect. Seeing your bottle opened adds to the sense of anticipation and the subsequent pleasure as you taste the wine.

2 Open white and sparkling wines when the customer is ready to drink them.

3 Red wines can be opened after they have been approved.

4 The cork is sometimes left with the customer, on a small plate or in the wine basket if the wine is left on the table, or in the ice bucket.

5 Pour the wine from behind the customer, standing at the customer's right shoulder. In a more informal situation, you might be able to fill everyone's glass standing in one position at the table. What you should try and avoid is having to stretch in front of anyone.

6 Offer the person who ordered the wine the opportunity to taste a little before you begin pouring. Hold the bottle so the customer can see the label.

7 Do not allow the neck of the bottle to touch the glass as you pour the wine (for hygiene and safety reasons). Twist the bottle slightly just as you lift it away after pouring each glass. This helps prevent the wine dripping on to the table. It is also advisable to wipe the neck of the bottle with a napkin after each pouring.

8 Fill the glass of each customer who requires wine. To allow the bouquet to be enjoyed, no wine glass should be filled more than two-thirds full. Some experts recommend between one-third and one-half full.

9 When everyone has been served, place the bottle in the insulated wine cooler on the table if it is to be kept chilled (returning the wine to an ice bucket may result in it being over-chilled – see box on previous page). Red wine can be placed on the table, usually standing on a coaster or small plate, or lying in a basket.

10 From time to time, return to the table to refill glasses.

11 When additional bottles of wine are requested, each bottle should be presented and, once opened, a little poured in a clean glass for approval. If the wine is different, everyone should be given a clean glass. When it is another bottle of the same wine, some restaurants will provide clean glasses.

12 Empty bottles should be taken away promptly.

Opening a bottle of still wine

1 Remove the top of the plastic or metal capsule which covers the cork. Use a small sharp knife (the blade of the waiter's knife is ideal – in use in the photographs). Do not rotate the bottle – with experience you will be able to cut round the capsule in one movement.

2 Wipe the top of the bottle with a moistened napkin.

3 Pinpoint the centre of the cork with the tip of the corkscrew, then raise it directly above the bottle.

4 Keeping the corkscrew upright, twist firmly twice.

Step 1. Cutting through the capsule. The ring of the bottle provides a natural guide for the knife blade.

Step 2. Wiping the top of the bottle. With older wines the top of the cork can be quite dirty.

Step 3. The tip of the corkscrew is dead centre to give a stronger grip and reduce the risk of the cork fragmenting, when small bits will fall in the wine.

Step 4. Twist in a clockwise direction twice.

5　Hold the lever of the waiter's friend against the rim of the bottle. With the other hand, lever the cork out a short distance. Then give the waiter's friend another two turns and lever the cork a second time until it is almost out of the bottle.

6　With your fingers, pull the cork out gently and quietly.

7　Remove the cork from the corkscrew.

8　Wipe the neck of the bottle with a moistened napkin.

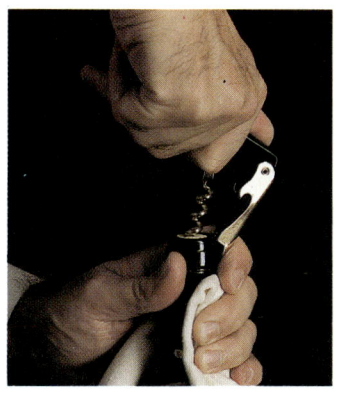 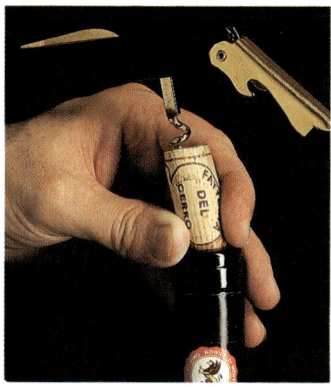

Step 5. Hold the end of the waiter's friend firmly against the rim of the bottle so that it provides an effective, safe lever.

Step 6. The cork should not make a sound as you pull it out of the bottle.

Opening a bottle of sparkling wine or Champagne

Safety should be your first consideration. People have lost an eye through carelessness when opening sparkling wine. Always keep the top of the bottle covered with a napkin. If the cork won't budge, don't peer at it – it's likely to hit you in the eye.

1　Grip the bottle firmly with one hand. Hold the bottle at an angle of 45°, pointing away from anyone or anything that might be damaged should the cork suddenly shoot out.

2　Locate the ring of the wire muzzle with the fingers of the other hand.

3　Untwist the wire muzzle to break it.

4　Take a firm grip of the top of the cork (with the muzzle and foil still in place) with one hand. With the other, firmly grip the bottle. Gently twist the bottle in one direction, the cork in the other.

5　As you feel the cork begin to move, ease it out between your finger and thumb. Continue to hold the napkin over the top of the cork. The cork should come out with a hiss.

 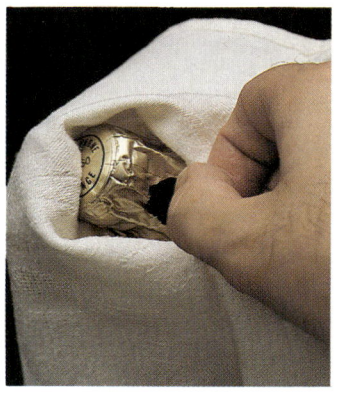

Step 1. The thumb is held over the cork, while the fingers have a firm grip around the neck. The napkin will catch the cork if it flies out.

Steps 2 and 3. Breaking the wire muzzle. There is no need to remove the foil before this step, although some people prefer to do so.

Step 4. Twisting the bottle and cork in opposite directions is easier than trying to twist the cork alone. And there is less risk of the cork breaking.

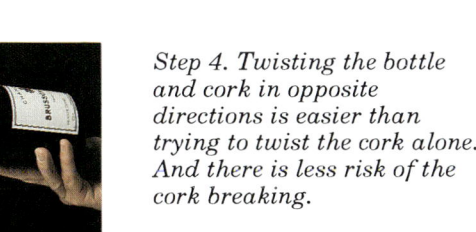

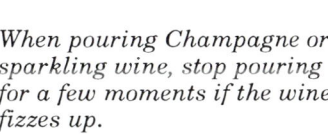

When pouring Champagne or sparkling wine, stop pouring for a few moments if the wine fizzes up.

Dealing with a faulty wine

By knowing what to look out for, you can often prevent a faulty wine being served, or at least being tasted by the customer. But if it is the customer who first notices the fault, a knowledgeable response from you will keep the customer satisfied.

These are the general rules:

1 Apologise and remove the faulty wine and any glasses into which it has been poured.

2 Offer another bottle of the same wine or invite the customer to choose a different wine.

3 Bring fresh glasses with the new wine.

4 Recork the faulty wine or seal the bottle with clingfilm, and put aside for your manager to deal with. Generally the offending bottle will be returned to the supplier.

The condition of the bottle

Any sign that wine has leaked out (e.g. stickiness around neck) indicates a faulty cork. Do not serve.

If the wine has been stored in a damp cellar, the label will looked aged. This is not usually a problem, unless there is doubt over the identity of the wine.

The appearance of the wine in the bottle

In a mature red wine, some natural sediment is to be expected. Wines of this age are often decanted.

Crystals (of tartar) in white wine are harmless and do not affect the taste. They probably mean the wine has been stored at very low temperatures at some stage.

If a still wine appears to be fermenting in the bottle (small bubbles form, especially when it is moved), do not serve. Remember that some wines are made to sparkle slightly in the bottle (e.g. Lambrusco, Vinho Verde).

If the wine is cloudy, stand the bottle upright. If it does not clear within 24 hours, it should not be served.

The top of the cork

Mould on the top of the cork, underneath the capsule, does not harm the wine, and is easily wiped off.

The end of the cork

Crystals on the end of the cork are harmless.

A dry cork on an older wine is a sign that the bottle has been stored upright. This will not necessarily spoil the wine, but the cork may be difficult to extract cleanly.

If the cork is very dry and has shrunk so much you think air has got to the wine (which will ruin it), get another bottle, or recommend a replacement.

The cork smells musty

Smelling the cork is more of a ritual (which few people insist on now) than a guaranteed test.

The wine itself smells unpleasant

Some wines give off a mildly unpleasant smell after the bottle is first opened. It is the result of many years of storage in the bottle and should disappear quickly, leaving the wine unaffected. With some red wines the smell in these first few moments is dank, while some white wines smell of sulphur.

A genuine 'corked wine' is rare (although some people use the expression incorrectly, to describe wine which has pieces of cork in it). It has a strong, pungent and unpleasant dank smell of mushrooms. The smell may go after the wine has been opened for a short time, but if not, do not serve.

The wine will also taste unpleasant if the glass it is served in has not been polished correctly (see page 28).

Appearance of the wine in the glass

If a still wine fizzes or has bubbles (not noticed before the bottle was opened), do not continue serving.

If the wine is darker in colour than it should be, this is a sign of oxidisation (excessive exposure to air, e.g. because the cork has dried out and shrunk, letting in air).

If crystals, sediment or bits of cork have got into the glass, remove the offending glass with an apology.

Customer finds the wine faulty on tasting it

Report it to your manager who will pour a little into a clean glass, smell and if necessary taste the wine. If the wine is faulty, it will be replaced without question.

NVQ svQ RANGE CHECKLIST

LEVEL 2

2C6.1 Prepare and serve bottled wines

provide information on these
- [ ] flavour
- [ ] price
- [ ] origin
- [ ] food complements

serve these wines
- [ ] red
- [ ] white
- [ ] rosé
- [ ] sparkling/Champagne
- [ ] fortified
- [ ] dry
- [ ] medium
- [ ] sweet
- [ ] vintage

using these
- [ ] ice buckets or wine coolers
- [ ] wine cradles
- [ ] carafes or decanters
- [ ] cork screws
- [ ] serving cloths

Introduction

In counter service customers collect their own food from a counter or table and take it to an eating area. There are three main variations.

Fully-assisted

Everything is served for the customer. As many customers enjoy the freedom of helping themselves, this style of service is not so much about luxury as:

Speed – skilled staff are faster at serving, so the throughput of customers is greater

Portion control – with staff serving this can be precise, while giving customers good value.

Partly-assisted

Some items are served, while customers help themselves to others. Usually the items served are the more expensive, and staff can give the right portion.

Staff will also serve food which has to be carved at the counter, or where the elaborate presentation might be spoilt if customers serve themselves.

Letting customers serve themselves to certain dishes encourages a feeling of value for money.

Portion sizes may be unrestricted, with no charge for extra helpings. More usually, control is indirect, by:

- using plates of a certain size
- offering standard size items, e.g. 200 g baked potatoes
- pre-portioning the food, e.g. individual trifles
- charging per item, e.g. rasher of bacon 75p
- weigh and pay, e.g. 120 g container of salad for 50p.

Un-assisted

Customers help themselves to everything. Portion control methods are similar to partly-assisted service.

Units and elements covered in this section

LEVEL 1

1C3 Prepare and clear areas for counter service
- 1C3.1 Prepare counter for service
- 1C3.2 Prepare customer dining areas for customer service
- 1C3.3 Clear dining and service areas after food service

1C4 Provide a counter service
- 1C4.1 Serve customers at the counter
- 1C4.2 Maintain counter and service areas

Contents guide

Contract catering firms (Gardner Merchant is an example) provide the catering services for a wide range of companies and institutions. If you work for a contract caterer, the customers are the staff and management of the client company or institution. Competition in contract catering is strong, and if your customers are not satisfied with the service or the food, the contract may be lost to a competitor.

Customers' satisfaction is increased when food is presented well, and customers who are satisfied are likely to return. This in turn may encourage them to recommend the restaurant to their friends – all of which leads to increased sales and therefore higher profits.

Preparing counter for service `LEVEL 1`

The care and attention you put into your various preparation tasks will prove well worthwhile when the busy service period gets under way.

Try and develop a routine to suit you and your workplace. The aims are to:

- approach each task methodically

- tackle things in the best order

- minimise the risk of forgetting or overlooking something

- avoid having to rush particular jobs because time has run out.

General procedure

1 Check crockery, cutlery and glassware for chips and cracks, and to ensure that it is clean.

2 Refill the plate warmer and put piles of cold plates on the counter as necessary.

3 Place cutlery, glassware, napkins and trays at the appropriate places.

4 Switch on all appliances in time to reach the right operating temperature. Report any faults to your supervisor.

5 Display the day's menu. If the menu includes items which do not vary from day to day, e.g. soft drinks, fruit juices, salads, are the prices correct? Is the spelling correct?

6 Stock the counter with non-perishable items, e.g. individual packets of sauce.

7 Arrange promotional displays.

8 Bring cold food from the kitchen and display in the chilled cabinets. Portion any sweets or starters (unless this has been done in the kitchen).

9 Immediately before service, collect hot dishes from the kitchen. If service is over an extended period, these will usually be cooked in batches.

10 Position ladles, spoons, carving knives and other serving equipment required for the day's range of dishes.

11 Check that there are plenty of back-up supplies of crockery, cutlery and food items to replenish during the serving period.

12 Check sneeze screens (given this name because they protect the food should a customer sneeze or cough in the direction of the display) and glass display cabinets for smears or other unsightly marks.

Loading counters

Do not overload food service counters. The food will look more appetising if displays are not overcrowded. With hot dishes, it is better to replenish regularly with freshly cooked food.

Do not block the intake or outlet air vents of refrigerated displays with dishes of food or decorations.

Keep doors of food display counters and storage cabinets closed to ensure the temperature is kept at the correct level. Both hot and refrigerated equipment will lose efficiency if doors are left open.

Refilling the plate holder (sometimes called a lowerator).

Loading the counter with cold foods – salads, meats and desserts.

Stocking up checklist

1 All counters and display units always cleaned and polished before service.

2 All products presented with selling to the customer in mind.

3 All products placed in correct position and held at correct temperatures at all times.

4 Presentation standards maintained throughout time when re-stocking.

5 Hygiene rules and regulations adhered to.

6 Supervisor informed when stored stock is running low.

7 Stocks rotated correctly by moving old stock to the front for use first.

ACTION   42

Visit a range of supermarkets, delicatessens and other shops selling food and drink in your area. Study the methods used to present their products. Draw sketches of the best, with comments to show how they might be adapted to suit your workplace.

Promoting sales

One of the advantages of counter service is that customers can see the range of foods available, without the need to rely on menu descriptions.

Effective and attractive presentation depends on:

Colour – the imaginative use of colour on the counter can be very effective. Contrasting colours help to offset each other, e.g. placing carrots between two containers of green vegetables.

Shape – a variety of shapes will add interest, e.g. placing trays of filled rolls next to trays of sandwiches.

Texture – good balance requires variety, e.g. apple crumble next to rice pudding.

Portion size – match portion size and plates. An overcrowded plate looks messy and too large a plate makes the portion look mean.

Impact – there is almost no limit to the ways in which you can lift a display from being dull and rather ordinary to something that really attracts customers' attention. However you should remember that you are dealing with food. Don't:

- mix cooked and uncooked items, e.g. a fresh trout surrounded by fillets of smoked trout

- put plants or fresh flower arrangements where they might come into direct contact with uncovered food

- display food in containers which cannot be properly cleaned, e.g. bread rolls in a wicker basket

- use artificial food items in arrangements which might lead customers to think that it is fresh food, available for sale, e.g. a plastic apple among the cheeses.

Using chalkboards and posters effectively

GARDNER MERCHANT

Consider where they will be placed:

- well-lit: smaller print, more details
- badly-lit: larger print, fewer words
- easily visible: dynamic and stimulating.

Light, bright colours give an impression of fun.

Deep colours give an impression of quality.

Use plain, clear lettering – simple and bold. Fancy printing styles are sometimes hard to read.

Plan the layout carefully so that letters are evenly spaced, and there is sufficient space between all words.

Let one or two people read it before it goes out.

Watch that spelling!

Selling ideas

GARDNER MERCHANT

Take products from their usual position and create a special 'impact' display.

'Pile it high' to make a bold display – but don't overdo it and confuse the customer.

Group and display related products together to encourage a second purchase, e.g.:

    sandwich, yogurt, drink

    salad, bread roll, butter

    filled roll, fruit, drink

With 'mix n' match' displays: balance colours together and strive for maximum eye appeal.

While your customers are waiting, catch their eye at the till – with confectionery, home-made jams, recipe books, etc. Think of the things you decide on impulse to buy at a supermarket, as you queue at the till.

People relate to people and like to know things were made **personally** by the chef or cook. 'Julie's Special' or 'Alan's Dish of the Day' sounds much more friendly than 'Chef's Special'.

Don't just have a chilled display cabinet. Do something with it. Change the name to 'Eskimo's Larder', 'Arctic Shop', etc.

ACTION   43

Food and drink companies spend millions of pounds creating and advertising their latest slogan. Which of these products are sold in your workplace, and how can you get in on the act?

Here is an idea, from Ealing Hospital, to get your mind working. Sketch a suitable display. Or, with your supervisor's permission, make up a display on the counter.

Pukka Cuppa
You have heard it on the radio
You have seen it on TV
Now come & join us for
A pukka cuppa tea
Now on sale in the restaurant
Buy individually or a box of 50 tea bags
Assam or Darjeeling

Preparing dining areas

Food and drink is much more enjoyable when the surroundings are pleasant. Your attention to every detail, from the arrangement of napkins to the general comfort of the room, will show the customers that you have their satisfaction at heart.

Even where it is not possible for you to take action directly, e.g. replacing a carpet which is frayed and likely to cause an accident, you are in a good position to notice such problems. Reporting them promptly will help get the matter attended to.

General procedure

1 Refill or replace sauces, mustards, salts and peppers.

2 Lay place mats or tablecloths, if used.

3 Position table decorations (e.g. flowers), menus and promotional items.

4 Set tables with cutlery, plates, drink glasses, napkins, ashtrays, etc. as appropriate.

5 Fill cutlery trays and napkin dispensers.

Preparation of dining area

Avon
COUNTY COUNCIL
FOR SERVICES YOU NEED

1 Tables must be wiped clean with a solution of hot water and bactericidal detergent before use, between each sitting and at the end of service.

2 Chairs must be placed around the table using a chair trolley.

3 Cutlery may only be handled using the handles.

4 It is expected that when cutlery is required to be placed on the table, it will consist of a knife and fork for the main course and a spoon and fork for the sweet course.

5 Mugs and a jug of fresh drinking water must be available. The water must be replenished after each service.

6 Salt and pepper pots must be refilled and wiped before being placed on the table.

7 A trolley must be placed in a suitable position in the dining room to receive the empties. Receptacles for food waste (with a scraper), paper waste, mugs and cutlery must be provided.

8 At the end of service the tables must be folded and stacked. The chairs must be stacked in piles of 8.

9 The floor must be swept and any spillages wiped clean.

ACTION	44

The diagram below (from Gardner Merchant's *Good Ideas Book*) shows 'hot' and 'cold' spots in a typical servery area.

Products placed in hot spots become fast sellers, because these locations are:

- highly visible
- in the mainstream flow
- where most customers stand
- where most customers pass slowly.

Cold spots are less visible, out of the mainstream flow, or most customers pass quickly.

On a sheet of graph or other suitable paper, draw a diagram indicating the hot and cold spots in your workplace for the main meal service.

Then discuss with your manager which products might be promoted in the hot spots.

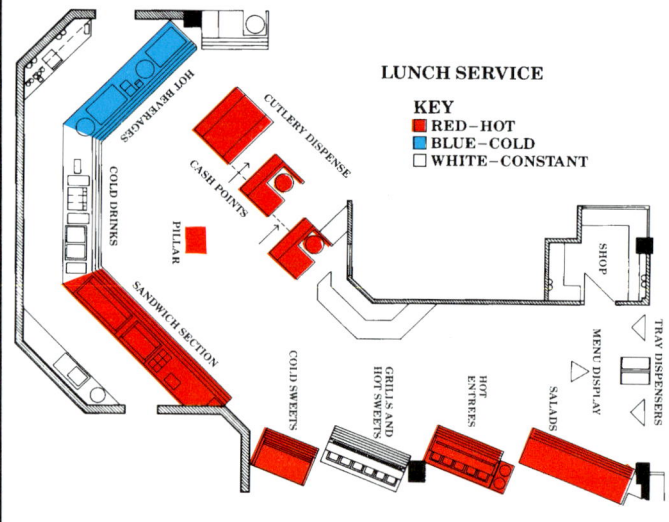

LUNCH SERVICE

KEY
- ■ RED–HOT
- ■ BLUE–COLD
- □ WHITE–CONSTANT

Table lay-ups in counter service restaurants vary from nothing on the table to a full place setting to suit a 3-course meal.

Large trolleys like this help in clearing dining areas (see page opposite).

Clearing after service

The priority is to leave everything in a safe and tidy state, so that whoever is responsible for cleaning can do the job properly.

If you are working in a 24-hour operation, clearing will take place during quiet periods when sections of the counter and dining areas can be closed off with minimum inconvenience to customers.

Clearing dining area – general procedure

1 Remove rubbish from floors, tables, etc.

2 Wipe down surfaces, tables and chairs with the appropriate cleaning and sanitising solution. Check furniture for chewing gum, other sticky substances and stains.

3 Collect trays, wipe clean and stack at the appropriate place.

4 Empty rubbish bins, clean and return to their correct places.

5 Empty ashtrays into a covered metal bin (or other suitable fireproof container), wash and dry before replacing.

Clearing service area – general procedure

Return food items to the kitchen or storage area without delay. The chefs will probably deal with menu items which are left over from service, but you may be responsible for returning to storage packets of butter, fruit juices, canned drinks, etc.

Treat such stocks with care so that:

• everything is used on a first in, first out basis

• stocks of a different age are not mixed up

• nothing is allowed to pass its use-by or best-before date unnoticed

• proper storage temperatures are maintained at all times.

Clear the counter of display trays, serving equipment, etc.

Return packaged, non-perishable items, such as cans of soft drink, to the correct storage area.

Dispose of rubbish.

Switch off equipment, as instructed.

Daily cleaning schedule for restaurant after service

1 Refrigerated display counters emptied and cleaned, switched off.

2 All food locked in fridge. Fridge doors cleaned.

3 Stainless steel counters washed and polished.

4 Hot counters emptied and cleaned top and bottom, and clean covers put on.

5 Coffee machine emptied, coffee jugs washed. Trolley cleaned, replenished with spoons, sugar, coffee ready for morning and locked away.

6 Orange dispenser cleaned and switched off.

7 All sinks cleaned.

8 Floor swept and washed.

9 Tables in restaurant cleaned and left ready for morning service.

10 All cutlery checked and put away.

11 All cleaning cloths washed and put to dry. Buckets emptied and washed. All mops put in solution, then rinsed, dry squeezed and put to dry.

12 All bins emptied, cleaned and new bags put in.

SAFETY

Always use CAUTION or CLEANING IN PROGRESS signs to indicate hazardous areas.

Always use protective clothing where advised.

Never mix detergents/cleaning fluids.

Always follow manufacturers' instructions when using cleaning products.

Keep fire exits clear.

Dispose of broken glass safely.

Ensure cleaning equipment is kept in safe condition and report any disorders to supervisor.

Dispose of used/diluted cleaning solutions in outside drain.

Clean all equipment after use and before storage.

Store equipment and cleaning products safely, preferably in a specific designated area under lock and key.

Only store cleaning materials in their original containers.

Serving customers

Your situation is not unlike that of politicians or members of the Royal Family on a walkabout. Faced with an ever moving queue of customers at the counter, your challenge is to convey in the few moments' contact you have, that warm, genuine human touch that makes all the difference to your customers' eating and drinking experience.

Providing what customers want

The presentation of the food remains important until it is actually eaten by the customer. A beautifully presented dish may persuade someone to choose that dish, but if the food looks unappetising once served on to the plate, the effect will be completely wasted.

- Position food on the plate carefully, with consideration for what the customer is choosing. Vegetables should be placed next to each other and not on top of the meat. If it is a dish with rice, the rice might be positioned in a circle, so that it surrounds the main item, or to one side.

- While serving foods, place the container lids below the counter to enable customers to see the dishes. Replace lids during quiet periods to keep the food hot.

- If customers change their minds – 'Oh, may I have the flan instead of the lamb?' – start again with a clean plate. Don't scrape the unwanted food off the plate.

- Use the correct serving equipment for each dish. A perforated spoon would be wrong with fruit salad, because the syrup is part of the enjoyment of the dish.

- When customers are not familiar with a particular dish, they will expect you to be able to describe how the dish has been made and its main ingredients.

- You will also have the opportunity to promote special dishes and drinks. You can play a key role in encouraging customers to choose additional or alternative items which add to their enjoyment of the food and drink and increase sales.

- If a certain dish is no longer available, inform the customer and recommend some alternatives.

- Know what accompaniments should be offered with each dish, e.g. Yorkshire pudding with the roast beef, ice cream or custard with the apple pie.

Special meal trays are used at this school. They are suitable for cold and hot food (as above).

Here are some one-liners from the Gardner Merchant *Good Ideas Book* – single sentences that can form part of your conversation with customers on any new idea.

☺ Don't forget our new roll service in the morning.

☺ The recipe is our own – try it.

☺ Go on spoil yourself.

☺ I bet you never get this at home.

☺ Don't forget the sweet to go with it.

Add 3 one-liners of your own, appropriate to your customers. Before writing them down, try each one out on colleagues and friends. Does it work? How can it be improved?

☺ _____

☺ _____

☺ _____

A cheerful smile is an important aspect of providing what customers want.

Portioning

Your customers expect to get value for their money – consistently. And they expect to get the same value as other customers receive.

The smooth running of your operation depends on accurate portion control:

- menu prices have been worked out on the basis of a particular size portion. Margins between sales and costs will decrease if over-sized portions are served, and this could lead to the closure of the business

- a specific quantity of food has been ordered and prepared to produce X number of portions. If too much is served to the first customers, the food will run out

- customers will complain if they get different size portions for the same price.

Some items may be offered in different size portions, according to the price, or there will be a standard size. Methods of portion control include:

1 Size of container in which the item is served, e.g. coffee cup, soup bowl, a certain teapot for 1 serving, a larger one for 2.

2 Use of a particular serving utensil, e.g. 25 ml ladle for sauce, scoop for French fries, 200 ml ladle for soup.

3 Metered dispense equipment, e.g. for soft drinks.

4 The way in which the food has been purchased or prepared, e.g. 175 g breast of chicken, 200 g piece of steak (uncooked weights), 50 g portion of cheese (pre-wrapped), 440 ml can of coke.

5 Presentation guidelines, e.g. a tray of roast pork, with slices clustered together with a piece of crackling.

6 Specific instructions, e.g. 3 boiled potatoes, 2 slices of roast lamb.

7 Pre-plating the food in the kitchen, e.g. a slice of pâté, garnished with lettuce, tomato, lemon slice and wrapped in clingfilm or cellophane.

Serving and presentation of food

1 Portion control adhered to.

2 Plates/cutlery, etc. checked for cleanliness before use.

3 Food arranged on plate to standard.

4 Food checked for quality and temperature when serving.

5 Appropriate cutlery supplied with each dish.

6 Condiments/relishes supplied and checked for freshness/sufficiency.

7 Opportunities used to sell desserts/coffee.

8 Customers questioned for their views.

9 Complaints handled politely and referred to appropriate person.

HYGIENE

Carry plates from underneath, or by the rim so your fingers or thumb do not come into contact with the food.

Pick up cutlery by the handle only.

Do not touch the rims of cups or put fingers inside cups.

Keep your hands scrupulously clean at all times. Money is a particular problem – it's filthy, having been in and out of pockets, machines, etc. So remember to wash your hands if you have handled money and then have to touch food.

Pay strict attention to procedures for monitoring temperatures (see page 17) and the length of time the food is on display.

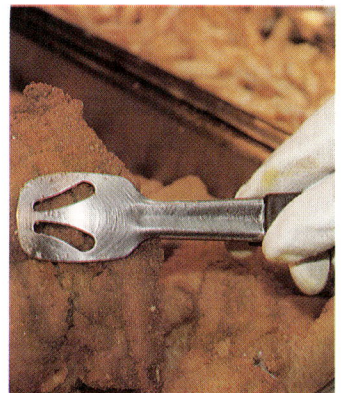 

Use the correct serving equipment to ensure accurate portion control and good presentation of the food.

The last customer is just as important as the first customer. Do keep the counter properly stocked. Don't get to the last spoonful of vegetables before asking the kitchen for more. Don't chase the last six chips around the tray.

The customers in this photograph are employed by Transmanche-Link on the construction of the Channel Tunnel. The counter service staff are employees of CCG Services, one of the catering contractors who provide catering services at the Dover construction site.

Serving drinks

In some counter service restaurants, drinks are served by the counter staff. In others, the customers serve themselves from vending machines on the counter or elsewhere in the service/dining area.

Cans, bottles and pre-poured glasses of cold drinks are often placed in a chilled cabinet for customers to select.

Hot beverages are either poured into the customer's cup or an individual pot is made to order for each customer.

When the cup method is used, the beverage is sometimes made in bulk, and served from a large pot. Alternatively, the beverage is dispensed from a vending machine located behind the counter.

Some general points to remember

1 If the beverage is made in a large pot and poured as the customer requests it, take care that the brew of tea or coffee does not stand for too long. Throw away old brews.

2 When the milk or cream is served by the counter staff, the customers should be asked whether they require it. In many counter service restaurants the milk and cream are individually portioned for customers to take as they require.

3 Be careful not to spill drinks into the saucer. If this occurs, provide a clean saucer for the customer. Do not overfill the cup, or it will be difficult to carry.

4 When a machine is used to dispense drinks, switch it on in advance of service to ensure that the drinks are served at the correct temperature.

You will find more information on drink service in sections 9, 10 and 13.

Preparing the counter for drink service – here, customers serve themselves to coffee.

Mixing packaged foods and cans of soft drinks makes an attractive display for St. Valentine's day.

Coffee dispensers

1 Turn off machine. Empty and clean coffee pots.
2 Fill water containers to indicated level. (Not necessary if the machine is connected to the water supply.)
3 Insert fresh filter.
4 Add correct measure of coffee. For Conas, the coffee is usually purchased in packets of the appropriate size.
5 Turn on machine when required for coffee service.

Start a new brew before the last pot is finished. Don't leave empty Cona pots on the hotplate, or they will crack. If the machine is one where customers help themselves, you will need to keep an eye out for empty pots.

Drinks dispenser checklist   **Butlin's HOLIDAYS**

1 Check drinks dispenser to ensure that it will not run out prior to service.
2 Ensure that sufficient quantities of various drinks mixtures are available for service, if required.
3 Ensure that correct drinks products are placed in correct containers.
4 Ensure water supply on and power supply on.
5 Empty slop trays frequently and clean down drinks servery.
6 Clean down dispenser at the end of each serving period in correct manner.

Still operation checklist

1 Clean still area and all appliances.
2 Switch on still in adequate time prior to service (20 minutes).
3 Display extreme care when handling receptacles with hot water in them to prevent injury to anyone.
4 Operate the still in the correct manner.
5 Know the methods to ensure the quality of product from the still is excellent.
6 Empty spillage trays frequently.
7 Maintain sufficient supply of tea pots, coffee pots, etc. for service period.
8 Touch only insulated handles when still is in operation.
9 Follow all health and safety requirements to the necessary standards.

Maintaining counter and service areas

Attractive counter displays and the skills of your colleagues in the kitchen will do much to create the right impression when the first customers enter the service area. What can be quite difficult is to maintain the level of presentation throughout service, so all customers get a good first impression.

Because there is a flow of customers throughout service, many of the general preparation and clearing procedures are equally appropriate for maintaining service. The difference is that the restaurant may be full of customers who:

- make access to some areas more difficult, e.g. the front of counters, or island counter displays

- can see what you are doing, e.g. if you absent-mindedly pick up a packet of biscuits which has dropped on the floor, and return it to the display, this will convey a poor impression to customers even though it may not be endangering the quality of the biscuits.

A tidy, methodical approach will always help. So will teamwork and good communications. Warn the kitchen staff when dishes are getting low. If a colleague is under pressure with a rush of customers, offer to help.

Replenishing stocks

Serve first dishes which were prepared first. Maintain a strict rotation of containers.

When replenishing counter containers, remove the nearly-empty/empty dish and put a fresh one in its place. Don't pour the food from one container to another.

Quiet periods during service are an ideal opportunity for replenishing stocks.

The tray-run should be wiped down if customers spill food on it during service.

Maintaining dining areas

With a busy throughput of customers it can be quite a difficult task to keep all the tables clear, the floor free of rubbish, and the waste bins neat and tidy. The job is an even greater challenge when customers leave behind a chaotic pile of dirty crockery, food wrappings, and trays covered with spilt drinks.

While customers may be prepared to leave chaos behind them, they certainly don't want to be faced with chaos when they arrive. Your role is to keep firm control of the situation, so that the surroundings remain pleasant for everyone.

Work quickly, but safely and quietly. Customers don't want a lot of noise from clattering crockery and cutlery.

Spend time stacking up items carefully, and sorting out what is rubbish and what is to be washed.

Clearing by tray

Keep the weight evenly balanced over the tray. Heavier items should be in the centre.

Place containers of liquids in the centre of the tray so that small spills will be caught in the tray rather than spill on you or the floor.

Never carry trays or equipment over the head of a customer or colleague. Be extra careful in the vicinity of boisterous customers.

Watch where you are going. Keep an eye out for tripping hazards: customer belongings, rubbish or spills on the floor, etc.

Clearing by trolley

Take care as you wheel the trolley around not to bump into customer belongings, or into furniture.

Stack like items together. Most trolleys are specially designed for this purpose, with racks to take cups and glasses, trays or containers for cutlery, bags for collecting rubbish.

Do not overload the trolley. Attempting to cram a lot on to the trolley will cost you time if something falls off on the way to the service area.

Self-clear

Even when customers do the clearing themselves – taking the used items and trays to a service point – you will need to wipe table surfaces and generally keep the dining area looking tidy.

ACTION 46

Think of the customers in your workplace and how you might provide better service to them. To remind yourself of the key points, produce your own: *10 golden rules on how to keep our customers happy.*

The 10 golden rules of Commercial Catering Group Services

1 You must know your menu.

2 Your counter display must look good – people eat with their eyes. Cold food is very easy to display, but don't forget to show the customers the hot food as well.

3 Take a few minutes before service to tidy up. Make sure your overall is neat and clean and always wear a cap.

4 Smile!

5 Never leave a customer waiting.

6 Never be too busy for a customer.

7 Get to know your different customers and cater for them.

8 Never eat at the counter.

9 If you think any portion of food is of a poor standard or looks cold, do not serve it – inform the manager.

10 Always keep food cabinets, bain maries, topped up. Remember – the last customer is as important as the first.

ACTION 47

Refer back to section 1, and in particular pages 8 and 9, and write two short checklists which would help you and your colleagues when serving customers who have:

1 mobility difficulties

2 communication difficulties.

Case study – customer care, Ealing Hospital

Customer: 'I am allergic to flour – is there any flour in your gravy?'

Server: 'I do not know, but I will fetch the chef who makes the gravy and sauces to speak to you'.

Enter chef: 'I must be honest with you madam, we use gravy thickening, which of course contains flour. However I could get you some unthickened gravy if you would prefer'.

The customer thanked the staff and went away satisfied that she had been dealt with correctly and honestly.

The Grand Union Restaurant at Ealing Hospital

NVQ SVQ RANGE CHECKLIST

LEVEL 1

1C3.1 Prepare counter for service

with these

- [ ] trays
- [ ] crockery or disposables
- [ ] cutlery or disposables
- [ ] glassware or disposables
- [ ] disposable napkins
- [ ] service utensils
- [ ] food containers
- [ ] hot and cold beverage dispensers
- [ ] display cabinets
- [ ] refrigerated units
- [ ] heated units   [ ] seasonings
- [ ] sugars and sweeteners
- [ ] prepared sauces and dressings

1C3.2 Prepare customer dining areas for customer service

with these

- [ ] ashtrays
- [ ] condiments and accompaniments
- [ ] promotional material

1C3.3 Clear dining and service areas after food service

Clear customer dining areas, food counters and other service areas, involving these

- [ ] trays   [ ] ashtrays
- [ ] crockery or disposables
- [ ] cutlery or disposables
- [ ] glassware or disposables
- [ ] seasonings
- [ ] sugars and sweeteners
- [ ] prepared sauces and dressings
- [ ] service utensils
- [ ] hot and cold beverage dispensers
- [ ] refrigerated units
- [ ] heated units   [ ] display units
- [ ] food containers

LEVEL 1

1C4.1 Serve customers at the counter

provide information on these

- [ ] items available
- [ ] dish composition
- [ ] prices, special offers and promotions

serving these

- [ ] pre-portioned dishes
- [ ] dishes to be portioned
- [ ] hot dishes
- [ ] cold dishes
- [ ] soft drinks
- [ ] hot drinks

to these customer groups

- [ ] adults
- [ ] children
- [ ] those with mobility difficulties
- [ ] those with communication difficulties

1C4.2 Maintain counter and service areas

involving these

- [ ] trays
- [ ] crockery or disposables
- [ ] cutlery or disposables
- [ ] glassware or disposables
- [ ] disposable napkins
- [ ] hot dishes
- [ ] cold dishes
- [ ] accompaniments
- [ ] soft drinks
- [ ] hot drinks

Take-away service

Introduction

A recent nationwide survey revealed that one-quarter of the 45 million adults living in the UK buy take-away food every week. This compares to one-seventh, or about 6.75 million, who eat out in restaurants every week.

According to the survey (by Gordon Simmons Research, published in *Caterer & Hotelkeeper*) the two most important considerations when choosing a restaurant for eating in or taking away were:

- cleanliness of the restaurant
- quality of the food.

For take-aways this was followed by:

- good value for money
- reasonable prices
- staff who serve you quickly
- friendly, helpful staff
- good service.

Your responsibilities will vary according to your role in the team, and the size and style of establishment.

 **Units and elements covered in this section**

Preparing customer and service areas

LEVEL 1

Careful attention to preparation tasks will do much to ensure that the service period runs smoothly.

General preparation procedures

1 Check that customer areas are clean, with furniture positioned correctly. Areas not in use should be clearly signposted so customers are not confused.

2 Check the less obvious places and hidden surfaces where rubbish can accumulate – under tables and chairs, behind plant arrangements, on shelves or high surfaces. If customers have left something behind, e.g. an umbrella, hand it to your manager explaining where exactly you found it. If it is a package which has been left behind, or anything which might be dangerous, do not touch it. Report the matter immediately to the manager. (See page 15 for dealing with suspicious objects.)

3 Refuse bins (inside and out) should be clean, with a new rubbish bag in place.

4 Top up brochure racks. If newspapers are supplied, check these are in place. Tidy noticeboards and displays of promotional material.

5 Check menu panels and price lists.

6 Refill napkin and drinking straw dispensers.

7 Collect more trays if necessary from the wash-up area. Replenish stocks of take-away bags and boxes, napkins, wet wipes or towelettes, salts, peppers, sugars, sauces, drink cups and lids, tea/coffee stirrers and other disposable cutlery, tray mats, etc.

8 If a special promotion is on, confirm that you have the appropriate vouchers/coupons, and that the advertising material is properly displayed.

9 Fill refrigerated display cabinets with drinks, trifles/ ice creams, etc. as appropriate. Put the new stock at the back of the display, so that the older stock is used first. Remove any products which have passed their sell-by or best-before date. Check operating temperatures.

Clearing customer and service areas

After the restaurant has closed for the day, everything should be left tidy, safely stored, ready for overnight cleaning (if applicable) and for the staff who will be on opening duties.

General clearing procedures

1 Clear up customer service areas. Sweep and if appropriate mop the floor.

2 Wipe down all surfaces using the correct concentration of cleaning/sanitising solution.

3 Tidy up or pack away napkins, drinking straws, disposable cutlery, take-away food packaging, salts, peppers, sugars, sauces, etc.

4 Empty display cabinets as required and return the contents to the main storage area. Check sell-by and best-before dates before returning products to storage – those that have exceeded the date on the packaging should be discarded and a record made. Always position old stock so that it gets used first.

5 Thoroughly wash and sanitise the tops and shelves of service counters, inside and outside surfaces and doors of display cabinets, food and drink dispensers.

6 Empty and wipe clean waste bins (internal and external). Check carefully for discarded cigarette ends which have not been fully extinguished.

7 Where appropriate, collect rubbish from outside car park, pavement, etc. Do not let your workplace get a poor reputation with the local community because customers leave their meal packaging everywhere.

8 If the rubbish is collected from outside the restaurant after closing, assemble bags, boxes, etc. as neatly as possible. Avoid obstructing pavements and roads. Check that bags are securely tied at the top. If the bag has burst, place it inside another. If liquid is leaking out of the bottom of the bag (e.g. from discarded drinks containers which have not been completely finished), it will cause less of a mess if the bag is placed inside a cardboard box, lined if necessary with newspaper.

9 Wash out mop heads and other re-usable cleaning equipment. Put away in the correct place.

From the customers' point of view, one of the attractions of fast food and take-away restaurants – particularly the ones with many outlets throughout the country – is the fact that customers know what they will be getting. That is, a consistently good product served in pleasant surroundings.

SAFETY △ △ △

Always report equipment, fixtures or fittings which are damaged or not working correctly. Never attempt repairs yourself. In October 1991 a 21-year-old employee of a fast food/take-away restaurant was electrocuted while investigating a fault with filtering equipment for the fryers.

Always position warning signs to indicate wet floors or cleaning in progress.

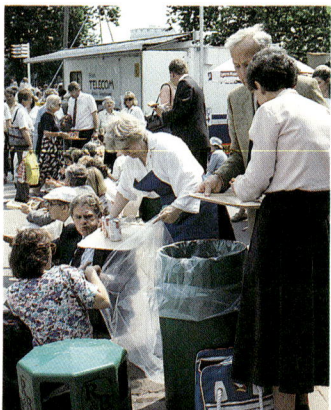

Take-away service is also popular at outdoor events. At many of these the equipment has to be brought to the site, marquees assembled, etc.

Taking and serving customer orders

With many people to serve and everyone expecting fast, efficient service, the most has to be made of your few moments with each customer.

Greeting the customer

Your company may have a standard form of greeting. Otherwise find your own collection of natural-sounding, friendly words which are appropriate to the various groups of customer – children, people of your age, those who expect a more formal greeting.

Remember that a warm smile can take the place of many words.

So does good eye contact. Looking at the person speaking shows your interest.

Taking the order

Looking at the person whose order you are taking also helps you. If you watch the lip movement and facial expression you will find it easier to understand what the person is saying, and how he or she is reacting to what you are saying. This is especially helpful if the restaurant is noisy, or the accent is one you are unfamiliar with.

If the customer has difficulty in speaking, or does not speak English well, be patient. Pointing out items on the menu can help establish what the customer would like. (There is detailed advice on dealing with customers who have mobility or communication difficulties on pages 8 and 9.)

Where necessary, clarify what the customer requires with an appropriate question:

'Would you like chocolate or strawberry flavour?'

'To eat in or take-away?'

'Cream or milk with your coffee?'

'Would you like vinegar with your chips? And salt?'

Repeat the order. This helps avoid mistakes or misunderstandings.

Tell the customer if there will be a delay over any items. Be as specific and helpful as possible:

'The cheeseburger will be about 2 minutes. Do you mind waiting?'

Or if the wait is longer:

'The cod will be about 8 minutes, I'm afraid. Would you rather order something else, haddock or plaice perhaps?'

Every second counts in your few moments of contact with customers.

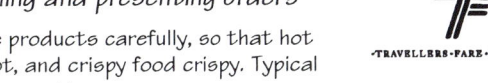

Assembling and presenting orders

Assemble products carefully, so that hot food is hot, and crispy food crispy. Typical order of assembly:

1 Cold drink.

2 Cold dessert.

3 Hot drink.

4 Boxed hot products (e.g. bacon and cheeseburger).

5 Pies.

6 Fries.

Pack products carefully so that items do not get squashed, or packets spill their contents.

1 Boxed products in the base of the bag.

2 Fries with napkin to one side.

3 Pie on top of boxed products.

4 Cold desserts in separate bag.

5 One napkin per cooked product.

Present products carefully. Logos on cups and packaging should always face the customer as you hand the order over.

Bags should be double folded away from logo, with a crisp, neat fold.

Selling by suggestion

Some customers come into your restaurant hungry, but not sure what food they want. No problem! You have a full range of products to tempt them with, and a few minutes to help them decide.

Other customers rush in, knowing basically what they want. No problem either. You have a few minutes to sell the products they want, and suggest others they might want but hadn't thought of or didn't realise were available.

Yet other customers really do know what they want. They will not usually object to you offering other products but may be offended by the over-sell.

With the right suggestive selling technique you can win new customers, and keep a regular customer coming back.

1 Look directly at the customer and smile. Everyone responds to a smile. Make it natural, and let the smile reach up into your eyes.

2 Make the food you are describing sound irresistible. Use phrases which will tempt your customer. On a hot day: 'Would you like a long cool drink?' sounds more refreshing than: 'Would you like a drink?'

3 Promote larger portions or sizes. Suggest that the customer might enjoy a large size product. He or she can only say no thank you.

4 Don't over-promote yourself. People don't like a pushy person to tell them what they want. Persuasion is a gentle technique. Be natural. People respond to this, they feel comfortable.

5 Treat every customer individually. Make each customer feel special. Don't use exactly the same words with every person in the queue, you are not a robot. To one say: 'Would you like a fruit juice with your breakfast?' To another say: 'We have freshly squeezed orange or grapefruit juice, may I get you one?'

6 Keep up the sales pitch. Continue to suggest products right through the order. Just because you get: 'No thanks' to the orange juice, that is no reason to think the customer would not enjoy a large coffee.

7 Don't make the customer feel rushed by saying: 'Is that all?' While you may need to ask if the customer has finished ordering, let the opportunity for doing this arrive naturally.

ACTION 48

These are some examples of how you could help promote sales in a take-away restaurant.

KEY: ☺ Customer ☺ Server/You

☺ Chicken and chips

☺ Would you like a large fries?

☺ Would you like coleslaw or baked beans?

☺ Beefburger with cheese

☺ Would you like a double-decker with cheese and onion?

☺ Would you like a hot apple turnover to finish your meal?

☺ Would you like a coffee, milkshake or soft drink?

☺ A coffee please

☺ Would you like a large coffee?

Now give some similar examples of how you could promote sales in your workplace.

☺ _____

☺ ....

☺ ....

☺ _____

☺ ....

☺ ....

☺ ....

☺ _____

☺ ....

☺ ....

☺ ....

Collecting the money

This is dealt with in more detail in section 4.

Remember to say aloud the amount of money the customer has given you, e.g. £5, and to count the change as you give it to the customer.

Serving the order

With the number of customers you have to serve, strict portion control is obviously important. The customers want to get the same value for their money each time. The business wants to make a profit and expand.

Always use the correct serving equipment and the right size food container for the portion size ordered by the customer.

Another thing customers expect, and successful businesses build their reputation on, is a consistent standard of presentation. Follow workplace guidelines exactly. If you have some good ideas for presenting the food more attractively, pass these on to your manager so that they can be considered for the company as a whole.

Thanking the customer

As with the initial greeting, some companies have standard closing remarks. Otherwise find your own expressions which will convey to customers that you:

- thank them for their custom
- want them to enjoy their meal/snack/drink
- are pleased to have served them
- would like them to call again.

Maintaining service areas

The general procedures are similar to those involved in preparing and clearing the service area.

If it is necessary to close off sections of the restaurant for thorough cleaning, position ropes or signs so that customers know where they may sit, and which areas they can only pass through, e.g. on their way to the toilets.

Always remember the safety of your customers. If you are in the middle of wiping a table, for example, and get called away for another urgent task, take your cleaning equipment with you. Otherwise the table may be occupied in your absence, or a child may start playing with the container of cleaning fluid.

Make the best use of quiet periods to restock with service items, to tidy and empty waste bins, etc. (Often waste bins look full, when in fact a customer has failed to push the rubbish into the bin properly.)

In wet weather, be prepared to clean the floor more frequently, and to wipe down surfaces where customers leave wet belongings.

You can promote sales as you listen to and check the order, e.g.: 'Would you like a large portion of fries?', 'Would you like an apple and cherry pie with your coffee?', 'Would you like to try one of our new range of side salads? There is a choice of dressings.'

You may also be able to help sell, and at the same time give the customer better value, by suggesting an inclusive meal, or drawing the customer's attention to a special promotion: 'There's free coffee or tea with our Sunshine Breakfast this month.'

ACTION   49

When you next visit a take-away restaurant as a **customer**, use the following questions to assess your experience. If possible, ask a friend to visit and assess your workplace in the same way.

Then write a brief report on the survey results – you may find it helpful to discuss them first with your friend. Here are some points you could comment on:

- What most impressed you/your friend about the restaurant? What least impressed you?
- In what areas does your workplace compare well/badly with the restaurant you assessed?

Finally, discuss the survey results with your supervisor. What could you personally do to give a better quality service to your customers?

☑ = yes   ☒ = no

SERVICE

- ❑ Did the server greet you pleasantly, politely and with a smile?
- ❑ Did the server help you make your selection?
- ❑ Did the server suggest other items in addition to those you asked for?
- ❑ Did the server repeat your order before registering your payment and taking the money?

  Write down the actual comment the server used when closing the sale:

  ....

  How long did you wait for your order, from the time of ordering to receiving:

  ....

- ❑ Were the other staff you saw carrying out their work in a businesslike manner?

CLEANLINESS

- ❑ As you approached the restaurant was there any rubbish in the surrounding area?
- ❑ Was the advertising material in the windows clean, tidy and correctly positioned where it was easy to read from the outside?
- ❑ Were any wastebins outside the restaurant dirty and full to overflowing?
- ❑ Were the outside lights and signs working properly?
- ❑ Was the initial impression one of cleanliness when you walked in the door?
- ❑ Had the server a clean and tidy appearance and uniform?
- ❑ Did the other staff you could see have a clean and tidy appearance and uniform?
- ❑ Was the customer area clean, tidy and free from rubbish?
- ❑ Was the menu display clean, tidy and the items and prices easy to read?
- ❑ Was the service counter clean and well organised?
- ❑ Were the tables and chairs provided for customers clean and free from rubbish?
- ❑ Were the wastebins inside the restaurant neat and tidy?
- ❑ Were all the lights inside the restaurant working properly?
- ❑ Were the toilets clean and tidy?

OTHER COMMENTS

Fish and chip shops – this is Harry Ramsden's in Guiseley, Yorkshire – are a great British tradition, one of the first examples of take-away service.

NVQ SVQ RANGE CHECKLIST

LEVEL 1

1C5.1 Prepare customer and service areas

involving these

- ❑ serviettes   ❑ straws
- ❑ take-away food packaging   ❑ disposable cutlery
- ❑ seasonings
- ❑ sugar and sweeteners
- ❑ convenience sauces
- ❑ service utensils
- ❑ display cabinets
- ❑ service item dispensers
- ❑ refrigerated units
- ❑ heated units

1C5.2 Clear customer and service areas

involving these

- ❑ serviettes   ❑ straws
- ❑ take-away food packaging   ❑ disposable cutlery
- ❑ seasonings
- ❑ sugar and sweeteners
- ❑ convenience sauces
- ❑ service utensils
- ❑ display cabinets
- ❑ service item dispensers
- ❑ refrigerated units
- ❑ heated units

1C6.1 Take and serve customers' orders

provide information on these

- ❑ items available
- ❑ dish composition
- ❑ prices, special offers and promotions

deal with these customer groups

- ❑ children   ❑ adults
- ❑ those with communication difficulties
- ❑ those with mobility difficulties

1C6.2 Maintain take-away service areas during service

involving these

- ❑ serviettes   ❑ straws
- ❑ take-away food packaging   ❑ disposable cutlery
- ❑ seasonings
- ❑ sugars and sweeteners
- ❑ convenience sauces

Introduction

Although you are unlikely to have the direct contact with your customers that is found in most other forms of food and drink service, your role is no less important for this. The convenience offered by vending depends on the work of efficient behind-the-scenes operators – that is, you and your colleagues.

Contents guide

Preparing & clearing dining areas for vending

LEVEL 1

The procedures are similar to counter service (see section 11), the main difference being that customers serve themselves from a machine rather than a counter.

General preparation procedure

1 Tables and chairs should be clean and in their correct position. Check under seats and table tops for chewing gum and other sticky substances left by customers.

2 Arrange ashtrays, placemats, salts, peppers, sauces, etc. on tables, as appropriate.

3 Restock tray racks, napkin dispensers, cutlery trays, crockery and glassware, etc.

4 Check that waste bins are clean and ready for use.

General clearing procedure

When staff are obviously taking trouble to keep dining areas looking pleasant, customers generally respond well. This makes your job easier.

1 Pay particular attention to table surfaces, counter tops, chairs, etc. Wipe down as necessary, using the correct cleaning and/or sanitising agent.

2 Keep floors free of litter. Mop up spillages promptly.

3 Empty waste bins regularly, and wipe down the lids and sides if they have become soiled.

4 Watch out for half-empty containers of liquid. The customer may not have put the lid back on securely, and if the container has been put in the waste bin, the liquid has probably spilled out. You could find a trail of wet patches behind you as you carry away the waste bag, or even worse, that you have soaked yourself in a mixture of milk shake, cold coffee, etc.

5 Empty ashtrays into the special metal bin which is provided, or a suitable container which will not burn or melt. Wipe ashtrays with a cloth reserved for that purpose, or preferably a disposable paper cloth, moistened slightly.

 **Units and elements covered in this section**

LEVEL 1

1C7 Prepare and clear areas for vending service
 – 1C7.1 Prepare dining areas for vending service
 – 1C7.2 Clear dining areas for vending service

1C8 Provide a food vending service
 – 1C8.1 Provide a food vending service

1C10 Clean and restock drinks machines/equipment
 – 1C10.1 Clean drinks machines/equipment
 – 1C10.2 Restock drinks machines/equipment

 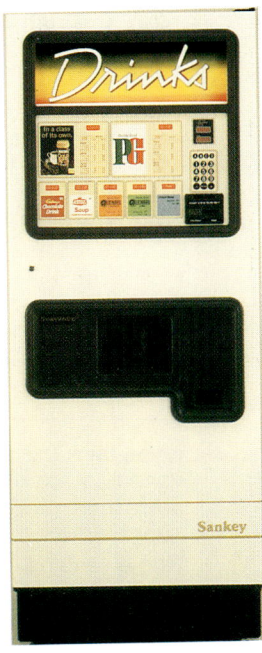

Vending machines provide customers with a choice of food and drink items in a wide range of situations, from staff restrooms in offices and factories to hotel corridors and the crew's quarters on an oil rig. In many cases the vending machine is there because it provides the only practical way of offering a catering service to the number of customers involved, over the hours they require the service.

Providing a food vending service

Vending machines are also used in counter service and take-away restaurants to increase the range of products available. In these situations you have much more of an opportunity to help customers.

LEVEL 1

Food vending machines fall into two types:

Snacks machines – used to sell packets of crisps, peanuts, biscuits, sweets, chocolate, etc. These products have a long shelf life and do not require storage under refrigeration. Some snack vendors are chilled to between 15°C and 20°C, so that chocolate bars, etc. do not become unacceptably soft in warm locations.

Cold food machines – designed to hold perishable foods at temperatures below 5°C: sandwiches, meat pies, pre-plated salads and desserts, dishes which require reheating in a microwave oven, etc.

General procedure for cleaning

1 Prepare cleaning equipment (see page 104 for more detailed notes).

2 Remove all out-of-date food from machine and place in reject food bag, ready for removal from premises.

3 Turn the machine off.

4 Thoroughly clean each compartment of each shelf, using the recommended cleaning solution and sanitiser, mixed to the correct strength. Wipe dry.

5 Wipe and dry the coin mechanism.

6 Clean air filters.

7 Clean and polish inside and outside of the door.

8 Restock with food.

9 Switch the machine back on.

Condensation sometimes builds up on the inside of the vending machine during loading. This should clear within a short time of the door being closed.

Personal hygiene checklist   Sankey Vending

- Are your hands clean?
- Are your overalls clean?
- Is your hair covered?
- Are all cuts, open sores, etc. covered with a clean waterproof dressing?
- Do not smoke while cleaning or restocking.

SAFETY ▲ ▲ ▲

- If you think the machine has been tampered with, or vandalised or is otherwise faulty (e.g. internal temperature too high), report the matter urgently to your supervisor.
- Some vending machines should not be turned off when they are opened to clean or restock. The safety cut out switch comes into operation when you unlock the door. Check that this has in fact happened before you start the cleaning or restocking procedure.
- Never wipe electrical parts with a damp cloth.
- Always use cleaning agents according to manufacturers' and workplace instructions.
- Never attempt to carry out any repairs for which you are not authorised.

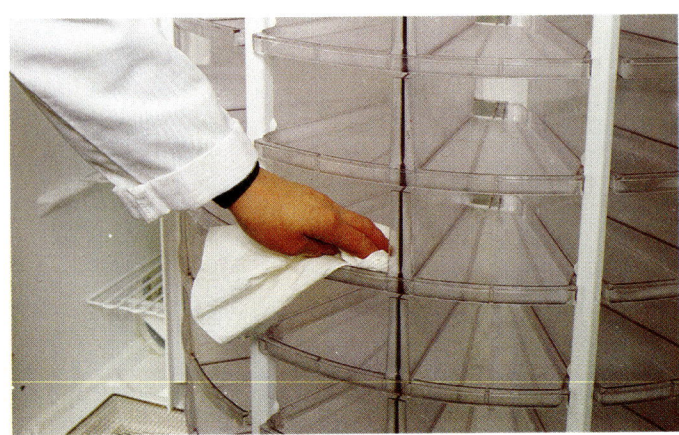

Take care when wiping the inside of the machine to get into all the corners where food debris can accumulate.

General procedure for restocking

The safe storage life of the different products will be indicated on the packaging by the use-by or best-before date. Pay careful attention to these and to hygiene (see box on page 102).

1 Before opening, check that the cabinet is operating at the correct temperature. Record the temperature on the appropriate form.

2 Put aside any products which have passed the date on the package, for returning to the supplier, or destroying as appropriate.

3 Also put aside any products which have damaged packaging.

4 Restock machines so that food which is already on the shelves or racks gets used before any of the fresh food. In other words, so that the food is dispensed on a *first in, first out* basis. With machines which allow the customer to select any product from the shelf, all the products are usually replaced with fresh products.

5 Ensure that chilled products are kept at safe temperatures during transportation and restocking of machines. This may involve the use of insulated containers.

6 Check that products are on the appropriate shelf and displayed correctly. Generally, there should be no empty compartments.

Inevitably the temperature in the cabinet will have risen during cleaning and restocking. The machine will be built to deal with this, and should restore the temperature to a safe level within 30 minutes or so. If this does not happen, some machines will cease vending and the lighting will go out.

Check the date stamp on all products before restocking.

All food machines will have a thermometer to enable the internal cabinet temperature to be checked as well as a health and safety cut-out (sometimes called a health timer).

Loading snacks machines

Poor loading is a frequent cause of selections not being available to customers. Attention to the following will help you avoid problems:

- always load from the back of the auger, otherwise gaps can be left
- lean products backwards not forwards
- do not push products into auger
- use the correct rails, guides or pushers for products which might slip out of position in the auger.

Stock and sales control

This will usually involve counting and recording the number of products:

- remaining in the machine before you clear or re-stock
- that cannot be sold because they are damaged or have passed their use-by date
- which you place in the machine as new stock.

Food display systems

Four main methods are used in food vending machines to ensure the product looks attractive and reaches the customer in good condition.

Drum and shelf – a series of shallow drums or round shelves which rotate to allow the customer to select the required item. The shelves come in various heights to suit the food, and each one can be divided into compartments of the appropriate size. These are particularly suitable for plated food, and delicate products.

Rotary conveyor feed – similar to a self-service counter display, with rows of like products together. The food containers are resting on a conveyor belt. When the product from the front of the row is selected, the others move forward.

Auger feed – similar to an open coil spring into which the bagged or wrapped food products are inserted. When a selection is made, the spiral revolves and the product drops out of the coil and down the dispense shoot.

Clip-in bagged conveyors – the packets of food are clipped to an overhead conveyor. Once the selection is made, the conveyor moves forward, the clip is mechanically opened and the product drops to the vend station.

Cleaning and restocking drinks machines   LEVEL 1

To protect the drinking quality of the product, machines require regular cleaning. In busy locations, for equipment like Conas, this may be several times a day. For vending machines, once a day is the normal routine.

General procedure for cleaning

Collect all the cleaning materials you need:

- trolley, spare canisters and machine parts
- plastic buckets for washing removable equipment
- disposable cleaning cloths and drying paper
- dusting brushes. On some machines, special brushes must be used to avoid damaging surfaces
- detergent solution and sanitiser. Use the right one in the correct concentration. Replace by fresh solutions if you are cleaning several machines
- polish and cloths for cleaning outside of machine
- rubbish bags.

Put on gloves to protect your hands, and an overall or uniform to protect your clothes.

Turn the machine off and remove the plug from the mains socket before starting to clean. Remember to switch on again before leaving the machine.

Premix machines

1 Empty the drinks container. You will usually have to measure and keep a record of any waste.

2 Wash the drinks container out with cleaning solution. Where necessary, soak removable parts in sanitising solution.

3 Rinse well. Air dry, or use disposable paper.

Postmix machines

1 Remove canisters ready to be refilled or replaced with spares. Cover dispense nozzle with cap, if supplied, to protect against spillages.

2 Dry-wipe all dust and powder spillages. Wet-wipe all areas of spillage and splash.

3 Remove for soaking in detergent/sanitising solution: mixing bowls, nozzles, troughs, whippers.

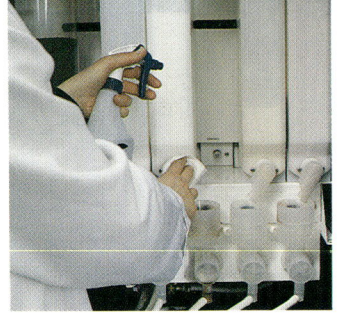

Step 2. Cleaning a postmix machine.

4 Replace parts with clean spares. Alternatively use the parts which have been soaked for at least 3 minutes.

5 Replace canisters.

6 Clean interior surfaces, cup station and chute.

7 Flush system with hot water from the machine.

8 Empty waste bucket and clean/replace. Check float or probe is in correct position, and working properly.

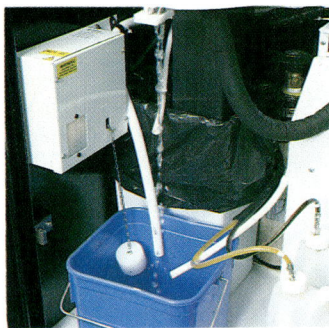

Step 8. Check the float of postmix machines.

In-cup machines

1 Clean the cup station and transfer arm.

2 Weekly (usually): remove cup stacks. Clean and dry carousel columns. Replace cup stacks.

3 Wipe the water nozzle.

4 Remove waste tray, empty and clean in detergent/sanitising solution. Dry before replacing.

The outside of machines

1 Clean and sanitise the delivery area for the products.

2 Wipe top, front and sides of machine.

3 Polish all exposed areas, particularly glass panels and doors to remove fingerprints.

Step 1. Cleaning the outside of the machine (the delivery area is shown here).

4 Clean the area around the machine and ensure that the waste bin is empty.

Final checking

1 Close and lock door of vending machines.

2 Ensure that power is on.

3 Test drinks for quality, quantity and temperature. If required, check coin acceptance.

4 Check that indicator lights are working and that product descriptions/labels are correctly placed.

General procedure for restocking drinks machines

1 Rotate stocks. Use stock on a first-in, first-out basis. Never use stock which has passed its use-by or best-before date.

2 Keep stocks in the correct conditions. For some items this will involve chilled storage.

3 When reloading with cups, avoid touching their rims. Some types of cups need to be loosened before they are stacked, otherwise they tend to stick together. Do not overload with cups, otherwise they can jam the machine.

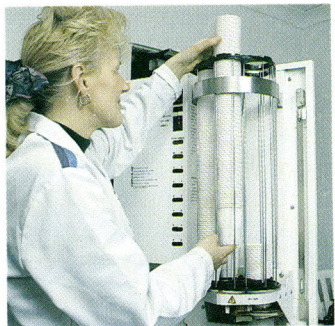

Loosening or feathering the cups to prevent them sticking together.

4 Take care to put the right ingredients in canisters. For example, a non-dairy creamer is used for whitening coffee, and milk compound for tea.

5 After restocking postmix and fresh brew machines, test vend to check quality and temperature of drinks.

Premix machines

Fill dispenser to required stock level, with drink diluted/mixed as per instructions.

Postmix machines

1 For powdered drinks, lightly tap canisters to loosen ingredients. Place cover over dispense nozzle and remove to refill or replace. Check levels of liquid concentrates. Replace as required. Replace coffee/tea filter paper if machine has a fresh brew unit.

2 Check CO_2 cylinder pressure gauge. If low, close the valve, depressurise the circuit, disconnect and replace cylinder.

In-cup machines

1 Fill cup magazines. Put the cups in the correct position for the type of drink they contain. Do not force cups together as this could jam the mechanism.

2 Cover the top cup of each selection with the lid to protect the contents against contamination.

3 If the machine is a table-top model, not connected to the water supply, top up water tank to correct level.

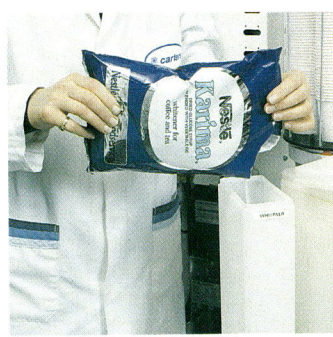

Replenishing powdered ingredients in a postmix machine.

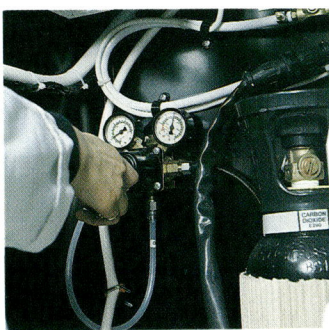

Checking the pressure of the CO_2 cylinder.

ACTION 50

This postmix vendor has a fresh brew unit. Identify the different parts. Some of the answers are given.

1 Brewer filter roll

2 _____

3 _____

4 Audit and test vend switches

5 _____

6 Coin validator mechanism

7 Cash box

8 Refrigeration unit for cold drinks

9 _____

10 _____

11 CO_2 gas cylinder for carbonated drinks

12 Brewer waste container

13 _____

14 _____

15 Brewer unit

16 Brewer ingredient canister (water heater is behind)

17 Door safety isolator switch.

Drinks machines

Premix – drink in bulk, ready to serve. For example, tea and coffee urns in a self-service staff restaurant, or fruit juice dispensers. The term premix is also sometimes applied to *in-cup* machines.

Postmix – the flavouring product is kept in concentrated liquid or powder form. At the press of the button, the ingredients are mixed in bowls by whippers, with hot water, iced still water, or, for fizzy drinks, iced carbonated water. The drink is then delivered in a cup, at the point of service. It can include a fresh brew tea/coffee unit, cappuccino-style coffee, brand name soft drinks.

Fresh brew – uses leaf tea and/or ground coffee instead of instant products. The infusion process requires more time for the drink to be made, and even longer if the machine actually grinds the coffee beans before brewing. Most fresh brew vending machines also offer postmix drinks made from instant ingredients, e.g. soup and hot chocolate.

In-cup – the required ingredients for each drink are already packed in the cup (in powdered form). The machine adds hot or cold water as required. The ingredients are kept fresh by the airtight stacking of the cups. Some machines have a bulk sugar canister for sweetening to taste.

Sachets – dry ingredients (enough for one cup) sealed in a foil-type package. When a drink is selected, the sachet is emptied into the cup and hot water added, or the water directed through the sachet into the cup.

Coffee machines – of various types. *Pour 'n' serve* or *cona* units generally hold 12 cups. This means fresh coffee can be made at regular intervals to keep pace with demand. Where appropriate, customers can serve themselves. (For cleaning of coffee dispensers see page 92.)

Espresso machines – high pressure boiler provides hot water and steam which is 'expressed' through a small amount of coffee to produce one or two cups at a time. Some models grind the coffee beans, infuse the drink and dump the waste grouts and filter paper into a container within the machine. A steam jet and hot water supply mean that tea and other hot drinks can also be prepared.

Cold drinks machines – popular for milk, soft drinks, mineral waters, fruit juices, as well as beers, wines and spirits. The products are stored and dispensed in cartons, cans or bottles.

Postmix dispense systems – concentrated syrups are piped to the point of dispense. When the tap is opened to pour the drink, the syrup mixes with water and carbon dioxide gas (from a cylinder) to make cola, tonic, etc.

Fault finding guide

No lights – machine switched off, door not closed, electrical fault.

Sold out sign shows – waste bucket full, no cups, cup turret/carousel not turning, disruption to mains water supply, ingredients canisters empty.

Cup delivery problems – cup carousel jammed, lack of cups, cups packed too tightly, wrong size (two different suppliers' cups used), cup chute wrongly assembled, cups fallen over in cup station, stabilising weight not in correct position.

Ingredient problem – canister not properly located, incorrect ingredients used or badly stored, blockage in system, water heating unit faulty, 'throw' adjustment required.

Condensation in machine – exhaust grill or steam extractor blocked.

Whippers leaking – incorrectly assembled, seal needs replacing.

Cold drinks warm – cooler not working.

Machine flooding – waste bucket float or switch not operating; waste bucket, pipes or housing not replaced correctly.

Carbonated drink problem – CO_2 cylinder empty, not turned on, not connected properly.

Fresh brew coffee/tea problem – filter needs cleaning or replacing, filter wiper jammed, canister not seated correctly, brewer unit not switched on.

ACTION 1   section 1, p.4

Some of the statements may have seemed a good idea, even though the details are not quite right for your workplace. Others would be totally inappropriate, but you can probably think of restaurants where they would be suitable.

In a more formal restaurant, the customers generally want efficient, knowledgeable service without being over-friendly. As the bar chart on page 5 suggests, many customers expect formal service: around 40% in The Butter Council survey, and 10% are impressed by formal service. By comparison, just under 30% expect to be treated as a friend, and 25% are impressed when this happens.

Case study – informality not always accepted

Recently Forte Posthouses tried a new approach to customer/staff communications. At a selected hotel, waiting staff took food orders kneeling beside the customers' table, or, if it was a single person dining, sat down beside the guest. The idea was that the guest was 'not looked down upon'.

Michael Stevens, Head of Forte Posthouses, explained that the new approach had not gone down well with the more traditional Posthouse guests. Other ways were being examined in which the traditional practices could be adapted to attract new customers. 'Communication is a vital part of good customer care.'

A senior Forte manager, who had joined the company recently, hadn't heard about the experiment, but recollected a similar experience:

'TGI Friday's use the "Puppy Dog Technique". The waiting staff have kneeling stools, or sit beside customers to take their food and drink orders. I was rather shocked when a pony-tailed young man slid on to the bench seat next to me. It was a few moments before I realised he was doing this to take my order!'

ACTION 2   section 1, p.5

What probably struck you about this survey was the high score given to anything which related to customer skills.

Further discussion points

Just under 40% of customers were impressed by the offer to hang their coat. And for each of the other aspects of service, a significant number of customers fell into the impressed category. Is this because they so often don't get staff who are knowledgeable, helpful, etc.?

Why is it that nearly one-in-ten customers don't like their glass being refilled frequently? Is it because they don't like feeling pressurised to drink more? How can you tell this?

Follow-up activity

If your workplace uses customer comment cards (see example on page 4), ask your manager if you may look through some of the replies. Discuss what you could do to make your customers' visit more enjoyable.

ACTION 3   section 1, p.7

Observing, listening and thinking are about taking note of, or paying attention to, what your customers are doing and saying. That doesn't mean being inquisitive. You shouldn't deliberately listen to customers' conversation, for example, but customers do say things in your hearing which give a clue to their needs.

There is a wider aspect to knowing what your establishment offers. A good knowledge of what's on the menu is important, and you should also be able to advise customers on which wines or drinks would go well with the various dishes, and what combination of dishes works best. To suggest to a customer that the prawn cocktail would make a delicious first course, and the King Prawns the perfect main course, shows lack of imagination.

Similarly, it is helpful to know that there are various degrees of vegetarianism. Some will eat fish, others won't (see page 39). If a customer tells you he or she is vegetarian, you can then ask further questions before recommending dishes from your menu.

For more on suggesting alternatives, see page 54.

Follow-up activity

If you are not planning to read section 11 because you do not work in counter service, read the industry box on selling ideas (page 87), then have a go at ACTION 43.

ACTION 4   section 1, p.9

Top photograph Many food and drink operations cater for customers of all ages, and elderly customers do not require any special help. But if you are working in a fast food restaurant (where this photograph was taken) you might find some elderly customers who haven't visited such a place before, and are not quite sure how to order, or do not know that they have to help themselves to drinking straws, for example.

Try not to sound patronising when you find customers don't know what is expected of them.

Centre photograph These customers have special needs because they are confined to a wheelchair. The text on page 8 gives suggestions on how you can help.

As children they have another set of special needs – they become bored easily. If the children are with adults, you might suggest some menu items which can be quickly prepared, and offer to bring those as soon as they are ready. Some restaurants have novelty items which are intended to amuse and entertain children.

Lower photograph People on their own in hotels, whether they are male or female, in a suite at The Grand in Brighton, where this photograph was taken, or less luxurious accommodation, should be treated with sensitivity and patience. Notice how this waiter is being friendly, yet taking care not to overwhelm the guest – he stands a respectful distance away.

Many prefer to eat and drink in their rooms rather than appear alone in the restaurant and bar. Some are talkative – but you can't chat for too long or you will be neglecting other customers. Some are demanding, and seem to be out to make your life difficult. Some are shy and reserved, and you can make their stay more enjoyable with a little warm humour.

Follow-up activities

Ask people you know who have special needs how, in their view, waiting staff could do more to help.

Alternatively, consider what waiting staff could do to avoid situations like these – told by Peter Osborne, who is completely blind and his wife Kate, who is 95% blind.

'Friends of ours were celebrating their first wedding anniversary. Always the romantic, the husband leaned across the restaurant table to give his wife a kiss, only to burn his chin on a lighted candle.'

'We love gâteau but hate it when it comes on a flat plate with only a pastry fork – you chop off a piece, the fork is too small to pick it up. You chase around the plate and the cream splurges everywhere.'

'Loud music makes it difficult to hear when the menu is read to us. Furthermore, a large part of the enjoyment of a convivial evening out with sighted or unsighted friends is conversation.'

ACTION 5   section 1, p.10

Complaints from customers about waiting staff

1 Being asked who has ordered what – see pages 39 and 42 for some tips on overcoming this problem.

2 Poor wine service – read section 10.

3 No order of service – see pages 40 and 44.

4 Being interrupted – quality service is unobtrusive, so it is important not to interrupt customers' conversations, or to keep returning to the table to ask how everything is – this suggests no notice is being taken anyway of how the customers are feeling.

5 Not being attended to on arrival – see page 37. Remind yourself of the statements to do with timing made in ACTION 1 on page 4.

6 Unfriendly/unhelpful staff – the importance of being helpful and friendly was noted in ACTION 2 on page 5.

7 Bread not fresh/warm – purchasing bread is not usually the responsibility of waiting staff, but if procedures for clearing after service are not followed yesterday's bread may get muddled with the fresh supply. If bread is meant to be served warm, and it is not, then either the serving staff have forgotten to put it in the hot cupboard, or they have allowed the bread to get cold before taking it to the customers' table. See step 5 of The Fox & Pheasant checklist on page 30.

8 Food not cooked to specification – this might indicate a problem in the kitchen, but with some dishes it is the responsibility of serving staff to ask how the customer would like the food cooked, e.g. steak, fried eggs, roast beef.

9 Poor tea/coffee – see page 69.

10 Plates cleared too soon – see page 51.

Complaints from waiting staff about their customers

1 Customers who think that waiting staff must be servile – the customer is always right even when wrong. It does no harm to get complaints about customers off your chest – providing you do so among colleagues and friends, and providing it helps you keep your approach to customers professional and uncomplaining.

2 Customers flicking fingers to get the attention – this shouldn't happen if you are keeping an eye on your customers. But if you are very rushed, and a customer does have to attract your attention in this way, respond promptly, even if only with a smile and nod of the head to reassure them that you have noticed.

3 Customers who don't bother to turn up – careful attention to reservations procedures will provide your manager with the information to take the matter further if required. See page 37.

4 Customers who reserve a table for 6 and then arrive with 4 or 8, without prior warning – the restaurant manager's response will depend on how full the restaurant is, and how easily the seating at tables can be adjusted.

5 Ladies who place their orders through their partners – something you learn to accept.

6 Customers who eat everything and then complain – this can be a ploy to get a free meal. This is why so much stress is placed on calling your manager in complaints procedures.

7 Customers who drink most of the wine, then complain – as 6. Corked wines are rare (see page 84), so the customer is on dodgy ground if planning to extract a free bottle from the restaurant.

8 Customers who smoke – this is why some restaurants have no-smoking areas, and others have a complete ban on smoking.

9 Customers who fail to observe dress code – many restaurants with a strict dress code have a supply of ties which they can loan gentlemen. If a lady guest is wearing trousers, and dresses are the rule, this can be more difficult to deal with. This is definitely something to refer to your manager.

10 Customers who try to intimidate staff – as 1 and 2.

Case study – changing views on dress

The 5-star Regent International which opened in London in 1993 has no dress code. 'Not everybody likes to be told you have to do things because that's the rule', Wolfgang Nitschke, the general manager, told *Caterer & Hotelkeeper*. 'I believe the client should be happy, and whatever makes the client happy I should provide'.

ACTION 6   section 1, p.12

Hopefully you will never see customers throwing food at one another in your workplace! At a more practical level, it is quite possible that you will have customers who lose their temper, or start having a row with each other in the restaurant. The first rule of course is to warn your manager. In the meantime, take care not to get involved yourself.

People who argue with each other in public sometimes try and recruit outsiders to support their point of view: 'Now waiter, wouldn't you agree that that's an absolutely stupid thing to say?' In this situation, waiters – and waitresses! – should give a neutral reply, e.g.: 'Well I don't think I can comment, really'.

ACTION 7   section 1, p.12

1 Pot pourri The example has been chosen to illustrate what totally unexpected (and amusing) things can happen. To avoid embarrassing the guest – providing he doesn't show any signs of ill health – you might explain that knowing he likes tea you have brought a packet of Oolong Black Dragon, Lapsang Souchong, or other speciality China tea which your establishment has in stock.

2 Separate bills You probably wished you had asked if they wanted separate bills at the beginning of the meal. But, the priority at this stage is to sort things out quickly. Ask the customers to confirm what each person had, and wants to pay for – for example, how are the drinks to be split between bills? Offer to call a taxi.

If the theatre is near, you might suggest that one of the customers pays the whole bill and returns during the interval or at the end of the show for the separate bills.

3 Ill child Hopefully you would be more sympathetic to the child's problem than the waitress in this case study.

There is nothing nice about cleaning up vomit, but a bucket of hot soapy water (depending on the floor surface), disinfectant and lots of absorbent kitchen paper will make it easier. Your supervisor will be able to take charge – it's important from everyone's point of view that action is taken quickly.

Follow-up activity

Make a list of more commonplace situations, and discuss with your colleagues how they should be dealt with. Here are some ideas: (1) customers ask for two sausages and no bacon with the all-day breakfast; (2) a single customer arrives and there is a choice between seating him or her at a corner table (which has just become vacant, but has not yet been cleared) or a table in the centre of the room; (3) a customer is waiting for the rest of the party to arrive before ordering. 15 minutes later, the customer is looking uncomfortable because they are so late.

ACTION 8   section 2, p.16

Unless you are a saint some of the items will have stars against them. It is all too easy in a busy workplace to take short cuts, or forget to do something because you are tired.

Follow-up activities

Repeat the exercise after a month, and see what improvements you have made.

Form a discussion group with some colleagues. Pick out one or two of the items from each category and expand on them so that they relate more closely to your workplace situation. For example, 'Get help to carry heavy items' might be changed to: 'Work in teams of two to carry banqueting tables. Never stack chairs more than 5 high as this is the maximum that can be carried safely.'

Ask your supervisor if you can look through the accident book to make a list of the accidents which have occurred. Use these to draw up a safety checklist for your workplace.

Collect together a set of all the safety procedures leaflets, procedures, etc. in use in your workplace. Have a look at noticeboards, as well as in the staff handbook and staff induction pack (if these are used). Make a list of any legislation which is referred to, with a note of the main requirements.

Draw a diagram of your work area showing the location of fire fighting equipment, and escape routes. Against each item of equipment, state its main use.

ACTION 9 section 3, p.19

These are some of the points you may have written if you decided to take the positive approach.

HAIR Kept clean and tidy, away from the face and away from food. Long hair should be tied back, loose hairs regularly brushed out.

COMPLEXION Clear skin and complexion. Any make-up used sparingly.

MOUTH Clean teeth and breath.

FINGERS AND HANDS Kept clean. Nails trimmed. Although some employers do not insist, it is preferable to avoid nail polish. Smokers should take special care that their hands are clean.

JEWELLERY Kept to the minimum.

BODY CLEANLINESS Any odour will be offensive to customers. Bath or shower frequently. Strong scents, perfumes, aftershaves, colognes, etc. should be avoided.

CLOTHING Clean, well pressed.

FEET Comfortable, sturdy shoes, with non-slip soles. Kept clean and in good repair. Heels of a practical height.

ACTION 10 section 4, p.26

There is a lot to remember when you accept payment. It is very important, nevertheless, not to skip the checking process. The bank or credit card company will refuse payment if any detail of the procedure has been overlooked.

Follow-up activities

The bank refuses to honour a cheque for £50 because the customer's card had expired. With your supervisor's help, work out how much money would have to be taken by the business to make up the lost profit.

Collect some menus from local restaurants. Ask a friend to order a meal and drinks from each: from one restaurant it might be for a meal for 3, from another for just one person.

Write down the food and wine order, as you would if you were working at the restaurant (some advice on this is given on page 38), then make out the bill. Use a calculator if you wish.

ACTION 11 section 5, p.29

This is a selection of Royal Doulton chinaware. Of course, there is enormous variety in designs of china, and some items are intended to be multi-purpose. The main purpose of this exercise was to get you thinking about shapes and purposes of so-called hollowware (see Glossary), and to demonstrate that some manufacturers produce items with a very specific use (e.g. the mint sauce boat and oatmeal bowl). From left to right:

Top: mint sauce boat, sauce boat, tea pot, coffee pot, jug.

Centre: crescent salad dish, soup cup, oatmeal bowl, soup bowl.

Bottom: ashtray, marmalade dish, covered sugar bowl, salt cruet, pepper cruet, mustard pot, bud (flower) vase.

Follow-up activities

Draw diagrams of all the different pieces of hollowware in your workplace with a note of their names and main uses.

Ask your manager if you can add details of the price of each item and whether a breakages chart would be useful. (Some establishments work out the number of items broken each week from stocktakes, and display the results in the service area as a reminder to staff.)

ACTION 12 section 5, p.31

On page 42 you will find some reasons why many food and drink operations lay the minimum amount of cutlery on the table. Practices also vary as to the position of the bread knife (on the right, on or by the side plate) and the dessert spoon and fork (both at the top, or the spoon on the right and the fork on the left).

Besides the general need for efficiency, it is important that customers have the right cutlery for their meal, and are not confused by a surplus of items. Some customers do not know what cutlery to use when the meal consists of several courses.

Further discussion points

Compare your drawings with those of colleagues, and discuss the reasons for any differences.

How can you best help customers who are not sure what cutlery to use for a particular course?

What should you do when customers use the wrong cutlery before you have had a chance to say anything?

ACTION 13 section 5, p.32

Preparing checklists like this one, and collecting examples of workplace checklists, will help show your NVQ/SVQ assessor the range of activities you are involved in doing.

Follow-up activity

Collect examples of work rotas/schedules which show the allocation of pre-opening tasks between members of staff. For those tasks which you are not involved in doing, but which appear on the range checklist on page 36, e.g. preparing trolleys, get as much information as possible.

ACTION 14 section 5, p.33

The photograph on page 21 shows the staff of St. Faith's School in Wandsworth, London, dressed for a Mexican day. In the employee feeding sector of the industry (providing the catering services to the staff of banks, insurance firms and companies of all sizes) theme events provide an effective way of introducing variety and boosting sales.

ACTION 15   section 5, p.34

These are the glasses you would need for the private party:

8	Martini cocktail	3	white wine
4	red wine	5	Champagne
6	brandy	9	water.

Principal use of the remaining glasses: (1) sherry (some sherry glasses are slightly larger); (2) white wine (manufacturers produce white and red wine glasses in various sizes); (7) fruit cocktail/dessert; (10) multi-purpose glass, could be used for water, beer, long cocktails, milk shakes, etc.

Follow-up activities

Draw a chart showing all the glasses in use in your workplace, and their purposes.

Ask the person responsible for buying glasses in your workplace what the reasons were for choosing the particular range. Make a note of these under such headings as cost, durability, overall design, conforming to regulations (this would apply to glasses used to measure draught beer, lager and cider, and wine sold by the glass).

ACTION 16   section 5, p.35

The illustration shows the tray set-up used at the Conrad Hotel. The photograph on page 52 shows the order being delivered to the guest.

Further discussion points

What are the reasons for any differences between the tray set-up at the Conrad Hotel and your own workplace?

Follow-up activity

Collect some examples of room service menus, if possible from a range of hotels including de-luxe or 5-star, 4-star, 3-star, country house, etc. Discuss with people working in the hotels concerned, what use their guests make of room service, and why the hotel has decided to offer that particular level of service.

ACTION 17   section 5, p.36

Hopefully the reference to a dance floor did not distract you from the effectiveness of this checklist, achieved through its simplicity.

Further discussion points

What notices need to be displayed in your workplace and why? Examples include: menus, drink price lists, the measures spirits are sold in. If the notice is a legal requirement, what is the minimum information it must give?

ACTION 18   section 6, p.40

The way the questions in this activity are divided into different categories is not important. But hopefully it did start you thinking about some of the usual questions you might get faced with.

Follow-up activity

If you still think customers are predictable, discuss this letter to *Caterer & Hotelkeeper* from Jean Nolan, manager of Ye Jolly Crofter in Horwich, Lancashire.

One of our bar staff recently came into the kitchen to ask if she could look in the soup kettle to see what colour the soup was.

'It's green,' I said. 'It's broccoli and ham.'

She came back to tell me the customer didn't like green so wouldn't be having the soup.

The customer ordered a salad instead!

ACTION 19   section 6, p.41

The basic information in the descriptions you and your colleagues gave should agree with the following:

Salade Niçoise – Tuna fish with anchovy fillets, French beans and potato, lightly tossed in vinaigrette and decorated with sliced tomatoes and olives. (Your workplace might omit the tuna fish.)

Pasta Carbonara – with garlic, mushrooms, smoked ham, cream.

Club Sandwich – toasted, three-layer sandwich with bacon, hard-boiled egg, lettuce, tomato, chicken and mayonnaise.

Grilled Salmon Steak with Hollandaise Sauce – salmon with a rich sauce of egg yolks, butter, white wine vinegar and seasoning.

Lamb Médaillon Marsala – tender slice of lamb (boneless) sautéed and finished with a rich sauce made with Marsala (see page 78).

Quorn and Spinach Lasagne – layers of spinach and Quorn, a vegetable protein product that is high in fibre and high in protein.

Potatoes au Gratin – potatoes baked in their jackets, halved, scooped out and mixed with grated Cheddar cheese and butter, returned to the jacket and cooked until golden brown.

Dutch Apple Tart and Custard – sugar pastry enclosing a delicious mixture of apple and sultanas, with a hint of cinnamon and lemon zest. Served with custard sauce.

ACTION 20   section 6, p.42

Host – add small knife and fork, add steak knife, keep table fork, remove table knife.

Pearls – add small knife and fork, keep table knife and fork.

Bow tie – add soup spoon and fish knife and fork, remove table knife and fork.

Silk – add fish knife and fork, keep table knife and fork.

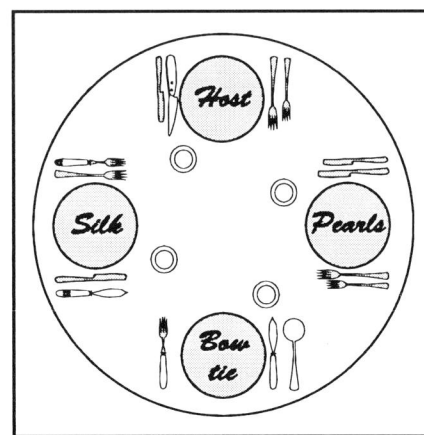

Further discussion points

The cutlery in the top illustration on page 42 has been drawn this way so that you can identify the different items. Is this the correct way to take cutlery to the table, or should the napkin/service cloth be folded over the knife blades, bowls of spoons, fork prongs, etc.?

Follow-up activity

Ask four friends to be the guests and demonstrate how each item of cutlery would be changed in a traditional restaurant.

Alternatively, describe the procedure in words. You might find the following example, based on the Royal Logistics Corps (Catering) procedure, helpful in starting you off. Note that it is based on changing a table d'hôte lay-up, so you will need to make some adjustments.

If soup is ordered the waiter/waitress will go to the right of the diner and remove the fish knife, then to the left of the diner to remove the fish fork. The server will then adjust the cutlery for the second diner, working in a clockwise direction around the table, or in the traditional order, women first, guests before host, etc.

What will be clear from this is that you should not stretch across the customer when adjusting the cutlery.

ACTION 21 section 6, p.43

These are the cutlery items on page 43, from left to right:

Knives: table/joint, small/dessert, steak, fish

Forks: table/joint, small/dessert, fish

Spoons: dessert, soup, teaspoon, grapefruit

Speciality forks: seafood cocktail, escargot (snails).

The cutlery requirements and those dishes suitable for vegetarians are identified below.

French onion soup – dessert spoon (as this dish is usually served in a small earthenware pot (marmite). Unless made with a vegetable stock (and then it is not true French onion soup), not suitable for vegetarians.

Deep fried brie with cranberry sauce – small knife and fork. Suitable for vegetarians.

Sauté of wild mushrooms – small knife and fork. Suitable for vegetarians. If butter was used in the cooking, you would need to check that this was acceptable to the customer (see page 39 for types of vegetarianism).

Country pâté – small knife and, depending on the garnish, small fork. Only suitable for vegetarians if made with vegetables.

Tapenade – fish knife and fork, with small knife for the French bread, but small knife and fork would also be acceptable.

Parma ham with melon – small knife and fork provided the melon was cut into suitable size pieces for picking up with a fork, otherwise a dessert spoon and fork. (Parma ham is quite delicate, so it can be cut with the edge of a spoon.) Vegetarians could be offered the melon on its own.

Smoked Scotch salmon – fish knife and fork.

Warm salad of goat's cheese, etc. – small knife and fork. Suitable for vegetarians, but not vegans.

Two eggs en cocotte à la crème – teaspoon – cocotte is the name of the small earthenware dish in which the eggs are baked. Not suitable for lacto-vegetarians or vegans.

Two shirred eggs with bacon – dessert spoon and fork – the eggs are cooked in a flat-bottomed ovenproof dish (known as a sur le plat dish); the bacon would be chopped up so there is no need for a knife. Not suitable for vegetarians, but you could probably ask if the chef could prepare a similar dish with a suitable garnish, e.g. mushrooms or asparagus.

Omelette of your choice – table fork, or sometimes large knife and fork. Vegetarians get bored with being offered omelettes because there is nothing else on the menu which is suitable (not the case with this menu).

Pasta piccante – dessert spoon and fork. As the pasta is in a tomato sauce with spicy sausage and chilli it would not be suitable for vegetarians.

Pizza napoletana – table knife and fork. With anchovies, tomatoes and black olives the filling is not suitable for vegetarians, but no doubt the chef could offer an alternative which would be suitable.

Braised tofu – table knife and fork. Tofu is soybean curd, high in protein. It has a fairly bland taste but readily absorbs the flavours of sauces and other ingredients in the dish. Ideal for vegetarians of all types.

King prawns – fish knife and fork – in many restaurants a finger bowl would also be placed on the table, half-filled with warm water to which has been added a slice of lemon.

Char grilled fresh tuna – fish knife and fork.

Poached salmon – as the tuna.

Char grilled lamb cutlet – table knife and fork.

Pork médaillon – as the lamb.

Bookmaker sandwich – table knife and fork, or small knife and fork – the sandwich filling is a grilled minute steak.

Ploughman's lunch – small knife, or depending on the amount and type of garnish, small knife and fork. Suitable for vegetarians who eat cheese and butter.

Follow-up activities

Photocopy a selection of menus and draw a diagram against each dish to show what cutlery would be required by the customer.

Identify the dishes which would be suitable for a vegetarian, and those which would be if the chef made minor adjustments to the ingredients.

Identify the dishes which a customer who is blind or nearly blind would find it difficult to eat (see page 8).

ACTION 22 section 6, p.45

If you were puzzled why this activity suggested the fish fork is removed from the left, and the knife from the right, the reason is to avoid stretching across the customer. In a more informal style of service, this is not necessary – in fact the customers might find it rather irritating.

You might also have taken issue with the suggestion that soup is served from the right. Some places do serve soup from the right, as it is a drink and drinks are usually served from the right. Others – and this includes hotels in the 5-star de-luxe Savoy Group – serve soup from the left.

ACTION 23 section 6, p.46

Tomato juice – Worcestershire sauce. Salt and pepper should also be available.
Lemon slice – can be offered with mineral water, may be used to decorate the tomato juice.
Cheese straw – served with some soups, e.g. mock turtle.
Tabasco sauce – one of the accompaniments with oysters. Some people enjoy it with tomato juice and with avocado.

Fresh grapefruit – caster sugar.
Ginger – melon. Caster sugar is also offered with melon.
Brown sugar – coffee (alongside a bowl of white sugar). Baked grapefruit is usually sprinkled with brown sugar before cooking.
White pepper – normally part of the table setting.

Smoked salmon – cayenne pepper, lemon wedge, buttered brown bread. Peppermill should be available.
Hot toast – pâté.

Prawn cocktail – buttered brown bread (and sometimes, lemon wedge).
Toast – potted shrimps.
Tomato sauce – usually included in the sauce for the prawn cocktail. Some customers enjoy tomato sauce with most dishes!
Freshly milled white pepper – some restaurants put peppermills for both black and white pepper on the table.

Spaghetti – Parmesan cheese, freshly milled black pepper.
Rye bread – makes a delicious accompaniment to stronger, sharper dishes, e.g. rollmops (herrings pickled in white wine vinegar with herbs and spices), gravlax (salmon which has been marinated with coarse sea salt, dill and brandy).
Cheese straws – sometimes put on the table for customers to 'nibble' at while they are waiting for their food.

Smoked trout – lemon wedge, cayenne pepper, horseradish, buttered brown bread.

Melon boats/sliced melon – caster sugar, ground ginger.
Brioche – soft roll or bread made from a very light yeast dough, slightly sweet. Can be offered as an alternative to bread rolls with soup.
Lemon segment – most deep fried fish dishes.

Minestrone soup – Parmesan cheese.
Poppadums – curry.
Melba toast – sometimes offered in addition to bread rolls. It is very thinly sliced, dried toast.

Fish fried in batter/bread crumbs – lemon wedge.
Tomato sauce – popular with fried fish.
Mayonnaise – many speciality fish restaurants offer mayonnaise as well as tartar sauce with fried and grilled fish dishes.
Tartar sauce – with fried fish coated in breadcrumbs.

Poached fish in a sauce – no special accompaniments.
Croissants – a favourite at breakfast.
Pitta bread – with taramasalata.
Croûtons – with soups.
Worcestershire sauce – with Irish stew.

Sorbet – sometimes a wafer or biscuit.
Hot chocolate sauce – with some desserts and ice cream dishes, e.g. pears Belle Hélène.
Water biscuits – with cheese.
Raspberry sauce – with some desserts and ice cream dishes, e.g. peach Melba.

Green or mixed salad – usually vinaigrette, but some customers prefer mayonnaise, others to make their own dressing with olive oil and vinegar.

Roast beef – gravy, horseradish sauce, English and French mustard.
Brown sauce – some customers enjoy this with eggs and bacon and with snack dishes.
Mint sauce – with grilled and roast lamb.
Dijon mustard – an example of a speciality mustard, which some customers appreciate being offered with grilled and roast meats.

Roast lamb – mint sauce or jelly and gravy.
Freshly milled pepper – might be on table. Should be offered with pasta dishes, smoked salmon, etc.
Cranberry sauce – roast turkey.
Redcurrant jelly – sometimes offered with roast and grilled lamb.

Roast pork – gravy, apple sauce.
Horseradish – roast beef, smoked trout.
English mustard – with beef, also enjoyed with grilled and baked ham, with sausages, and with cold meats.

Roast turkey – gravy, cranberry sauce, bread sauce.
Soy sauce – with stir fried dishes and some Asian dishes.

Grilled steak (beef) – French or English mustard.
Chutney – curry, Ploughman's lunch. Might be asked for with cold meat salads.

Béarnaise sauce – popular with steaks but not usually offered unless it is mentioned on the menu.
Parsley butter – with grilled/sautéed steak if mentioned on menu, also with grilled fish dishes.

Curry – grated coconut, orange segments and a whole range of other accompaniments depending on the policy of the restaurant, including chutney, nan bread, sliced cucumber, tomato.
Sliced beetroot – nothing, but beetroot juice is served with bortsch (a Russian and Polish soup based on beetroot).
Parmesan cheese – pasta dishes, minestrone soup.

Chateaubriand – a cut from the head of the beef fillet, usually serves 2 people. Normally Béarnaise sauce will be offered, and various mustards.
Bombay duck – a dried fish eaten with curries.
German mustard – might be requested by the customer. Would also be offered with frankfurter sausages, for example.
Gravy – with roast meats.

Pasta dish – grated Parmesan, freshly milled black pepper.
Ketchup – another name for tomato sauce (see above).
Tomato relish – as part of a relish tray with hamburgers.

Cheese – butter, rolls or biscuits, possibly fruit such as an apple, but not normally bananas (see page 50).
Sliced banana – curry.

ACTION 24 section 6, p.50

Which boxes you ticked will depend on the style of breakfast service you had in mind. The main purpose of this activity was to encourage you to think how breakfast service differed from other meals, and from one hotel or restaurant to another.

If guests help themselves to cold and cooked breakfast dishes from a buffet, you will probably only need to take their order for beverages, and to establish what room they are staying in (if it is a hotel), or collect payment. However if the breakfast menu is à la carte (each dish priced), a detailed order is obviously essential.

Customers do have definite preferences on when they like their beverage at breakfast. Many Americans, for example, like to be offered coffee immediately they sit down, and a glass of iced water.

Follow-up activity

Write out the order of service for a traditional, full English tea, as might be offered at a very fashionable tea room or a top class hotel. You may need to do some research first: visit or phone any of these places near you, have a look through past copies of *Caterer & Hotelkeeper* for articles on tea at The Ritz, etc., contact The Tea Council in London.

ACTION 25 section 6, p.51

The cutlery on the lower plate has not been stacked correctly, and the left-over food is scattered everywhere. You may also have noticed that there are 2 knives and 2 forks on the lower plate, a third fork in the server's hand – where is the third knife? On the floor, perhaps? Another mystery is why there are 7 plates in the illustration, but only 3 sets of cutlery.

ACTION 26 section 6, p.53

There will be two main areas in which your procedure for delivering a meal tray to an office will differ from the examples given:

Taking the order – as the activity referred to directors and senior management, it is likely to be their secretary who orders the tray. She or he will often know exactly what is required, but if one of the usual requirements for the person concerned has been omitted, it may be appropriate to ask, e.g.: 'Would Miss Merchant like the usual bottle of mineral water with her meal?'

The secretary will not want to keep disturbing the boss to ask whether this or that is required. But you may be asked before the order is placed to explain the choice available.

Delivering the tray – the tray may be delivered to the secretary, who takes it into the boss's office at the required time, or checks with the boss that it is convenient for you to enter. You should not enter an office without being invited to do so.

Further discussion points

What sort of dishes would you recommend for tray service in a situation like this? Bear in mind that the person probably wishes to continue working while eating.

ACTION 27 section 6, p.54

The Coppid Beech selling recommendations are based on offering the appropriate accompaniments to whatever the guest orders. For example, if a guest orders soup, the implication is that he or she wants a snack. Hence the suggestions of sherry, a salad and/or a beverage. This is likely to be more successful than an attempt to persuade this guest to order Champagne.

On the other hand, an order for Champagne suggests a celebration or special treat, and either strawberries or canapés would add to the occasion.

ACTION 28 section 7, p.56

1 A child is too short to see the buffet display – describe the dishes the child cannot see, asking questions to check what sort of food the child is interested in eating. If possible, lift down some of the dishes so that the child can enjoy the display.

2 A guest has mistaken the pudding – poor arrangement of food on the buffet might confuse guests in this way, but do not embarrass the guest by pointing out the mistake in a loud voice. A solution might be to offer to take the guest's plate, explaining that one of the dishes he or she has chosen is much nicer served with cream, and you will be happy to transfer it to a dessert plate.

3 A guest is in a wheelchair – ask the guest if you can describe what is available on the buffet and put some food on a plate for him or her. If the buffet is not busy with other guests choosing their food, it may be possible to offer to escort the wheelchair user to the food so that you can give a fuller description of what is available and show some of the dishes. Remember the advice on page 8.

4 A group of children misbehaving – don't threaten to beat the children with a stick, as the waitress did in the case study on page 12. Ask the children firmly, but kindly, if they will sit down. If the parents are not around, or unwilling to control the children, you might offer to get them some sweets or ice cream if they behave.

5 A guest has difficulty walking – offer to help escort the guest to the buffet table, and hold the guest's plate, or describe what is available on the buffet and bring the chosen dishes to the guest.

6 A guest's hand is very shaky – offer to hold the guest's plate. Done in a kindly way, this should not embarrass the guest.

7 A guest has severely impaired vision – offer to describe the dishes available, and to serve some for the guest. The guest may enjoy walking up to the buffet table to enjoy the tempting smells of the food, and the sounds of activity. Offer to accompany the guest, and either describe the dishes yourself, or preferably ask your colleagues who are serving at the buffet table to describe what is available. Remember the advice on page 8.

8 A breakfast customer has gone straight to a table – invite the person to make a choice from the buffet table, explaining briefly the range of dishes available. Either take the beverage order, or reassure the customer that your colleague will do so shortly.

ACTION 29 section 7, p.60

For a party of 20, the plan of the room suggests that the buffet table is quite spacious. Since it is a conference the time for lunch is probably restricted. Some delegates may wish to eat their meal quickly and have some fresh air, or make urgent telephone calls before the conference resumes. Others may not be very hungry, and will skip one of the courses.

For these reasons, all the food would probably be placed out on the buffet just before the delegates break for lunch, the hot dishes on warmers (or in réchauds, a special container for keeping food hot).

The menu suggests a four-course meal, so the arrangement of food should reflect this, with dishes 1 and 2 on the left of the table. The quiche and salads (4, 5, 6 and 7) might come next – on the basis of cold food before hot. But since there are only 20 people to be served, there is not much risk of the lamb (3) getting cold and it might be preferable to place the lamb and quiche to the right of the starters, then the salads, then the sweets (8 and 9) and the cheese (10).

Further discussion points

What are the advantages and disadvantages (to the customer and to the workplace) of a buffet for a function of this type and size, compared to a sit-down meal?

How many staff would be required to serve the buffet, and keep the tables clear?

What menus and style of service would be suggested to the company if they asked your workplace to arrange the meal?

Follow-up activity

Collect examples of menus from your workplace and elsewhere to include all types of buffet. Find out for each what the usual arrangements would be for serving the buffet.

ACTION 30 section 7, p.60

It takes a lot of skill to keep people's attention in a training session, and to find a meaningful way of breaking down the points you need to get across. Generally it is better to concentrate on just one or two key points.

If you have used the safety points suggested on page 60, some cartoons showing collapsed buffet tables, and dripping ice carvings might make the point very effectively.

ACTION 31 section 8, p.62

There are various reasons why silver service has been replaced with plated service in many establishments:

- new styles of cookery have put more emphasis on elaborate presentation of the food, with delicate arrangements of the sauce, intricate baskets of pastry, and so forth. These can only be done effectively on the plate from which the food will be eaten

- restaurants offering this style of food have become fashionable places – by contrast, silver service suggests a bygone era to some people

- a large array of serving dishes are required for silver service, and they are costly items to buy and maintain

- shortage of waiting staff with good silver service skills.

Fashions, of course, come and go. There is no doubt that silver service well done is impressive, and gives customers a degree of personal attention that plate service cannot.

Answers to activities

ACTION 32   section 8, p.65

If you are already skilled at serving food with a spoon and fork, try teaching a friend how to do it.

Further discussion points

What would you do if you spilt some food or sauce on a customer's clothes while serving?

How can you make sure everyone gets a similar size portion with a dish like peas?

What would you do, if at a large banquet you are just about to serve the first guest on your station the main course, and you suddenly realise the plates haven't been put down?

Follow-up activity

Write up a procedure or checklist to describe the service of accompaniments with the various dishes on your workplace menu.

Study this illustration and comment on the way the sauce is being served. Identify what is on the small plates to the left and right of the customer.

ACTION 33   section 8, p.66

Bread rolls at a banquet – serving spoon and fork. In some restaurants customers help themselves from a basket of rolls which you offer to each in turn.

Sliced smoked salmon at a buffet – serving spoon and fork.

Truite meunière to 1 customer at the table – two fish forks (see illustration on page 64), or two fish knives, or serving spoon and fork splayed out.

Truite meunière at a buffet, or from a side table or guéridon – here you have two hands free, so it is easier to use a serving spoon and fork without damaging the fish. At a buffet you might use a fish serving knife and fork.

Individual steak and kidney pies at a buffet – the pie server would be easier to use than a serving spoon and fork.

Curry presented in a circle of rice – for 1 customer at table: 1 serving spoon and fork. As you would serve the rice first, there is no need to use a separate set for curry and rice. With 3 customers at table you would definitely need a second spoon for the rice, otherwise by the time you reach the third person there will be little difference between the appearance of the curry and the rice.

Creamed potato, red cabbage and Brussels sprouts (in a 3-division vegetable dish) to 3 customers at the table – 3 sets of equipment, as each vegetable is a different colour, and the colours will easily transfer from one to another. A spoon and fork would be best for both the Brussels sprouts and cabbage, and a spoon on its own for the potato.

Roast potatoes, peas, grilled tomatoes (in a 3-division dish) to 2 customers at table – serving spoon and fork: with skill there is little risk of spoiling the appearance of the vegetables.

Fresh fruit salad from a sweet trolley – serving spoon. A fork would only be necessary if there were large items of fruit.

Gâteaux at a buffet – cake lifter. There is a danger of squashing the gâteaux if you use a spoon and fork.

ACTION 34   section 8, p.66

If your ideas were going to be used in a face-to-face training session, there is more scope for humour and the slightly off-beat.

ACTION 35   section 9, p.68

As the cafetière held two cups, the waitress might have suggested the two customers share a pot. She should have explained what to do with the plunger, and, better still, offered to push it down after delivering the coffee.

Consultation with the manager might have led to an offer to serve coffee by the cup, as requested. The coffee could have been made in the normal way in the service area, poured into two cups and delivered to the customers.

ACTION 36   section 9, p.70

People who have had too much alcohol do react in different ways. The person who becomes quiet is not likely to cause a disturbance, but you still need to warn your manager in case the customer continues drinking and gets you and your employer into trouble with the law.

Never accuse a customer of being 'drunk'. You could face legal charges for defamation of character. If it is necessary for you to say something, stick to the general expression 'had too much to drink'.

ACTION 37   section 9, p.72

Young, romantic couple – recommending Virgin Colada is likely to cause red faces all round. Besides that, the cream makes it rather rich for a pre-dinner drink. The other suggestions would be fine, the San Francisco if one of the guests did not want alcohol.

Business executives – as it is a working lunch, they may not want to drink alcohol, but you should not make assumptions. Tio Pepe, a very dry sherry, makes a good aperitif. Red wine is not usual as an aperitif, but that is no reason for discouraging customers from ordering it.

Middle aged couple – the tea or coffee would be acceptable suggestions. The Chocolate Monkey might be appropriate if they had had no dessert and wanted to spoil themselves with something sweet, rich and delicious. The Manhattan would not be suitable, in view of the alcohol content – customers sometimes ask for drinks they have heard of and think sound good without knowing exactly what is in them.

Couple shopping – the rosehip, Earl Grey (also tea) and lime juice would be suitable suggestions. If they surprise you by asking for the Gin fizz, keep a straight face, but this is not a recommendation you should make.

Lorry drivers – do your best to make them relax by suggesting drinks they are likely to be familiar with, e.g. tea, coffee, beer, soft drinks. They might ask for Irish coffee without realising what it is: explain carefully but not in a patronising way.

All-male party – they are probably not too worried about preparing their palate for the meal to come, as none of the drinks listed is suitable. Grolsch and other imported lagers are likely to be more acceptable than the Rob Roy. You might suggest the Peach Crush if one of the party did not want to drink alcohol. If you are an outgoing sort of person, and have established a lively, light-hearted relationship with the group, you might suggest the Slow Comfortable Screw.

All-female party – Bloody Mary is normally a pre-dinner or cocktail drink, too sharp for the end of the meal. The Crème de Menthe Frappé (green, peppermint-flavoured liqueur poured on to crushed ice) and Brandy Alexander would be popular suggestions, the Coke Floater (coke and ice cream) more suitable for children.

Parents with teenage daughter – anything to make the young lady feel special. The first two suggestions would probably be popular, the tea less so, and the Brazilian cocktail contains alcohol (Berro D'agua) so not a good idea.

Business person entertaining client – if they are to enjoy the subsequent wine, there is really only one recommendation: Champagne. If the host suggested the other drinks because he knows the client would really enjoy them, keep silent!

Elderly couple having a snack – the tea might be an appropriate suggestion, but it is not tactful to mention rheumatic pains. The Caribbean coffee might be interesting for them. The Bloody Mary was described early in the activity, so you will know it is vodka-based – unlikely to be suitable. Bucks Fizz (Champagne and orange juice) is not appropriate either.

Follow-up activity

Collect details of all the drinks sold in your workplace, and make notes which will help you deal knowledgeably with customer questions, promote sales, and serve each drink correctly.

Draft a procedure for the service of a specific range of drinks at table in your workplace, e.g. liqueur coffees. The Coppid Beech Hotel example on page 71 should give you some ideas. Include details of taking payment for the drinks (here you might want to refer back to section 4).

ACTION 38   section 10, p.74

Has your label given the required information? Is the design effective? Compare your work to the labels on the bottles on page 73.

ACTION 39   section 10, p.77

No. of region		Deliberate mistake	Correct region
6	Burgundy	Château Latour	Bordeaux (8)
11	Veneto	Réserve de la Comtesse	Bordeaux (8)
7	Rhône	Meursault Charmes	Burgundy (6)
10	Piedmont (Piemonte)	Crémant de Bourgogne	Burgundy (6)
2	Rhine (Rhein) Valley	Entre-Deux-Mers	Bordeaux (8)
5	Loire	Pouilly-Fuissé	Burgundy (6)
13	Tuscany and Umbria	Médoc	Bordeaux (8)
1	Mosel-Saar-Ruwer	Pouilly Fumé	Loire (5)
9	Languedoc and Roussillon	Vouvray	Loire (5)
3	Champagne	Châteauneuf-du-Pape	Rhône (7)
12	Emilia-Romagna and The Marches	Pinot Blanc	Loire (5)
8	Bordeaux	Nuits St-Georges	Burgundy (6)
4	Alsace	Fitou	Roussillon (9)

Follow-up activities

Draw a map showing the wine-growing areas of Spain and Portugal, and name some examples from each area.

Draw a map of the world and show all the wine-growing regions. Give some examples from each.

Compare the names of the examples you have listed with the grape varieties described on pages 75 and 76. Find out about any other grape varieties you come across and write a short description of their main characteristics.

Have a look in local wine merchants and supermarkets and note the names and prices of one or two sherries and ports of each style. Are there any sherries which do not match the style description, e.g. sold as 'cream' but which are light in colour? Find out as much as you can about those sherries and why they are described in this way.

ACTION 40   section 10, p.79

2, 3 and 4 – elgin glasses. The medium-sized and largest glass (a schooner) are often used for sherry and port, but the shape and the fact that the glasses are always filled to the rim does not allow the bouquet to be enjoyed. Another disadvantage is that they are difficult to clean and polish. The smallest glass is for liqueurs.

5 and 6 – brandy balloons. The short stem and wide bowl are suitable for cradling in the hands to warm the brandy so the full bouquet is released. The generous-size bowl in relation to the amount of brandy that is poured in the glass allows the brandy to be swirled around the glass, so the warming process is speeded up.

7 and 8 – Paris goblets. A very popular glass. The smaller sizes are not ideal for wine, as there is insufficient room for the bouquet to develop.

9 and 10 – tulip glasses, an ideal, all-purpose wine glass. Its wide bowl narrows slightly at the top, holding the aroma and allowing the wine to be swirled. It can be held by the stem so that the hands do not mask the appearance of the wine, nor alter the temperature of chilled wine. A wider-mouthed version is also available. Sherry and port can also be served in the tulip.

11 – Champagne flûte. Its narrow top and depth encourages and at the same time holds the bubbles of sparkling wine and Champagne. The shallow, wide-topped glasses (sometimes used for these wines) allow the bubbles to break up too quickly.

Follow-up activity

Compare your answer to the earlier activity on glasses (ACTION 15).

ACTION 41   section 10, p.80

Discuss your recommendations with your supervisor, and then try them out on some customers. Your answers will depend on the sort of customers you had in mind. If they are obviously not regular wine drinkers, but want a special treat, you should probably stick to the wines they are likely to recognise by name. It would also be sensible to ask some more questions before you recommend a particular wine – some people only enjoy sweet wines, for example, no matter what they are eating.

Further discussion points

Are there any wines sold in your workplace which should be decanted before service? If so, ask your supervisor to give you a demonstration of how this is done.

How many bottles of each wine are stored at serving temperature? Are there any examples where the number is too high in terms of the demand for that wine, with the risk that the wine will deteriorate in quality?

Follow-up activity

For each of the wines sold in your workplace, name the menu dishes which the wine would accompany. If there are dishes with which you would not recommend a wine, what drinks would you suggest?

ACTION 42   section 11, p.86

In deciding what displays you liked, did you consider the range of dishes served in your workplace, the preferences of your customers, and how long it would take to make up the display? Some of the more elaborate displays in supermarkets would simply not be practicable in a busy catering situation.

Follow-up activity

Study the photographs on pages 92 and 94. How could St. Valentine's Day (or other special occasion) be marked in your workplace?

ACTION 43   section 11, p.87

Did you notice in the Ealing Hospital chalkboard that customers could buy tea bags (to take home to make a pukka cuppa tea with)? Quite a few counter service operations now sell products outside the normal range of food and drink, e.g. confectionery, home-made jams and cakes.

Further discussion

Have a look at the photograph on page 1 which shows the use of a blackboard to list the dishes sold in a pub. What improvements would you suggest to the person responsible for writing the board?

ACTION 44   section 11, p.88

To do this activity scientifically you should have spent some time observing what your customers actually do as they pass through the counter service area.

Follow-up activities

Repeat the exercise for coffee or breakfast service, as appropriate.

When you are next having a meal in a counter service restaurant, e.g. at a motorway service area or department store, study the flow of customers as they move through the service area. What are the 'hot' spots? What ideas could be adopted in your workplace to promote sales?

ACTION 45   section 11, p.90

Did you come up with any one-liners that your colleagues and friends did not like? One of the examples originally listed was 'How many Yorkshire puddings would you like, one or two? They only cost Xp', but someone reading the text who has to be careful about what she eats pointed out that this could be offensive.

ACTION 46   section 11, p.94

Compare your checklist and the CCG Services example with the other industry examples given in section 1.

ACTION 47   section 11, p.94

It can be very difficult for wheelchair users to see the display of foods on a counter, as it is for young children. You can help by describing what is available, and perhaps by showing some dishes to the person concerned. You should also offer to carry the person's tray.

Compare your checklists with the answers you gave to ACTION 28 in *Carvery and buffet service*.

ACTION 48   section 12, p.98

Did you try and vary what you said each time? If not, remind yourself of point 5 in the text on page 98.

Were any of your examples suitable for particular times of the day, e.g. offering different breakfast combinations? If not, try and add some more.

Follow-up activity

With your manager's approval, try out your examples on some customers. If the response is disappointing, try varying the words or ideas until you have a collection that work well.

ACTION 49   section 12, p.100

Were any of your survey results affected by special circumstances? For example, it is difficult in very wet weather to keep the entrance looking tidy.

Make a checklist of the areas you decided you could do better. Ask someone to repeat the survey in a few weeks' time, so that you can judge where you still need to make improvements.

ACTION 50   section 13, p.105

2 Instant ingredients canisters

3 Cup magazine

5 Cup station

9 Waste bucket

10 Syrup canisters

13 Dispensing spouts

14 Whipper units and mixing bowls

Follow-up activity

Draw and label a diagram to show the parts of a drinks vending machine at your workplace/college. Alternatively get a brochure from the manufacturers which includes a photograph of the inside of the machine, and label that.

Further activities

ACTION   *Customer skills*

Adapt the following to suit your workplace situation more closely.

Advice to staff at Hudson's

Customer contact

There are a thousand different ways of saying 'Good morning, can I help you?' The secret is in your voice.

HUDSON'S
A Tradition of Excellence

If you are tired or have had a bad day, it will be noticeable in your voice and mannerisms and will probably affect the guest's judgement on whether to stay or not.

Understandably no one person can be on a high note every day or even all day, but it is very easy to discipline your reactions so that each time you greet a guest your welcome is warm and polite even if you are feeling under the weather. This sort of reaction generates sales and promotes a good working environment.

Telephone manner

A disciplined, warm response is essential. Many people who have good social skills tend to neglect these when answering the telephone. This can be attributed to the fact that you cannot see the person on the end of the telephone line so why should you be welcoming and polite.

You must remember that a lot of people making enquiries about Hudson's Coffee Houses have never been to one, therefore your telephone manners go a long way to helping that person to build up a mental picture of the business and once again you can make or break a person's decision on whether to come to Hudson's or not.

Acceptable greetings

Good morning Sir, how can I help you?

Obviously the greeting depends on the time of day and the customer's gender.

If the customer is visibly below the age of 18 then the sir/madam may be dropped from the greeting.

ACTION   *Customer skills*

Agree with your colleagues what are the most important skills for someone who is serving food and drink. Here are some thoughts from the *Caterer & Hotelkeeper* to get the discussion going.

The waiter/waitress of the 1990s will have to be versed in the additional skills of communications, human relations and salesmanship. He or she will be the person at the point of sale with the opportunity to increase every 'spend'.

CATERER
& Hotelkeeper

To do this, according to Peter Sloyan (general manager of the Gosforth Park Thistle Hotel), the waiter/waitress will have to learn to use 'body language and human psychology, as well as pacing – that is matching your attitude and your tone of voice, your rhythm of speech, to that of the customer. Creating a rapport.'

Bruno Rotti, restaurant manager at Claridge's, put the argument for sensitivity. 'Of course he is a salesman. Of course he understands the psychology of the customer. But he also needs sensitivity. When it is right to 'sell' and when he should never interrupt with a drinks trolley or cigars; and when a client likes to be chatted to and when absolutely not – perhaps he is talking business or wants to be left alone to enjoy his partner's company.'

 Eve Jones, 1 December 1988.

ACTION   *Safety and security*

Below is the fire alarm procedure issued to the staff of Hudson's Coffee House in the Plaza Shopping Centre, Birmingham.

After studying it, arrange to visit some of the catering outlets in a shopping centre near you, or a similar, large multi-centre complex such as an airport. Explain you would like to learn about their fire procedures, and any special problems and priorities.

Use what you have learned to give a brief talk to your colleagues on the importance of knowing what action to take in the event of a fire.

FIRE ALARM PROCEDURE

1 If you discover or suspect a fire, go immediately to one of the nearest fire call points, situated by every fire exit, and activate the alarm.

   If it is safe, contact Control and inform them of the fire location (XXX XXX).

2 On activation of the alarm, you will hear intermittent fire bells which are backed up by an alert message on the public address system.

   All staff should await further instructions. No evacuation is required at this stage.

3 If found to be a false activation, an all-clear message will be given over the PA system twice saying "please note the emergency has now been cleared".

4 If it is a full alarm situation then the alarm system will proceed to continuously sounding bells. An evacuation message will be played through the PA system.

5 All members of staff must evacuate the building.

   The lifts should not be used.

   Staff should assemble at St. Phillips Churchyard.

   The Emergency Coordinator will wear a yellow jacket for easy identification.

6 The Senior Fire Officer will only allow a return to the building when he is satisfied that it is safe.

   No attempt to return should be made until this assurance has been given.

ACTION   *Security*

Personnel in the armed forces are particularly vulnerable to acts of terrorism. On the basis of these detailed procedures from the Army for dealing with suspicious object and bomb threats, and the industry example on page 15, draw up a checklist which could be used by the staff of a restaurant in an airport terminal or similar, high security area.

SUSPICIOUS OBJECTS

You must always endeavour to ensure that the mess members do not leave objects such as briefcases, suitcases, shopping bags and parcels lying about. Should you come across any such item in suspicious circumstances and with no name visible on it on no account attempt to move it, put it in water, etc. Clear the area and inform the security personnel as rapidly as possible.

TELEPHONE BOMB THREATS

If you receive such a threat over the telephone, the main priority is to keep calm. Elicit as much information as possible from the caller, putting down what you can into note form, the main points being as follows:

- location of the bomb
- time it is due to detonate
- what it looks like
- how it is fused
- who the caller is or which organisation he/she represents.

At the same time as trying to get this information, try to assist the security forces in tracing the caller by making a note of the following important points:

1 Was any code name or number given? If so, write it down.
2 What sort of accent did the caller have?
3 Did the caller sound natural or was the accent put on?
4 Was the caller calm, excited or possibly drunk?
5 Was there any noticeable speech defect?
6 Were there any background noises evident?

Once the caller has rung off, or earlier if you can attract someone else's attention, contact the security personnel and carry out the evacuation programme for your mess. Make sure you are easily found by the security personnel when they arrive.

ACTION   *Hygiene in serving*

Devise a quiz along the following lines. The theme of the quiz is personal hygiene for food and drink serving staff.

Decide on the words you wish to use. Keep sentences brief and punchy.

Re-write the sentences, omitting one or two words in each and leaving a blank space.

Make some copies of the quiz and try it out on some colleagues.

Change any sentences which seem too difficult or too easy.

For example, if this was one of your sentences:

Never lick the fingers

you might omit the word 'lick', so the sentence reads:

NEVER ---- THE FINGERS

ACTION   *Clearing after service*

You have been asked to compile a checklist to suggest improvements in the method for waste disposal in your workplace, with particular emphasis on hygiene and safety.

Below is the procedure used at the Clementine Churchill Hospital.

Waste disposal

1 Food wastage from a main meal (hot or cold) is returned to the kitchen in the hot trolley on its original plate.

2 Food wastage such as biscuits and sandwiches must be placed in the black disposable polythene sack (in the servery bin).

3 Yogurt wastage must be rinsed out from the coup and the coup washed in the servery dishwasher. The same applies to cream and clear soup wastage. Solid particles in soups such as vegetables must be spooned out into the servery food bin and liquid wastage rinsed.

The Clementine Churchill Hospital

4 During kitchen working hours, 7 am to 8 pm, black wastage sacks must be sent downstairs via the service lifts after each meal service. Staff on late duty must take their wastage sacks downstairs on their way home and place in bin marked 'Catering' beside the kitchen doors.

5 Glass, china and sharp objects must be placed in the boxes provided in the sluices.

6 Empty boxes and empty milk pergals must be taken downstairs and put in the blue bin marked 'Catering'.

ACTION   *Taking payment*

Describe briefly how you would deal with each of the following situations:

1 You work in England or Wales, and a customer hands over a Royal Bank of Scotland £10 note.

2 You work in Scotland and a customer hands over a Bank of England £50 note.

3 A customer refuses to accept a 50p coin you have given in change, because it is Irish.

4 Every customer seems to have nothing but large denomination notes, and you have run out of change.

5 Your colleague asks you to take over the till for a few minutes while he/she goes to the toilet.

6 A customer asks you for change to use the telephone, and there is no other reason to open the till at that point (i.e. the customer is not paying for something at the time of the request).

7 An elderly customer is having trouble finding the right money, and seems to be getting confused between the different notes.

8 The customer is carrying a white stick, and hands over his/her purse on reaching the till.

9 You have twice said the amount due, but the customer does not seem to have heard.

ACTION   *Cheese service 1*

You have presented a colourful cheeseboard (shown immediately below). Your customer is appreciative but unsure of the varieties offered. Name the cheeses shown below.

Top left	Top middle
Top right	Centre right
Bottom right	Bottom middle
Bottom left	Centre left

ACTION   *Cheese service 2*

Your workplace is having a French theme day. You have been asked to help brief your colleagues on the day's cheese board (shown in the picture on the right, below).

1	2
3	4
5	6
7	8
9	10
11	12

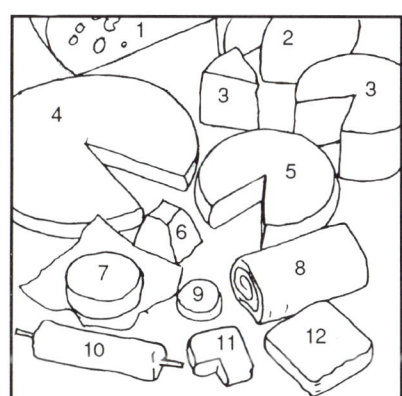

Cheese service 1: Top left: Stilton; top middle Huntsman; top right: Stilton with peppers; centre right: matured Cheddar; bottom right: Somerset Brie; bottom middle: Buxton Blue; bottom left: Pencarreg; centre left: Red Leicester.

Cheese service 2: (1) Emmental; (2) Pyrénées; (3) Roquefort; (4) Brie; (5) St. Paulin; (6) Goat's cheese pyramid; (7) Camembert; (8) fresh cheese with pepper; (9) fresh cheese with herbs and garlic; (10) Goat's cheese log; (11) Carré de l'Est; (12) Pont l'Eveque.

ACTION   *Selling wine*

Successful establishments respond to the ever-changing needs of the customer by devising new ways of presenting their wares.

These are some of the ways in which wine sales can be increased. Consider their relevance to your workplace, and mark the list accordingly:

- ☑ already used
- ★ should be considered
- ☒ a good idea but not appropriate to your customers

Then discuss your assessment with your manager. If possible, try and arrange to be involved in the sales promotion, e.g. by contacting the tourist office for the country concerned to get material to help make an attractive display of the country's wines.

- ☐ *selling wine by the glass*
- ☐ *special menus priced to include wine*
- ☐ *increasing the range of half bottles*
- ☐ *running promotions on a particular theme*
- ☐ *joint promotions with suppliers*
- ☐ *special wine offers/wine of the day with display cards on tables/in menus*
- ☐ *suggesting a wine for each dish on the menu*
- ☐ *letting staff taste the wines, so they know what they're selling*
- ☐ *offering a sweet white wine from the dessert trolley*
- ☐ *choosing high quality house wines of good value*
- ☐ *displaying wines prominently and attractively*
- ☐ *keeping wine prices competitive with other drinks*
- ☐ *changing the wine selection frequently*
- ☐ *putting the same mark-up on all wines regardless of price, e.g. £4, rather than 100% – this gives customers better value on the more expensive wines, and on a long-term basis can increase wine sales*
- ☐ *using more attractive wine glasses*
- ☐ *producing own-label wines*
- ☐ *redesigning the wine list to give more information on each wine*

119

ACTION *Knowledge of your workplace*

This is the checklist used at Hudson's, a prestigious coffee house in Birmingham's City Plaza shopping centre, of which *The Birmingham Post* writes *Tables get moved, names are remembered, nothing too much trouble.*

For the purposes of this activity, the checklist questions have been split into three categories. **Part A** contains those questions specific to a coffee house type operation. **Part B** contains the more general questions which are likely to suit your establishment. **Part C** are tasks which you should demonstrate.

1   Ask your supervisor, trainer or tutor to amend the questions in Part A (and if necessary Parts B and C) to make them appropriate to your workplace.

2   Answer each question in the space provided.

3   Demonstrate the tasks specified.

4   Discuss your answers and how you have performed the tasks with your supervisor, trainer or tutor.

PART A ·······································

State the components of a French breakfast.

State the ingredients for a health cocktail.

Recommend a coffee which we sell that is:

weak

strong

Name three herbal teas that we sell.

What does the afternoon tea consist of and how much does it cost?

If a food and beverage item is ordered for which there is no till code/number, how do you ring it up?

Why is the _____ Room named so?

How long does the preparation of a speciality sandwich take?

PART B ·······································

What is the correct greeting when you first meet a customer or party of customers?

What is the house mineral water and its country of origin?

Identify and describe two desserts which make a higher than average profit

Where are the till rolls stored?

What information is required for taking a reservation?

Why should a waiter/waitress never stand with his or her back to the seating area?

Why should dirty covers by cleared quickly?

Which way should a coaster be placed on a table/saucer?

How much does a pot of house coffee for one person cost?

What is the correct manner in which to answer the telephone?

Why should jewellery (other than a plain wedding ring) not be worn in food preparation or service areas?

PART C ·······································

Demonstrate the changing of a till roll.

Lay a lunch time cover for one person.

à la carte – menu giving a selection of individually priced items.

Accompaniments – something traditionally offered or served with a particular dish or drink, e.g. buttered brown bread with smoked salmon.

American service – another name for **plated service**. In a variation, used in some holiday centres and schools, the plates are taken to table on a special carrier like a large afternoon tea cake stand (see photograph on page 14).

Bain-marie – a container which keeps food hot.

Bill – statement of what the customer is due to pay, usually itemised.

Bin number – the number of that part of the cellar/wine store where a particular wine is kept. When used on the wine list, it offers customers an alternative to saying, and staff an alternative to writing down, a long name.

Buffet service – food is displayed on tables or counters. Has similar variations as **counter service**, i.e. fully, partly or unassisted service.

Bussing (Transatlantic term) – clearing, laying tables, fetching and carrying for other serving staff.

Butler service – customers serve themselves from flats or dishes held at their side by the server. In other European countries, called French or Continental service.

Cafeteria – self-service restaurant. Term not much used now, as it tends to be associated with poor standards.

Canapé – mouth-sized snack offered at cocktail parties, or with drinks before a meal.

Carafes – open-topped container (usually made of glass and fairly plain) used for serving wine and sometimes other drinks.

Carvery service – joints of meat are carved at the counter when customers have made their choice.

Chef de rang – station waiter/waitress in a traditional restaurant team. He or she will be responsible for serving a number of tables, usually with the assistance of a **commis**.

Choice service – the food is assembled on the plate by, or at the direction of, the customer. The basis of self-service (including partly-assisted self-service) or **offer service**.

Cocktail – mixed drink, traditionally with alcohol base, served before the meal to stimulate the appetite. Now enjoyed in their own right, and many places offer a huge range of flavours from very sweet to very dry, some without alcohol.

Commis – assistant waiter/waitress in a traditional restaurant team. Will help a more senior colleague serve, doing much of the fetching and carrying.

Condiments – any spice or sauce which people might wish to flavour their food with, e.g. salt, pepper, mustard.

Continental service – another name for **silver service** and for **butler service**.

Corkage – a charge (per bottle usually), when customers bring their own wine to drink in a licensed restaurant.

Counter service – customers collect their own food from a counter or table and take it to an eating area. *Fully-assisted:* serving staff serve all customers' requirements; *partly-assisted:* customers help themselves to some items; *un-assisted:* customers serve themselves to everything.

Cover – the place setting for each customer, including crockery, cutlery, glassware and napkin. Also refers to the number of customers expected/served, e.g. 50 covers.

Cover charge – set amount per customer added to the bill in some restaurants. By law it must be clear to customers before they order their meal that a cover charge is added, i.e. by a statement on the menu.

Crockery – plates, saucers, cups, bowls, dishes, etc.

Cruets – small containers for the table which hold ground salt and pepper, and sometimes mustard, oil, vinegar – which customers may require to add flavour to their food.

Crumb down – brush crumbs and debris from table between courses.

Cutlery – strictly, knives and other cutting implements, but generally used to include spoons and forks.

Decanter – container used to serve wines, fortified wines and sometimes spirits. Usually made of glass, with a narrow neck and stopper, and can be quite ornate.

Doily (also spelt doyley or doyly) – used to enhance appearance and presentation. Placed on or under dishes, glasses, cups, food, etc. Available in all colours.

Drive-in service – customers order and collect their food without having to get out of their car.

du jour – of the day, e.g. soup du jour.

Dumbwaiter – various meanings: (1) the sideboard in a restaurant or dining room used for preparation and storage; (2) elevator or lift used for carrying trays of food, crockery, etc. (but not people) between floors; (3) revolving circular tray placed on the dining table, so that customers can easily serve themselves to a variety of dishes.

English service – another name for **silver service**, and, confusingly, for **family service** (from the tradition of the head of the family carving or portioning and serving everyone at table).

Family service – food is placed on the table in serving dishes from which customers help themselves. Variations include: (1) meat/fish/main item plated, customers serve themselves to vegetables; (2) as (1), but server offers vegetables to each customer in turn.

Fast food service – customers select, order and collect their food from the counter. The food is packaged so that it can be eaten in the restaurant (when it is usually put on a tray), or taken away (when it is usually placed in a bag).

Finger bowl – small bowl of warm water with either a lemon slice, flower petals or perfume, placed on the table for the convenience of the customer when dishes have to be eaten with the fingers (e.g. King prawns).

Finger buffet – food is served in small pieces suitable for eating without the need for cutlery.

Flat – large, flat serving dish, usually oval or round, with a shallow rim.

Flatware – two meanings: (1) all forms of spoons and forks; (2) plates, soup bowls, saucers, etc.

Float – a sum of money, coins and sometimes notes, placed in the till at the start of service so that change can be given to customers. At the end of service, the value of the float is deducted from the takings and removed for safe-keeping to be replaced at the start of the next session.

Fork buffet – food is of the sort (or cut into small pieces) that can be eaten with a fork only, the other hand being required to hold the plate.

Frappé – drink served in a glass filled with crushed ice, e.g. Cointreau frappé. Also food served on a bed of crushed ice, e.g. melon frappé.

Free flow system – form of counter service (also called echelon or scramble service). The counters are arranged (e.g. staggered at an angle, or arranged informally around the room) so that customers need only go to the counter holding the items they wish to order.

French service – another name for **butler service**. In America it is the name for **guéridon service**. Also another term for **silver service**.

Garnish – decoration (e.g. slice of lemon) to enhance the appearance of a dish. Also aids digestion of certain foods (e.g. quarter of lemon with battered, fried fish), and compliments the texture and flavour of a dish (e.g. stuffing with roast chicken).

Gratuity or **tip** – money left by customers in appreciation of good service. Depending on the procedure of the establishment, it is either kept by the individual who receives it, or pooled to be divided among the staff.

Guéridon service – two meanings: (1) food presented on serving dishes, then placed on a trolley by the customers' table and transferred to each customer's plate using a spoon and fork (or other appropriate cutlery); (2) cooking or finishing of the dish is done on a trolley in view of the customers, e.g. boning a whole Dover sole, cooking speciality steak.

Hollowware (also spelled holloware) – any item made from silver or stainless steel apart from flatware and cutlery, e.g. teapots, milk jugs.

Hors d'oeuvre – dish served as an appetiser, the first course of a meal. There may be one item, or a selection on the plate, trolley or buffet table.

Maître d'hôtel – restaurant manager.

Mise en place – literally, to 'put in place', refers to the pre-service preparation, including setting the tables with cutlery and crockery and filling the sideboards.

No show – person who fails to honour a reservation (for a table at the restaurant).

Offer service – takes two forms: (1) when the food is presented to the customer on a salver or flat, and the customer serves him or herself; (2) Continental or silver service, when the server transfers the food from the salver on to the diner's plate.

Part-plated service – the more expensive meal elements or more complex components are placed on the plates before meal service commences.

Plated service – food is completely portioned and plated, usually in the kitchen, then brought to the table by serving staff.

Rocks – ice cubes, e.g. as in whisky on the rocks.

Russian service – originally a form of butler or family service. As used in small shooting lodge hotels in Scotland, the dishes of food are placed on the sideboard on hotplates or in réchaud dishes (with spirit warmers underneath), and guests help themselves. In France **guéridon service** is sometimes called Russian service.

Salver – small, round tray used to carry small items, and for the service of drinks.

Savoury – in food and drink service it usually refers to a dish which is not sweet in flavour. Also the name for dishes served at the end of the meal after or as an alternative to the dessert, e.g. devilled kidneys on toast.

Service charge – an extra charge for service of a set percentage (usually between 5 and 15%). The menu must clearly state that such a charge will be added (or that prices include service). Leading restaurateurs have campaigned for service charge to be abolished, since the money does not always go to staff. Tips are a more direct form of rewarding good service, they argue.

Service cloth – cloth used to hold hot dishes, as a support under trays, for polishing cutlery and crockery, for helping in the service of wine, etc.

Show plate – decorative plate placed in the centre of each cover, to enhance the table setting.

Side table service – another name for **guéridon service**.

Silver service – food transferred to the plate in front of the customer, from a flat or serving dish using a spoon and fork or other appropriate utensil such as a ladle.

Silverware – general term used to describe cutlery and metal flatware and hollowware, whether they are made of solid silver (very rare), silver-plate (e.g. EPNS electro-plated nickel silver), or stainless steel.

Slip cloth – placed over the normal tablecloth to cover the top of the table. It is quicker and easier to change and launder a slip cloth rather than the full tablecloth.

Smorgasbord – Scandinavian style buffet, offering customers a variety of hot and cold savoury dishes as a starter or main course.

Sommelier – traditional title for the person responsible for serving wine in a restaurant or hotel. Nowadays more often called the wine waiter/waitress.

Spritzer – drink of half white wine, half soda water.

Station – the tables allocated to a particular member of staff to serve.

Still room – traditional name for the area where teas and coffees are made, toast, butters, milks, fruit juices, etc., prepared.

Sweetener – sweetening agent, for coffee, tea, etc., made without sugar.

Table d'hôte – fixed price set menu of two or more courses, with a choice for each course.

Table linen – tablecloths and napkins which form part of the table setting, made of any textile, not necessarily pure linen.

Take-away service – customers select, order and collect their food from the counter, packaged to eat elsewhere.

Tray service – food is taken to the customer on a tray with the required cutlery, napkin, salt, pepper, etc.

Underliner – plate or saucer which is placed underneath something. There are 3 purposes: (1) to protect the tablecloth from spills, e.g. a plate under a finger bowl or jar of marmalade; (2) to help carry the item hygienically and safely, e.g. a plate under the soup bowl; (3) to enhance presentation, e.g. a plate under the coffee cup and saucer.

VAT – value added tax. A charge on many goods and services, paid to the government. Businesses with a large enough turnover have to be registered for VAT, and their prices must be shown on menus and wine lists inclusive of VAT.

Vending service – customers make their choice from a selection displayed in a machine.

Vintage – the year when the grapes which made a particular wine or fortified wine were picked (harvested).

Wine list – list of the names and prices of wines from which customers can make their choice. Other details should include the alcoholic content by volume (e.g. 12%), vintage, country and region of origin (if not clear from name). Some lists give a short description of the wine and recommend dishes to accompany it.

Index